D1590062

The Poem and the Book

NEIL FRAISTAT

The Poem and the Book

Interpreting Collections of Romantic Poetry

The University of North Carolina Press

Chapel Hill and London

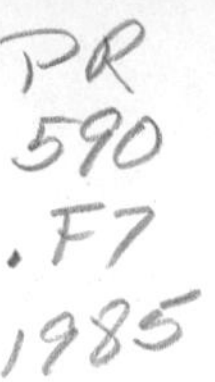

Manufactured in the United States of America

Library of Congress Cataloging in Publication Data

Fraistat, Neil, 1952–

The poem and the book.

Bibliography: p.

Includes index.

1. English poetry—19th century—History and criticism.

I. Title.

PR590.F7 1985 821′.7′09 84-10381

ISBN 0-8078-1615-9

The author is grateful for permission to reproduce passages from the following:

Robert Frost, "A Servant to Servants" from *The Poetry of Robert Frost*, edited by Edward Connery Lathem. Copyright 1930, 1939, © 1969 by Holt, Rinehart and Winston. Copyright © 1958 by Robert Frost. Copyright © 1967 by Lesley Frost Ballantine. Reprinted by permission of Holt, Rinehart and Winston, Publishers. The British Commonwealth rights are held by Jonathan Cape Limited, 30 Bedford Square, London, WC1B3EL, England.

William Carlos Williams, *Paterson*. Copyright 1946 by William Carlos Williams. Reprinted by permission of New Directions Publishing Corporation.

For Louis Fraistat and in memory

of Shirley C. Fraistat

Contents

Preface

Some thirty-five years after informing Joseph Cottle that the individual poems of *Lyrical Ballads* (1798) were "as stanzas" of an ode, Coleridge noted with admiration that Shakespeare's "extraordinary sonnets form, in fact, a poem of so many stanzas of fourteen lines each." Relatively few modern readers, however, have been as quick to grasp the fundamental interrelations between the poems in Coleridge's own collections, or in those of his contemporaries. In fact, although we now generally perceive the major Romantics as self-conscious in all things poetic, most of us continue to read their poems in editions arranged chronologically, even when the poets supplied their own purposeful organizations. This study, therefore, intends to offer the first extensive look at the Romantics' use of the poetic volume as an integral unit.

A few words ought to be said about the structure of this book. In order to outline the theoretical problems involved in reading a poetic volume as a whole and to furnish relevant historical contexts, the introductory chapter examines paradigms of organized collections—with special attention to Dante's *La vita nuova*, Petrarch's *Canzoniere*, and Milton's *Poems upon Several Occasions*. The second chapter moves the theoretical concerns of the first into the framework of the Romantic period itself, providing a foundation for full readings of three of the most important and complexly unified volumes of the age: Wordsworth and Coleridge's *Lyrical Ballads, with a Few Other Poems*; Keats's *Lamia, Isabella, The Eve of St. Agnes, and Other Poems*; and Shelley's *Prometheus Unbound, with Other Poems*.

For obvious reasons I have been forced to limit the historical scope of Chapter 1, which might otherwise have encompassed everything from the Bible as collection to any number of significant individual volumes. So that such a history might be rendered more expansively than was possible here, I am currently editing a book of essays that will range from Classical to contemporary collections, to be called *Poems in Their Place*. Similarly, I have chosen to offer full readings of only three Romantic volumes because, as will become evident, this process requires detailed analysis of the constituent poems. In Chapter 2, I have tried to suggest fruitful approaches to several other Romantic volumes, but much work clearly remains to be done. Substantial ground is still to be broken, for instance, on the subject of Byron's collections and Coleridge's *Sibylline Leaves*. Wordsworth's various orderings and reorderings of his books, as well as his pairings, suites, and sonnet sequences await further explication. So, too, Shelley's *Alastor* collection, Keats's *Poems*, and the books of Blake, Burns, and Clare all merit sustained critical attention. In large measure, then, this study is intended to engender debate not just on the interpretations offered in the last three chapters, or on the methodology developed herein, but, more broadly, on the way we as readers approach Romantic texts.

My research has been supported by grants from the Henry E. Huntington Library and the University of Maryland General Research Board, as well as a Fellowship for Recent Ph.D. Recipients from the American Council of Learned Societies, which was in part made possible by a grant from the National Endowment for the Humanities. The University of Maryland General Research Board also generously granted me a Book Subsidy Award. While conducting research, I have had the pleasure of working at libraries distinguished for the depth of their collections and the resourcefulness of their staffs. Chief among these are the Henry E. Huntington Library, San Marino, California; the Bodleian Library, Oxford University; the Library of Congress, Washington, D.C.; and the Charles Patterson Van Pelt Library of the University of Pennsylvania. I am especially grateful to Virginia Renner and Mary Wright of the Huntington Library for their unfailing good spirits and their many kindnesses. For permission to reproduce material in their collections, I would like to thank the Newberry Library, Chicago, and the Special Collections Division, Library of Congress.

Several teachers, colleagues, and friends have contributed substantially to the genesis and development of this study. Nina Auerbach, Houston Baker, Vincent Carretta, David DeLaura, Theresa M. Kelley, Lawrence Kramer, Malcolm Laws, Elizabeth Bergmann Loizeaux, and William Loizeaux have all read the manuscript either in part or in an early version, and commented helpfully upon it. To Leopold Damrosch, Jr., S. K. Heninger, Jr., Leonard S. Goldberg, Earl Miner, and William A. Ringler, Jr., I am grateful for sound advice and for conversation that was always as enthusiastic as it was enlightening. For his counsel and encouragement, I am deeply indebted to Joseph A. Wittreich, Jr., whose many fine suggestions are reflected throughout these pages. Donald H. Reiman and Robert Gleckner read the entire manuscript with dispatch and penetrating insight, generously sharing with me their formidable knowledge of the Romantics. Most of all, to Stuart Curran I am grateful for his first encouraging me to undertake this study and for the constant help that is responsible for much that is best here.

Finally, to my wife Rose Ann C. Fraistat goes my heartfelt gratitude for her cheerful involvement in every stage of the composition and production of this book—involvement, I might add, that continued unabated even while she was busy preparing her own book for the press. It was our joint wish that this volume be dedicated to my father Louis Fraistat and to the memory of my mother Shirley C. Fraistat.

College Park
18 January 1984

Abbreviations

BL Samuel Taylor Coleridge, *Biographia Literaria*

EY Ernest De Selincourt and Chester L. Shaver, eds., *The Letters of William and Dorothy Wordsworth: The Early Years, 1787–1805*

LC Earl Leslie Griggs, ed., *The Collected Letters of Samuel Taylor Coleridge*

LK Hyder Edward Rollins, ed., *The Letters of John Keats, 1814–1821*

LS Frederick L. Jones, ed., *The Letters of Percy Bysshe Shelley*

MY Ernest De Selincourt, Mary Moorman, and Alan G. Hill, eds., *Letters of William and Mary Wordsworth: The Middle Years, 1806–1820*

Owen W. J. B. Owen, ed., *Wordsworth and Coleridge: "Lyrical Ballads" 1798*

Poems Jack Stillinger, ed., *The Poems of John Keats*

Prose Roger Ingpen and Walter E. Peck, eds., *The Complete Works of Percy Bysshe Shelley*

PW Ernest De Selincourt and Helen Darbishire, eds., *The Poetical Works of William Wordsworth*

The Poem and the Book

CHAPTER 1

Ideas of Poetic Order and Ordering

Another vol. will clear off all your anthologic, morning-postian and epistolary miscellanies—but pray dont put Xtobel *therein.—dont* let *that* sweet *maid come forth attended with Lady Holland's mob at her heels. Let there be a separate vol. of Tales, choice tales, ancient Mariners &c.*

Charles Lamb to S. T. Coleridge

Yes, I do think of the construction [*of a book of poems*] *in a certain way. Frost said somewhere . . . that if there are twenty-five poems in a book, the book itself ought to be the twenty-sixth poem.*

James Wright

4 · *The Poem and the Book*

[1]

No doubt, as Charles Lamb warns Coleridge in the letter quoted above, the "*sweet* maid" "Christabel" would have ill suffered the unwashed and unruly company of Coleridge's ephemera as she made her public debut. Thus, with characteristic levity and acuity, Lamb brings home a telling point: poems published within the same volume inevitably interact. A poet can either attempt to control the chemistry of that reaction or passively accept the results.[1] Whenever discrete poetic "texts"—etymologically, something woven—are organized by their author (or coauthors) into a collection, they form what I shall call a "contexture," a larger whole fabricated from integral parts.[2] In other words, Frost's "poem" that is the "book itself" is the contexture of the twenty-five poems it contains. For most major Romantic poets, as we shall see, the organization of a book became a further—and significant—stage of composition.

Unhampered by the need to publish in mass-produced editions, William Blake could experiment with the variety of meanings and effects produced by differing patterns of organization. Each of the twenty-one copies of the *Songs of Innocence*, for example, has a distinctly different structure. Moreover, when Blake joined the *Songs of Innocence* with the *Songs of Experience*, he moved four poems from the former to the latter and created nineteen varying arrangements of the poems in the twenty-seven known copies.[3] Here in its most unadulterated form is the Romantic urge not only to structure, but to restructure, contextures. Wordsworth similarly alters the organization of *Lyrical Ballads* (1798) in 1800, and again in 1802, while the contents and structure of Coleridge's 1796 *Poems on Various Subjects* change both in 1797 and in 1803. New juxtapositions of poems allowed for such rich and varied permutations that one can only speculate upon the sundry shapes the other Romantics might have given their collections had they been in Blake's position.[4]

That Blake's peers did have to reckon with the demands of publishers, however, was a not-so-poetic fact of their literary lives. After all, there are very real constraints on a poet who can publish a collection of lyrics or a long poem only after producing enough material to fill a volume. Yet, if this pressure has forced some poets to publish pieces better left in manuscript, it has also fostered in many a sense of selectivity and purpose: "It is my intention to wait a few years before I publish any minor poems," John Keats wrote to his brother and sister-in-law in January 1819, "and then I hope to have a volume of some worth—and which those people will realish [*sic*] who cannot bear the burthen of a long poem."[5]

If not every one of a poet's works merits printing, neither is it always appropriate to place all publishable poems within the same volume. Coleridge, who apparently heeded Lamb's advice about the presentation of "Christabel," voices a similar concern in a letter to Southey. Should "Christabel" be published as the opening poem of Southey's *Annual Anthology*, says Coleridge in 1799, "it would . . . not harmonize with the *real-life* Poems that follow."[6] Shelley likewise writes to his publisher Charles Ollier: "If I had even intended to publish 'Julian and Maddalo' with my name, yet I would not print it with 'Prometheus.' It would not harmonize." Shortly thereafter, Shelley sent Ollier "poems . . . to print at the end of 'Prometheus' better fitted for that purpose than any in your possession."[7] In the next chapter, we will examine how Byron, with his flair for turning himself into the subject of his own poetry, used discrete but harmonizing poems to fashion a persona from the ensemble.

Of all the Romantics, though, no one had a greater penchant than Wordsworth for what might be called "contextural architecture." In Wordsworth's well-known comparison of his canon to a "gothic Church," *The Prelude* serves as "antechapel" to the main body of *The Recluse*, while his minor works, "when they shall be properly arranged," may be "likened to the little cells, oratories, and sepulchral Recesses, ordinarily included in those edifices."[8] Wordsworth's trope invites the reader to view his works synchronically, as parts of a contextural whole greater than the sum of its parts. The huge recesses of the canon/cathedral not only supply ample room for poems as yet unwritten but also entice the appreciative and curious reader to "enter." Wordsworth even provides a temporal program for the reader's "movements": one must first pass through the "ante-chapel" of *The Prelude* before gaining access to other parts. As poet, priest, and architect, then, Wordsworth creates from his *oeuvre* a sacred edifice, consecrated to the worship of the human imagination.

Of course, Wordsworth's elaborate organization of *Poems* (1815) and his canon as a whole were not without precedent. Since the Alexandrians, if not before, Western poets have recognized that texts are partly determined by their contexture, that the selection and arrangement of poems into collections are important steps in the poetic process. Although a complete historical survey of poetic collections lies far beyond the scope of this study, a brief sketch, with special attention to Dante's *La vita nuova* and Petrarch's *Canzoniere*, will help illuminate the contextural practices of Romantic poets and introduce a number of relevant theoretical issues.

[II]

To a great extent, the physical configuration of the first Western volumes of poetry—Hellenistic book-rolls—dictated the manner in which poems could be read and conditioned the way they were arranged, establishing a set of expectations for both the reader and the poet that is still largely in force today, long after the advent of the codex.[9] One read these earliest poetry books in sequence, carefully locating the beginning and end of each poem in turn, so that at any one time all the lines comprising a single poem would be open to view. After finishing the first poem, the reader rolled up all of its columns except for the last—which presumably included the start of the next poem—and then continued unrolling new columns until the end of the second poem was reached. He then read that poem, repeating the process again and again until the close of the final poem.

The reader's sequential progress through a book-roll encouraged Alexandrian poets to create meaningful juxtapositions, contrasts, and continuities among the poems. Any such effects would be especially heightened once the reader had reached the conclusion of the book and began to rewind the roll. For as he rolled back, the reader's original diachronic understanding of the poems was augmented by a synchronic perception of the book as a whole: "Return," explains John Van Sickle, "would enhance awareness of sequentiality, of the similarities and contrasts among the segments, beginnings, ends, in short of what makes the contents of the roll an articulated ensemble—a book."[10]

Callimachus, who is probably the first Western poet to advise the reader about the shape of his canon, also seems the first to use sophisticated techniques to unify his individual books.[11] In both *Iambs* and *Aetia* (i.e., "legendary origins"), he chooses poems to serve as prologue and epilogue to a larger collection, which itself displays other structural symmetries as well as thematic and imagistic resonance among the poems.[12] Nor is Callimachus the sole Alexandrian author to attend to the selection and arrangement of his poems. *Soros*, an anonymous early book of epigrams, suggests through its title that its diverse poems, like winnowed grain, have been sorted and organized, with all of the chaff removed. Even *The Garland* of Meleager, a selection of poems written by others, shows signs of sophisticated arrangement.[13] In fact, by the time of the Augustans, in "light of what was 'normal' in the making and use of books," poets could have presumed that good readers would as a matter of course respond "to sequential variation, enjoy the play of contrast in return of theme, admire a felicitous change, sense the import of positioning—proximities and deferrals, beginnings, articulations, ends."[14]

It has long been known that Augustan poets such as Horace, Virgil, Propertius, Tibullus, and Ovid were concerned with the structure of their books. Yet while most Augustan books tend to be more homogeneous in meter, subject, and tone than those of the Alexandrians, Horace in the *Odes* (bks. 1–3) appears just as interested as Callimachus in achieving coherence primarily through artful arrangement rather than through uniform selection.[15] In *Odes*, Horace utilizes many Alexandrian organizational strategies, including structural framing and symmetries, as well as the development of thematic progressions and verbal echoes among the poems. Indeed, centuries before Petrarch and Dante, Horace—and his predecessor Catullus—had shown how a recognizable narrative of love could emerge from a collection of discrete lyrics arranged in temporal sequence.[16]

Dante's *La vita nuova* is, however, a new kind of poetic aggregate: the first fictive work blending prose with poetry to provide not only a connective narrative fabric between the poems but also a critical and "autobiographical" commentary upon them. Although most of the thirty-one poems were probably composed before Dante conceived of the book itself, he was able to generate substantial unity in theme and plot by interposing prose passages between carefully organized groupings.[17] Of the thirty-one poems in *La vita nuova*, twenty-eight are sonnets (or short poems) and three are canzoni. From these, Dante devised a symmetrical structure by interspersing each of the canzoni between groups of the shorter poems, so that the book begins and ends with a group of ten short poems and has at its midpoint a single canzone (anticipating Beatrice's death), which is buttressed by a group of four shorter poems on either side.

Both *La vita nuova* and Petrarch's *Canzoniere* were generated by attempts to make from the sonnet's contracted tensions a more expansive statement, elaborating and exploring concerns that as a single unit the sonnet could only imply.[18] To grow, a sonnet needed to be linked with other sonnets and even other forms. Hence, Petrarch followed Dante's break with tradition by mixing a variety of genres in the *Canzoniere*. He, however, increased the mixture greatly.[19] Commingled with the 317 sonnets of the *Canzoniere* are 4 madrigali, 7 ballate, and 29 canzoni, with the last spread throughout to join themes and images introduced in the preceding poems.[20] By merging the perspectives on the world gained from these varied generic "sets" into a larger collective vision, Petrarch created a loosely structured analog to the long poem, which opened up both the generic and thematic range of the sonnet sequence. Thus, in the English Renaissance sequence, although sonnets continued to dominate, they were frequently joined by other companionable kinds. Such poets as Turbervile, Daniel, Barnes, Lodge, Sidney, and Spenser incorporated into their sequences a variety of lyric forms, including epitaphs, epigrams, songs, odes, elegies, and anacreontic verse.[21] Petrarch's positioning of the *Trionfi* at the end of the *Canzoniere*, moreover, provided a model for the later sequences ending in long narrative poems.[22]

Although a great deal has been written about the influence of *La vita nuova* on the *Canzoniere*,[23] the contextural strategies of Dante and Petrarch diverge in important ways. There is a considerable difference, after all, between Dante's grouping of thirty-one short poems with connective prose and Petrarch's arrangement of 366 lyrics into a meaningful whole. Moreover, *La vita nuova* is a work Dante designed once, early in his career, and never subsequently rearranged, whereas the *Canzoniere* continually evolved: Petrarch reorganized it some nine separate times—adding poems, deleting others, and revising the order of the contents. Even its "final" form at Petrarch's death appears to have been left open for additions. Whereas Dante considered *La vita nuova* to be a finished work—a stable contexture—Petrarch conceived of the *Canzoniere* as an elastic form that allowed him to shape and reshape all of the shorter poems he wished to acknowledge publicly within an overarching, if continually refocused, vision.[24] Ultimately, then, although Petrarch bequeathed to later sonneteers a limited and easily exhausted set of conventions, he also left behind a strikingly flexible structural model in which—through a series of heterogeneous short poems written at different times—a poet could maintain shifting, even contradictory, perspectives and, above all, an openness before experience.

[III]

The Petrarchan paradigm had implications for succeeding poetic collections whether or not they were designed as sonnet cycles. For it had shown definitively how a collection of diverse poems might itself aspire toward the complexity and variety of a long poem. After such notable experiments with contextural form as those conducted by Spenser in *The Shepheardes Calendar* and the *Complaints* volume, by Jonson in *The Forest* and *Underwoods*, by Herrick in *Hesperides* and *Noble Numbers*, and by Herbert in *The Temple*,[25] John Dryden produces in *Fables* what Earl Miner has termed "the epic as *cento*." Miner additionally suggests that *Fables*, "unified by links among the individual poems and by repeated treatment of several motifs and subjects," is consciously structured by Dryden as an epic answer to Milton's epics.[26]

There are probably few who agree with Poe that in *Paradise Lost* "what we term a long poem is in effect, merely a succession of brief ones," yet even they might acknowledge that at times the dividing line between a long poem and a poetic aggregate can be thin indeed.[27] For example, not only were each of the four sections of James Thomson's *The Seasons* composed separately, but "Winter" itself, which he wrote and published before the others, appears to have been originally a group of discrete pieces.[28] The distinction between poetic parts and wholes blurs further in what two critics have recently identified as the "major modern genre" in English poetry: a form that is "neither 'long poem' nor 'linked series' but 'sequence.'" As defined by M. L. Rosenthal and Sally M. Gall, the "modern sequence" is a "grouping of mainly lyric poems and passages, rarely uniform in pattern, which tend to interact as an organic whole."[29] Yet by grouping under the rubric of "modern sequence" such diverse works as Emily Dickinson's hand-threaded fascicles, Whitman's *Leaves of Grass*, Pound's *Cantos*, Eliot's *Waste Land*, and Lowell's *Life Studies*, these critics do not help us differentiate between a long poem and a well-integrated aggregate.[30] Under which category should we classify *La vita nuova*? Or *The Shepheardes Calendar*? Or *The Seasons*? Or, for that matter, Byron's *Don Juan*?

We might begin to distinguish a long poem from an aggregate by hypothesizing that, like dependent clauses in a sentence, the parts of a long poem do not have integrity as discrete wholes. However, one could point to sections from works such as *Paradise Lost* or the *Iliad* that can be read as separate poems—say, for example, any of the hymns that frequently appear in each. In fact, there are books in Homer or Virgil and cantos in *Don Juan* that could stand alone as integral "wholes." Perhaps we ought to stipulate instead that unlike the parts of a long poem, *each* part of a contexture must by definition stand as a discrete poem, which would retain its integrity if rearranged within or even removed from the larger whole.[31] Yet if this distinction negates Poe's polemical attempt to classify *Paradise Lost* as a collection and similarly excludes even the episodic *Don Juan*, it nonetheless remains for us to explain how collected individual poems come to be perceived as the parts of a larger whole.

No doubt, the very fact that a poet gathers certain of his works into a single book or collection grants them unity of a sort, implying that the poems share common ground (if only because they are his creations) and that they ought to be read together. However, as Floyd H. Allport's theory of dynamic structuring would suggest, there are many kinds of unity possible in a contexture. Allport conceives of each object in an aggregate as having both an "inside meaning," comprised of its own internal "object character," and an "outside meaning," created when the object is "structured in" as part of a more inclusive order. The "inside" structure of the object itself tends to be stable, predictable, and permanent. But whereas the "outside" structure might also be predictable and relatively permanent, it is more frequently subject to shifts, since an object can be moved readily from one "outer" structure to another. Allport notes as well that inner and outer structures "are not usually operative with an equal degree of energy ('conscious or attentive clearness'): one may be increased at the expense of the other according to circumstances."[32]

Allport's theory, applied to poetic aggregates, would simply suggest that the "outside" meaning of the poems increases in rough proportion to the poet's efforts to unify his collection. He may accomplish this, as we have seen, by carefully arranging poems compatible in subject, theme, image, or voice —or through any number of additional means, including the choice of an appropriate title or epigraph; the composition of poems or prose specifically to preface, open, or close the book; and the use of poetic or prose links between the poems. Perhaps the strongest formal unity is achieved when the poems of a contexture are organized so that each "follows" logically or temporally from the other: presenting a plot, advancing an argument, or appearing in some pattern of serial arrangement (e.g., calendrical, liturgical, numerological). In such arrangements, the "inner" energy of each poem is displaced "outward," and an identifiably unified, progressive structure is generated throughout the collection.

Since outer meaning can be increased only at the expense of inner meaning, the poems in a weakly unified collection are likely to seem disparate as well as discrete. In most sonnet sequences and in collections such as Whitman's *Leaves of Grass* or Herbert's *The Temple*, the inner and outer structural energies approach equilibrium: we are aware of the poems both as discrete units and as members of the larger set they collectively shape. Although such highly unified works as *La vita nuova* or *The Shepheardes Calendar* may tend to lose much of their identity as "collections," it is equally possible that the individual sections of loosely unified "long poems" such as *The Seasons* or Hart Crane's *The Bridge* may acquire enough "inner" meaning during a particular reading to appear virtually as integral poems within a larger collection. Indeed, if received tradition as well as the author's own statements about its structure play a large role in conditioning our perception of the unity characterizing a poetic aggregate, other significant circumstances may vary not only from reader to reader but also between readings.

[IV]

As Stanley Fish might remind us, the "facts" of a text never speak for themselves: we speak for them. And the methodological problems involved in reading a single poem are necessarily compounded in the reading of a collection, because we must account for both the "inner" and "outer" meanings of each poem. Our past experiences as readers of poetry, of particular poets, and of poetic collections all affect what gestaltists call our "set to perceive." We are not likely, therefore, to begin most books of poems expecting to find the kind of formal unity we normally seek in a long poem. After all, we know that poets are under no constraints to unify their collections, nor do they as a rule provide linear sequence or plot in their books. In fact, because the individual poems in a contexture are rarely written to fill a specific place in the whole, the continuities between them are more likely to be associative than causal—and the discontinuities may sometimes be sharp.

As readers, we gather data about the cohesiveness of a volume not only from explicit prefatory material or cues such as titles and epigraphs, but from our growing awareness of the formal and thematic repetitions and modulations among the poems. Thus, our perception of unity in a book depends upon the process Barbara Herrnstein Smith has labeled "retrospective patterning." That is, in the movement from poem to poem, "connections and similarities are illuminated, and the reader perceives that seemingly gratuitous or random events, details, and juxtapositions have been selected in accord with certain principles."[33] The ending of each poem, therefore, is apt to serve as what Fish would call a "perceptual closure," a moment in which inferences about the overall structure of the book can be reevaluated and adjusted. Like the opening poem, which generates our initial expectations, the concluding poem will have special significance in our understanding of the whole, because (as Smith says about the ending of a poem) "it is only at that point that the total pattern—the structural principles which we have been testing—is revealed."[34]

Regardless of whether readers proceed consecutively from beginning to end—presumably the order chosen by the poet—or out of sequence, by the end of the work they are likely to have noted the import of positioning and the relationships between the poems (e.g., common genre, themes, imagery). In books without plot or linear sequence, a reader may even have hypothesized some principles of formal unity to be tested and confirmed by subsequent readings. However, as Fish duly notes, once "the criterion of formal unity is dictated . . . it in turn dictates the setting up of a procedure designed to discover and validate it." In other words, our assumptions as readers and critics have a tendency to be self-fulfilling: we "discover" whatever unity we have presupposed, since "only ingenuity limits the ability of the critic to impose unity of either a cognitive or purely formal kind on his materials."[35] This danger looms largest when we are uncertain that a poet has given attention to the organization of the volume. Even ingenious accounts of the patterns within or the "unity" of a volume may falter before the discovery that the poems were placed at random or selected and arranged by someone other than the poet. Nor is it settling to recognize that the articulation of any pattern in a book will inevitably be at the expense of other, perhaps equally conceivable, schemes. For, as Wolfgang Iser observes, "The moment we try to impose a consistent pattern on the text, discrepancies are bound to arise."[36]

A poetic contexture is thus liable to present a mass of complex data, both tempting and defying the reader to articulate its structure. But before we busy ourselves with plotting coordinate image patterns or mapping the intricate angles of intersection among the poems in a book, we should be careful, in Matthew Santirocco's words, not to sacrifice "texture for architecture." Similarly, while noting that "Homer, Virgil, Catullus, Ovid, Propertius and doubtless others have been explicated with complex diagrams and numerical ratios," Charles Segal warns that the danger in developing abstract analytic or numerological patterns to explain a work is that they, "in their abstractional purity, lead us farther and farther away from the primary experience of the work as poetry . . . [and] if developed beyond a certain point, lack any connection with either our fictions or our lives."[37]

In fact, we must reckon with the possibility that a poet has deliberately avoided neat patterns of any kind in assembling a book. It is clear, for instance, that there are verbal and conceptual links among the poems in Herbert's *The Temple* that add to the larger unifying pressure of the book's metaphoric title. Nonetheless, Rosalie Colie points out shrewdly that the volume as a whole "resists schemes to organize it into a consistent structure." Colie argues that all attempts to do so—and there have been many—not only risk distorting the poems but invariably miss Herbert's reason for avoiding a rigidly articulated structure: "in good Protestant form, [Herbert] planned to call upon a reader's ever-revived capacity to contribute to his own revelation."[38]

In a similar way, Robert Gleckner hypothesizes that William Blake is attempting an "anti-book" in *Poetical Sketches* by militantly avoiding cycle or sequence in arrangement and by refusing to give the book as a whole strong closure, though the poems throughout are related thematically and imagistically. Blake's purpose in such an arrangement, according to Gleckner, is to deter "casual perusal and 'normal' reader expectation," thereby forcing the reader to comprehend imaginatively the "allusive intertextuality" of the whole.[39] In other words, by rejecting any overall sequential patterns, Blake insists that his volume be understood as a synchronic structure whose unity is perceivable only to the reader approaching it on what he calls elsewhere the "fiery wings of Contemplation."

Dissatisfied with past readers' attempts to force rigid structure on resistant material, both Colie and Gleckner might themselves be accused of finessing structural problems in *The*

Temple and *Poetical Sketches* by providing such cogent rationales for the absence of consistent patterns. Although their accounts seem conformable to the "facts" of the books as well as the vision of each poet, neither Colie nor Gleckner is completely free of the kind of ingenuity that Fish warns against. Nor, for that matter, is any critic. Yet, if by forswearing silence a critic is bound to "falsify" somewhat the complexities of a text or collection, then Colie and Gleckner at least demonstrate that, when a critic treats data responsibly and imaginatively, the process of delimiting need not be merely limiting.

[V]

As readers we tend to bestow unity of a sort on a volume even when no formal principles are apparent. Jonathan Culler notes that while reading a single poem our "major device of order is . . . the notion of the person or speaking subject . . . and even poems which make it difficult to construct a poetic persona rely for their effects on the fact that their reader will try to construct an enunciative posture."[40] It is true, furthermore, that we are wont to synthesize the subjects, themes, and genres of a contexture into the preoccupations and perspectives of a "speaker" (present or implied) who is responsible for them all. This speaker's voice is "revealed" to us in the verbal and imagistic echoes among the poems as well as in their individual rhetorical, metrical, and grammatical structures. S. K. Heninger has shown, for example, that the twelve eclogues of the *Shepheardes Calendar* "taken in their entirety are a comprehensive projection of Spenser himself in 1579."[41] That is to say, as we read a volume by a single poet, part of the outer structural energy of each poem will be directed toward fashioning and reflecting an image of the poet.[42]

By placing his poems in a book united primarily by his own presence, then, a poet may create a coherent perceptual field. Alphonse De Lamartine's reliance on this premise is demonstrated vividly in the Avertisement to the *Harmonies poetiques et religieuses*:

> Here are four books of poetry written just as they were felt, not arranged into any particular order or sequence: like nature, which has an order without showing it; genuine poems, devoid of pose, the testimony less of the poet than of the human being, the intimate experiences day by day, pages from his inner life, prompted on occasion by sadness, at others by joy, by solitude and by the world, by despair or by hope, at times of sterility or inspiration, of fervour or perfidy.[43]

However purple his prose, De Lamartine's insight is sound. Poets can literally "publicize" themselves in their books, fashioning a public identity through the process of selection and arrangement. English poets as diverse as Spenser, Jonson, Milton, Pope, and Byron were all adept at using the poetic volume as a form of self-fashioning and self-advertisement.[44] For instance, William Riley Parker observes that Milton published his first collection, *The Poems of Mr. John Milton*, in 1645, "when he had felt dirtied by the unexpected notoriety of his divorce tracts, and worried about his public image." Parker asks rhetorically, "Was it only coincidence that in 1673, when he was chafing at the latest attacks upon his reputation, he decided to bring out a second edition of his minor verse?"[45] Important for what they can tell us about Milton's sense of himself as poet and the way he wished to be perceived by his contemporaries, these two volumes are also significant as paradigms of how miscellaneous poems, written on several occasions (as we are told on both title pages), can nonetheless present a coherent perceptual field, unified by a distinct persona, resonant effects, and structural symmetries.

With original verse in four languages as well as a wide range of subjects and kinds, *The Poems of Mr. John Milton* represents its author as a learned and urbane poet, who, as the inserted commendatory verses by Manso, Salzilli, and others indicate, is already admired by prominent European contemporaries. These poems, which comprise most of Milton's minor verse written before 1645, are divided into two sections with separate title pages: the first contains the English and Italian poems, the second the Latin and Greek. Within each section poems are grouped primarily by genre and then, within each grouping, by rough chronology.[46] Yet through variations from this pattern and in the larger thematic and generic progressions in the collection, Milton is able to fashion a statement about his own ascent from youthful pastoral poet to maturing poet-prophet. "The whole volume," as Louis Martz remarks, "has been arranged to convey a sense of the predestined bard's rising powers."[47]

The Virgilian nature of this project is highlighted by the epigraph on the initial title page, culled from Virgil's seventh eclogue and referring to the singer as a "predestined bard" —"Baccare frontem / Cingite, ne vati noceat mala lingua futuro."[48] Moreover, both the opening and closing poems have been positioned out of chronological sequence to establish a frame for the book. Indeed, read within the context of the volume, the opening "Ode on Christ's Nativity" concerns both the birth of Christ as man and that of Milton as the poet destined to explore in his work the full implications of Christ's life and death.[49] And "Epitaphium Damonis," the closing poem, becomes not only a look backward, "a farewell to . . . the pleasures of pastoral poetry,"[50] but also an anticipation of the great prophetic poetry to come, so ably foreshadowed in the central grouping of the book—"Arcades," "Lycidas," and "Comus"—all of which, as Joseph Wittreich has shown, involve the transformation of pastoral poetry into visionary forms.[51]

In 1673, when Milton revised *Poems* into *Poems upon Several Occasions*, he dropped the epigraph—his emphasis had shifted from preparation and ascent to arrival and mission. Thus, "Ad Joannem Rousium," a new concluding poem, is added, which playfully assesses the earlier volume as "shining with unlabored elegance which a hand once young imparted —a careful hand, but hardly that of one who was too much a poet" (ll. 2–3).[52] The matured poet, assured of his own place "among the sublime names of authors who were the ancient lights and the true glory of the Greek and Latin race" (ll. 70–72), is already an embattled prophet calling for the regeneration of vision in England: "What deity will summon our fostering studies and recall the Muses who have been left with hardly a retreat anywhere in all the confines of England?" (ll. 30–32).

As if in support of his plea, Milton nets into the collection, as its final piece, the prose essay "Of Education," with its program for liberating the visionary energies of English youths. Fittingly, then, *Poems upon Several Occasions* concludes with a public and hortatory piece that resolves those tensions between pagan classicism and English Protestantism signaled by the book's very division into two sections and made apparent by the contrasts between the Nativity Ode and "Elegia Sexta" as well as "Lycidas" and "Epitaphium Damonis." The hierarchical scheme outlined in the essay subsumes the classics within a larger system of learning whose final issue is an understanding of "what religious, what glorious and magnificent use might be made of poetry, both in divine and human things" (p. 637). Emphatically British and Protestant in its vision, "Of Education" calls for all the Lord's people to be prepared as prophets, "fraught with an universal insight into things" (p. 637).

In both *Poems* and *Poems upon Several Occasions*, especially in such paired poems as the Nativity Ode and "The Passion," and "L'Allegro" and "Il Penseroso," Milton would seem to insist that the poet-prophet needs double vision: aware of deep joys, he must also be aware of abiding sorrows, of loss.[53] By adding in 1673 "On the Death of a Fair Infant" and "Methought I Saw My Late Espoused Saint" to an already formidable array of elegies and epitaphs, Milton highlights the radical losses to which humanity is subject and helps to underscore the thematic centrality to the whole book of "Lycidas," its single most profound meditation on loss and restoration.[54]

In fact, when Geoffrey Hartman comments upon Milton's achievement in "Lycidas," he could just as easily be describing the volume within which it is published: "In *Lycidas* Milton is also concerned with the destiny of the poetical spirit, its relation to the classics and the Bible, and with the role of an English poet in that destiny. It is he who linked the themes of liberty and poetry; and it is also he, in *Lycidas* as elsewhere, who associated poetry and the spirit of prophecy."[55] Whereas we now recognize precisely these interlocking themes as an important part of Milton's legacy to tradition and, particularly, to the Romantics, we rarely note that they were first joined on a large scale in Milton's 1645 collection. Ever the master of his craft, Milton fashioned his miscellaneous books into profound explorations of the appropriate roles for poetry and the poet, while at the same time seizing the opportunity they afforded him to become his own creator—to invent and publicize his own identity as poet-prophet.[56]

[VI]

The title Petrarch himself chose for the *Canzoniere—Rerum vulgarium fragmenta* (Fragments of vernacular poetry)—most fully illuminates the special nature of the poetic aggregate. For if the radical incompleteness of any one short poem as an act of vision renders it essentially a "fragment," Petrarch implies that such fragments can be gathered and assimilated into the multiplicity comprising the collection as a whole. As evidenced by the title of his *Sybilline Leaves: A Collection of Poems* (1817), Coleridge shared Petrarch's view. "The following collection," he writes in the preface, "has been entitled Sibylline Leaves in allusion to the fragmentary and widely scattered state in which they have been long suffered to remain" (p. 4). And, as Coleridge expected his reader to know, to piece together the scattered leaves of the Sibyl is to discover the contents of a prophecy. Indeed, the chance to build a poetic whole from disparate "fragments"—to fashion, to adapt Coleridge's term, a kind of unity from multeity—had special significance for the Romantics, who were themselves exploring the meaning of life within a world that seemed increasingly fragmented.

Robert Durling, observing that Petrarch may have been the first to use the term "fragment" to describe a work of art, perceives the collective form of the *Canzoniere* as reflecting the "provisional, even threatened nature of the integration of experience possible for natural man."[57] The fact that the poetic book could be used as a vehicle through which the vision of one poem could be supported, qualified, or supplanted by the next, made it—to many Romantics—more than just a mere necessity for publishing their poems. Robert Gleckner has recently commented upon the "Romantic poets' habitual clustering of reciprocally active poems."[58] Yet, with the exceptions of *Lyrical Ballads* and *Songs of Innocence and of Experience*, critics have failed for the most part to consider the arrangement of Romantic poetry in volumes. Even critics of *Lyrical Ballads* tend to focus on the issue of its contemporaneity or on selected individual poems rather than on questions about the poems as a unit. Nor, despite the frequency with which Romantic poets themselves discussed such issues, is there a study of their contextural practices. As readers, we are poorer for this neglect. For until we better understand these practices and begin reading poems within the structures devised by their authors, we will, in a real way, continue to misread them—losing, in effect, the "poem" that is the "book itself."

CHAPTER 2

Forms of Coherence in Romantic Poetic Volumes

[T]o arrange . . . and fit [The Warrior's Return, and Other Poems *(1808)*] *for publication has been the amusement of many hours of retirement.*

Amelia Opie

. . . for him who reads with reflection, the arrangement [of Poems *(1815)*] *will serve as a commentary unostentatiously directing his attention to my purposes, both particular and general.*

William Wordsworth

[1]

Spurred by hopes of profit and of critical success, so many poets assembled volumes for the press during the Romantic Period that by 1809 a somewhat imperious John Cam Hobhouse complained that "the world at present suffers from a glut of [poetic] books."[1] No less remarkable than the sheer number of volumes issuing at the time from presses is that their authors spanned virtually the entire social spectrum, from rustics and tradespeople to bluestockings and aristocrats. And given the nettlesome critics of the day, most contemporary poets, regardless of their social standing, were justifiably worried about the reception of their books.[2] A young Lord Byron speaks for many when he prefaces *Hours of Idleness* (1807) with the assertion, "I have hazarded my reputation and feelings in publishing this volume" (p. vi).

Through good judgment in the selection of poems, a poet could be shown publicly to best advantage. Ian Jack notes, for instance, that whereas the poems selected for *The Village Minstrel* were "apparently intended to demonstrate the sheer bulk of Clare's output," *The Shepherd's Calendar* volume was organized to emphasize instead "the types of poetry at which he excelled."[3] Yet publishing a collection instead of a single long poem had other recognized advantages as well. Anticipating Poe by several years, Joanna Baillie remarks in the preface to *Metrical Legends of Exalted Characters* (1821): "I have made each Legend short enough to be read in one moderate sitting, that the impression might be undivided, and that the weariness of a story, not varied or enriched by minuter circumstances, might be, if possible, avoided" (p. xiii).

Contemporary poets were discovering firsthand the truth of Coleridge's dictum about the necessary "organic" relationship obtaining between the "pleasures" of the parts and the pleasure given by the whole.[4] Moreover, they were conscious that many readers would not abide the tedium of a long poem and that critics especially would be quick to squelch those poets with pretensions to writing epics. After *Endymion* had failed with the public and inspired reviewers to notorious excesses,

Keats hoped yet to produce a collection that would win popular acclaim.[5] John Clare, who shared the same publisher as Keats, also shared a similar conviction. He wrote to John Taylor: "I think a series of little poems connected by a string as it were in point of narrative woud [*sic*] do better than a canto poem to please critics."[6]

On a wider scale than ever before, poets were now self-conscious about their contextural practices, and their fear of critics played a significant role in establishing this awareness.[7] Nonetheless, the kind of preconceived linearity that Clare describes to Taylor is rare in collections of the period. More frequently, it would seem, poets grouped together and arranged works that were initially written as discrete entities—some poets with little apparent care about the integrity of their volumes, others with a clear sense of purpose. With dilettantish pleasure, Amelia Opie comments upon her "amusement" in selecting and arranging the poems for *The Warrior's Return, and Other Poems* (1808). George Dyer speaks more earnestly of his attempts to control the "subject and design" of *Poems* (1800), a volume that "pursues a track of reading not hastily entered upon, nor to be relinquished at random" (p. lviii). Wordsworth's own pains to explicate the organization of *Poems* (1815) for the "attentive Reader" is but one telling example of the self-consciousness with which the major poets also assembled their books.

Much in the preceding chapter would suggest that we have overlooked the integrity of important Romantic collections simply because we have not known what kind of coherence to seek. A more detailed look at typical contemporary strategies for shaping collections will elucidate the kinds of poetic aggregates the best poets were fashioning in their books. Such a study will, in addition, provide the backdrop for our further consideration of three great—and largely neglected—Romantic achievements in contextural form: Wordsworth and Coleridge's *Lyrical Ballads, with a Few Other Poems* (1798), Keats's *Lamia, Isabella, The Eve of St. Agnes, and Other Poems* (1820), and Shelley's *Prometheus Unbound, with Other Poems* (1820).

[II]

An anatomy of Romantic collections might usefully begin by considering the two types most prominent early in the eighteenth century: "Works" and "Poems on Various Subjects." "Works" generally designated collections by classical authors, recent modern authors with an assured place in literary history, and well-established living authors near the end of their careers. By contrast, "Poems on Various Subjects" was used for collections by poets as yet unestablished, posthumous collections of minor poets, and collections admittedly containing juvenilia. In sum, the title "Works" is associated with canon formation and implies that the poet is sufficiently important to have established a public canon. "Poems on Various Subjects" is a more modest title, indicative of selected miscellaneous pieces that are intended to show a poet's mastery over a range of genres and subjects.[8] The former announces that a poet is securely at home in literary tradition, the latter that he is knocking at the door.

Such a distinction still largely remained in force at the beginning of the nineteenth century. Although the first authorized edition of Byron's *Works* was published in 1815, neither Shelley nor Keats lived to publish a "Works," and both Wordsworth and Coleridge waited until relatively late in their careers before doing so. In fact, given the canon-making status of Wordsworth's 1815 *Poems* and Coleridge's 1817 *Sybilline Leaves: A Collection of Poems*, both collections are modestly titled—though, as we have seen, Coleridge's title has its own important implications. In comparison with the major poets, Leigh Hunt manifests his own pretensions by publishing a three-volume *Poetical Works* in 1819. The popular, if facile, Barry Cornwall similarly reveals his sense of self-importance by printing a *Poetical Works* in 1822 (at the age of thirty-five), whereas Walter Scott—perhaps to show the secondary role he ascribed to his poetry—simply titles his collected verse *Miscellaneous Poetry* (1820).

Purposely heterogeneous in genre and subject, the most typical volume of the day was entitled "Poems on Various

Subjects" (e.g., Coleridge, 1796, and Byron, 1807), or merely "Poems" (e.g., Wordsworth, 1807 and 1815; Keats, 1817).[9] Because relatively distinguished verse might appear in volumes so named, several minor poets resorted to meeker, even self-deprecatory titles in order to offset criticism (e.g., "Parnassian Trifles," or "Poems, by an Amateur"). Byron's own first volume was rather timidly called "Fugitive Poems," and Blake's appeared as "Poetical Sketches" (though Blake himself apparently did not choose this title). Conversely, "Poems Original and Translated" was a more ambitious title for this sort of miscellaneous book, produced usually by poets eager to flaunt their erudition or—as it often turned out instead—their public school education.

Another common type of volume was built around one long piece, meant to be impressive, followed by a miscellaneous group of poems that frequently were little more than filler, as, for instance, in George Darley's 1822 *The Errors of Ecstacie: A Dramatic Poem, with Other Pieces*, and Barry Cornwall's 1820 *A Sicilian Story, and Other Poems*. This kind of format, used characteristically by Shelley, received its most ingenious development in his *Prometheus Unbound, with Other Poems*, where the title poem forms an integral and complex unit with the poems that follow. A related but somewhat less common format consisted of two set pieces plus filler, as in George Croly's 1820 *The Angel of the World: An Arabian Tale; Sebastian: A Spanish Tale, with Other Poems*. One might well wonder if the title of Keats's 1820 *Lamia, Isabella, The Eve of St. Agnes, and Other Poems* was meant to suggest the unusual depth of the collection, since three pieces were rarely singled out in the title of a book unless they comprised its entire contents. In any case, Keats's 1820 volume, like Shelley's, is remarkable for the complex interrelations among its apparently miscellaneous poems.

Many contemporary volumes more homogeneous in subject, genre, or style than those we have so far considered derived their coherence from the poet's conscious interplay with his audience. That is, to a great extent, popular taste, as well as contemporary debates over issues moral and political, exerted their pull on the shape of Romantic volumes. For example, the unity of subject in William Sotheby's *Farewell to Italy, and Occasional Poems* (1818) is fashioned by the contemporary fondness for travelogues, while books such as Felicia Hemans's devotional *Scenes and Hymns of Life, with Other Poems* (1834) were designed to appeal to popular religious sentiments.[10] With the revival of poetic genres in full swing by the end of the eighteenth century, poets by the score capitalized on the seemingly insatiable contemporary appetite for sonnets or antiquated ballads. Anna Seward's 1799 *Original Sonnets on Various Subjects* and W. H. Ireland's 1801 *Ballads in Imitation of the Antient* are but two of the many collections uniform in genre.[11] A book such as *Lyrical Ballads, with a Few Other Poems* was, of course, capitalizing on such generic trends, while simultaneously countering a spate of volumes epitomized by Robert Bloomfield's later *Wildflowers: Or Pastoral and Local Poetry* (1806), which treated—to the sentimental delight of urban audiences—rural poverty as pastoral idyll. "It will be observed," notes Bloomfield in the preface, "that all my pictures are from humble life, and most of my heroines servant maids" (p. vii).

The passion for rural subjects and peasant bards, which was responsible in the eighteenth century for the astonishing popularity of Stephen Duck's *Poems on Several Subjects* (1730) and many subsequent imitations, continued later as a rage for "original geniuses" and "untutored bards" like Ossian. Although this trend guaranteed a host of truly artless and shapeless collections, it also helped to make an instant success of more sophisticated efforts, such as Burns's 1786 *Poems, Chiefly in the Scottish Dialect* (commonly referred to as the Kilmarnock edition) and Clare's 1820 *Poems: Descriptive of Rural Life and Scenery*. Clare's volume, like Burns's, ends with a glossary, indicating that the cosmopolitan English reader has entered a world from which he is at least partially cut off—a world whose integrity is symbolized by the very language used to depict it.

Even without the sullen didacticism of a Thomas Tompkins, who edits *Poems on Various Subjects; Selected to Enforce the Practice of Virtue* (1795), several poets attempted through their collections to "improve" or educate their readers. James Montgomery's 1809 *Poems on the Abolition of the Slave Trade* is unified by the impassioned argument sustained throughout the individual poems, as is Joseph Cottle's earlier, and slightly less cohesive, antiwar *Poems* (1795). Cottle, in fact, claims to be presenting his collection to the public "not from a fond persuasion of its merit, but from a belief that it is the duty of every man to inspire the . . . abhorrence [of war] in the breasts of others" (p. ii).[12]

Patrick Brontë's 1811 *Cottage Poems* results from an attempt to edify and educate "the lower classes of society" (p. viii). Both in subject and style, these poems typify the sentimental condescension with which the poor were increasingly treated. Seemingly without conscious irony or arrogance, Brontë writes in the preface: "For the convenience of the unlearned and poor, the Author has not written much, and has endeavoured not to burthen his subjects with matter, and as much as he well could, has aimed at simplicity, plainness and perspicuity both in manner and style" (pp. vii–viii). When Shelley contemplated assembling a collection written in a plain style, he had in mind a larger, more openly dissatisfied audience than Brontë's tractable "unlearned and poor." Writing from Italy in 1820, Shelley asks if Leigh Hunt knows of "any bookseller who would like to publish a little volume of *popular songs* wholly political & destined to awaken & direct the imagination of the reformers."[13]

In general, minor poets—particularly those publishing by subscription—wrote for a limited audience, composed primarily of friends, acquaintances, and well-wishers; and they selected their poems accordingly. Thus, the Reverend John Anketell included a rather lame group of acrostics in *Poems on Several Occasions* (1793), "merely from an idea that they are the property of my subscribers, which, therefore, common honesty requires me not to with-hold from them" (p. xxiii). Elizabeth Bentley even went so far as to conclude *Genuine Poetical Compositions on Various Subjects* (1791)—which garnered 1,931 subscribers—with "Lines Addressed as a Tribute of Gratitude to the Subscribers in General." One presumes as well that there is no coincidence in Bernard Barton's inclusion of the adulatory "Verses to William Wordsworth" in *Poems, by an Amateur* (1818), a volume to which Wordsworth himself subscribed.[14]

[III]

Our evidence reinforces what logic would suggest: works in the collections of most minor poets were not selected with any profound concern for the unity of the whole. Yet all contemporary poets, as M. H. Abrams has shown, could expect their poetry to be read as an index of their own personalities;[15] and if this sometimes made for acute anxieties, it also provided special opportunities. Even without any elaborate organizational scheme, for example, a collection could easily acquire unity through the voice and persona of the poet. The more a poet brought himself to the reader's attention—say, in a preface or notes—the more his miscellaneous poems appeared to be related statements of his own preoccupations and talents.

Thomas Moore exploits this fact in his 1801 *Poetical Works of the late Thomas Little, Esquire*, while simultaneously deflecting attention away from his own personality. That is, in creating a fictive author responsible for these diverse lyrics, Moore gives a conceptual unity to the whole: each poem ostensibly reflects the mind of a poet who, as Moore in his guise as an editor explains at the beginning of his preface, "died in his one and twentieth year," never intending his poems "to pass beyond the circle of his friends." Clearly, here, too, is a means of protecting from harsh criticism a miscellaneous collection of light-hearted and amatory verse that represented in fact much of Moore's own juvenilia.[16]

More straightforward, George Dyer remarks in the preface to *Poems* (1800), "I have studied to make my volume as miscellaneous as possible, and am, indeed, frequently sportive, or dramatic outwardly, when I am inwardly sad or serious." Although his poems are varied for the pleasure of his audience,

Dyer hastens to apprise the reader that his own personality informs them all: "I have sometimes taken the poet's liberty, by introducing fiction, and speaking in a feigned character, though I no where sacrifice *sincerity* to fiction" (p. xxxvi). Dyer's comments would suggest that some other ordering or selection of poems might open his volume to charges of "insincerity." After all, when the integrity of a volume becomes equated with the integrity of the poet's personality, "sincerity" may well become an evaluative criterion and, even, an organizational principle. What then of the poet who purposely organizes his poems as a means of self-fashioning and self-promotion? We have already seen the skill with which Milton fabricated a public image through a collection of miscellaneous poems; a poet such as Byron was no less adept.

On the one hand, Byron counted on the reader to understand his first published collection, *Hours of Idleness*, as a sincere reflection of his own personality, and through references in the poems and notes to circumstances in his own life, he actively encouraged such a perception. On the other hand, however, sincerity was largely irrelevant to Byron's aim of designing the collection as a medium for self-dramatization. "The most significant fact about *Hours of Idleness*," says Jerome McGann, "is that in it we observe Byron trying to organize a series of disparate lyrics into a coherent self-portrait."[17] To insure that this self-portrait was sufficiently flattering, Byron worked hard at revising its form, producing a total of four different versions. For instance, after hearing complaints that his initial effort *Fugitive Poems* (1806) was too ribald, Byron revised the contents and reordered the whole, producing a markedly chaster version in *Poems on Various Subjects* (1807).[18] Still dissatisfied, he reorganized the collection twice more within two years, first in *Hours of Idleness: A Series of Poems Original and Translated* (1807), then in *Poems Original and Translated* (1808).[19] In this final version Byron sophisticated his image by dropping all the lighter pieces as well as the preface with its defensive posing, while adding five poems that intensify what Robert Gleckner has called the "aura of loss" in the volume.[20] The sometimes ironic, disillusioned voice ultimately emerging from the entire collection nonetheless seems both noble in its aspirations and almost tragically haunted by its own past: Byron thereby incarnated himself as the original Byronic hero.[21]

However adolescent yet as a poet, Byron was unquestionably successful in making himself the focal point of his collection, as the following excerpt from the *Critical Review* for September 1807 demonstrates: "Valuable, as this little collection [*Hours of Idleness*] is, from its intrinsic merit, it is rendered much more so by the mind which produced and pervades it" (p. 53). In effect, the volume served to introduce Byron as a public figure as much as to announce his arrival as a poet, allowing him to establish and experiment with his own personal myth.

Perhaps Burns's Kilmarnock edition, of all important contemporary volumes, comes closest to Byron's in the way it mythologizes the poet himself. Commenting shrewdly upon Burns's desire for the reader "to perceive a larger psychological unity obtaining among his disparate lyrics," McGann notes that the volume "amounts to one man's observation upon himself and his culture, and achieves a coherence by means of a mythic personality very dear to the nineteenth century—one 'bred to the Plough, and . . . independent.' "[22] The epigraph to the Kilmarnock edition portrays Burns as a "Simple Bard, unbroke by rules of Art, . . . / And if inspir'd, tis Nature's pow'rs inspire" (ll. 1–3). Burns thus appears full-blown upon the poetic scene, already an inspired, if "Simple," bard at the height of his powers.

Whereas a "natural" genius such as Burns had no call to shape his book to emphasize his poetic development, both of Keats's collections work to dramatize the poet's growth and self-discovery. Jack Stillinger has observed, for instance, that throughout *Poems* (1817) Keats probes his own identity as a poet.[23] This investigation, moreover, proceeds specifically as a consideration of the pleasures and insufficiencies of pastoral, climaxing in "Sleep and Poetry," the final poem of the volume, in which Keats dedicates himself to forsaking pastoral for a poetic that will openly encounter "The agonies, the strife / Of human hearts."[24] In other words, *Poems* depicts Keats as a rising bard, much along the Virgilian pattern of generic ascent followed by Milton in *Poems* (1645) and Pope in *Works* (1717).

The progression from pastoral piper to prophetic bard is also charted in Blake's *Songs of Innocence and of Experience*, if in less immediately personal terms. There, through the use of dramatic personas, Blake fashions his own fiction of poetic ascent, moving from Piper to Bard until—in seven of the eight last copies—he ends by speaking as the Ancient Bard, in a prophetic voice transcending the limitations of both the pastoral world of innocence and the disillusioned world of experience.[25]

One finds this same pattern more broadly articulated in Coleridge's 1796 *Poems on Various Subjects*, an admitted collection of juvenilia, which ends in the prophetic mode of "Religious Musings." "By its location," James Averill says of the concluding poem, "this Miltonic rumination on things past, present, and to come promises the reader that the author is an ambitious poet who will produce greater things in the fullness of time." Coleridge himself believed that such contextural dramas of growth might be further developed by poets who arranged their collected works chronologically: "After all you can say," he told Henry Nelson Coleridge, "I still think the chronological order the best for arranging a poet's works. All your divisions are in particular instances inadequate, and they destroy the interest which arises from watching the progress, maturity, and even the decay of genius."[26] A canon so arranged, it seemed to Coleridge, shapes the collective significance of its individual poems into a narrative concerning the rise and fall of the poet's imagination. The poems themselves thus cohere as an extended self-portrait of the poet.

Wordsworth strongly objected to chronological arrangement on just these grounds. According to R. P. Graves, Wordsworth said that "such a proceeding would indicate on the part of the poet an amount of egotism, placing interest in himself above interests in the subjects being treated by him, which could not belong to a true poet caring for the elements of poetry in their right proportion, and designing to bring upon the minds of his readers the best influences at his command in the way best calculated to make them effectual."[27] One might well pause over such a statement, considering that it issued from a man who had written the longest poem in English literature about the growth of his own mind.

Yet there is important substance in Wordsworth's remarks. Whereas *The Prelude* is expressly designed as self-portraiture—a verbal picture to preface the canon—Wordsworth's collected poems themselves are elaborately arranged to deflect attention away from the poet's personality and toward the thematic core of the poems themselves. This deflection may have been prompted, as Jared Curtis believes, by critical attacks on the more personal poems in the 1807 collection.[28] It may even have been a means of psychological self-defense for Wordsworth, a way of distancing himself from the reader (and potential critic). The autobiographical *Prelude*, after all, was only to be published posthumously. But the fact remains that Wordsworth was a self-styled poet-prophet: his contextural strategies, insofar as they are self-reflexive, tend to emphasize office rather than personality.

In Wordsworth's view, the "true poet" is most concerned with the affective properties of his work, the influence he can bring to bear upon the reader's mind. As prophet, he is necessarily a public figure whose private emotional life and self-glorifications might serve only to distract the reader from the real significance of his poetry or even trivialize its import—prophecy, in essence, is an impersonal art. However, if in this elevation of office over personality Wordsworth's contextural practices are distinguishable from those of a poet such as Byron, the difference is in degree rather than kind. All of the major Romantics used their collections as a means of self-fashioning, and the distinctive personalities they projected through their books worked as shaping and unifying forces—even when other structural principles played more important roles.

[IV]

Unlike many of his contemporaries, Wordsworth was not satisfied with arrangements simply based on chronology or principles of contrast and variety. As he expanded *Lyrical Ballads* into two volumes, however, he must have discovered that the arrangement of so many small pieces posed a special challenge for one who wished to control the reader's experience of the whole.[29] In such collections, one poem "stands in the way of the other," as Wordsworth later complained to Sir George Beaumont in November 1806. "They must either be read a few at once, or the Book must remain some time by one before a judgement can be made of the quantity of thought and feeling and imagery it contains . . . and what variety of moods and mind it can either impart or is suited to" (*MY*, 1:95).

To solve this problem, Wordsworth experimented in his 1807 *Poems, in Two Volumes* with a system of subsections, each of which maintained its own integrity. As Wordsworth explained to Lady Beaumont in a letter written 21 May 1807, the poems within each section were to be valued not only in themselves but for their context within the larger group. The sonnets on liberty, for example, "each fix the attention upon some important sentiment separately considered . . . [but] at the same time collectively make a Poem on the subject of civil Liberty and national independence, which, either for simplicity of style or grandeur of moral sentiment, is, alas! likely to have few parallels in the Poetry of the present day" (*MY*, 1:147).

But such a "Poem" was only marginally connected with those formed by the other sections. In order to create a "legitimate whole" from "poems apparently miscellaneous," Wordsworth developed a more elaborate system of organization in *Poems* (1815), whereby poems were first arranged according to subject, genre, chronology, or even the mental faculty most prominent in their inception (e.g., "Poems of the Fancy," "Poems of the Imagination"). For the sake of providing the collection with the "three requisites of a legitimate whole, a beginning, a middle, and an end," these groups were then ordered internally to simulate a temporal progression "corresponding with the course of human life, . . . commencing with Childhood, and terminating with Old Age, Death, and Immortality" (pp. xiii–xiv). In this way, Wordsworth evolved for his numerous short pieces a structure that not only was coherent but would also, he hoped, direct the reader to his "purposes, both particular and general."[30]

Though several other Romantics organized their poems by categories, no one developed an aesthetic plan matching Wordsworth's in sophistication or conceptual unity. The poems of *Sybilline Leaves*, published two years after Wordsworth's 1815 collection, were grouped primarily by subject and genre. More often, as in Bryan Waller's *Poems on Several Occasions* (1796), poems were arranged within a book according to genre alone.[31] However, chronology could add further structure to a generically organized group: for instance, George Dyer (referring to himself in the third person) comments that the odes in *Poems* (1792) "are printed in the order as nearly as he can recollect, in which he wrote them" (p. vii). As one might also expect, some books were organized solely by chronology. Charles Lamb, who proofread and arranged for Longman the 1803 edition of Coleridge's *Poems on Various Subjects*, writes to the author: "Longman wanted the Ode [i.e., "Ode to the Departing Year"] first, but the arrangemt. I have made is precisely that mark'd out in the Dedication, following the order of time."[32]

Occasionally poets ordered their poems in a linear pattern suggested by their subject matter. In *Walks in a Forest; Or Poems Descriptive of Scenery of a Forest at Different Seasons of the Year* (1796), Thomas Gisborne, prompted perhaps by Cowper's organization of *The Task*, divided his volume into six walks spanning the course of the year, beginning with "Walk the First: Spring" and ending with "Walk the Sixth: Winter —Frost." Thomas Moore in *Epistles, Odes, and Other Poems* (1806)—a book of poems composed during a trip to North America—apologizes to the readers "for intruding upon their notice a mass of unconnected trifles, such a world of epicurean atoms as I have here brought in conflict together" (p. x). To organize and loosely unify the whole, Moore arranges the poems to follow the order of his travels. Many explicitly refer to their settings, and a series of numbered and dated epistles (e.g., "Epistle III, Bermuda, January 1804") are spaced throughout as structural pillars—much like the canzoni in Petrarch's *Canzoniere*—gathering and developing the themes and images appearing in the preceding poems.[33]

Many contemporary books, including those that otherwise have little coherence, contain pairs or clusters of interrelated poems. These poems, to take a few well-known examples from Wordsworth's canon, may "answer" each other thematically like "Expostulation and Reply" and "The Tables Turned" in *Lyrical Ballads* (1798), or constitute a suite of formally and thematically related works like the twenty-six "Sonnets Dedicated to Liberty" in *Poems* (1807), or even tell a "story" like the five "Lucy" poems in *Lyrical Ballads* (1800). John Anketell's *Poems on Several Subjects* includes two other typical suites: one on the ages of man—"On Age," "On Life," and "On Death"; the other on the diurnal rhythm—"On Morning," "On Noon," "On Evening," and "On Night."[34] Nor did spatial contiguity alone govern the relationship between poems. A few thoughtful poets developed structural symmetries and synchronic connections in their books by spreading thematically related pieces throughout, just as Moore does in *Epistles, Odes, and Other Poems*—or as Blake in *Songs of Innocence and of Experience*, where paired poems are routinely placed apart.

Even the most randomly ordered collections of the day usually followed certain principles of arrangement. At least some attention was given to the choice of an opening and, often, closing poem.[35] In a typical volume, the two longest or most impressive pieces were placed first and last, positions most conspicuous to the reader. Samuel Rogers's *Poems* (1816), for example, a collection of thirty-five miscellaneous pieces, begins with "The Pleasures of Memory: A Poem in Two Parts" and concludes with the twelve cantos of "The Voyage of Columbus"—by far the two most ambitious works in the book. When Joseph Cottle expanded his second edition of *Poems*

(1796) into *Malvern Hills, and Other Poems* (1802), he added several poems composed by his brother Amos but reserved pride of place for his own works, which are printed first and last, enveloping those by his brother.

True pride of place went generally to the opening poem, which often supplied a collection with its title. Byron, who first published *Lara* with Rogers's *Jacqueline* as a companion piece, explains in the Advertisement that he had tried vainly to convince Rogers that *Jacqueline* "should occupy the first pages of the . . . volume" and "regrets that the tenacious courtesy of his friend would not permit him to place it where the judgment of the reader, concurring with his [i.e., Byron's] own will suggest its more appropriate station."[36] As a rule, Byron chose the opening poems of his collections quite deliberately. Through all four versions of *Hours of Idleness*, for instance, "On Leaving Newstead Abbey" remains first, though the order of several other poems is changed and still others are dropped from the book.[37] Similarly, according to Frederick Shilstone, "One of the very few instructions Byron was able to give Nathan [about the arrangement of *Hebrew Melodies*] was to place "She Walks in Beauty" at the beginning of any edition."[38]

Just as careful attention was given by many to the concluding poem of their books. Barbara Herrnstein Smith observes that the "most casual survey of the concluding lines of any group of poems will reveal that in a considerable number of them there are words and phrases such as 'last,' 'finished,' 'end,' 'rest,' 'peace,' or 'no more,' which, while they do not refer to the conclusion of the poem itself, nevertheless signify termination or stability."[39] Such references—though they may not refer specifically to the conclusion of the volume itself—are often located in a final piece whose tone further contributes to the reader's sense of closure. Leigh Hunt thus underscored the festive tone of *Foliage: Poems Original and Translated* (1818) by punctuating the whole with "The Nuptial Song of Julia and Manlius," which itself ends: "Close the doors, ye virgins, now; / 'Tis enough. But you, your vow, / Keep, ye link'd in love and beauty, / And fulfill your age's duty"

(p. 111). On a less elevated note, James Montgomery ended *Prison Amusements, and Other Trifles* (1797) with "A Tale—Too True," whose last stanza opens, "But now at the death of our long-winded song, / The Readers their night caps may take" (p. 200). Due perhaps to their strong closural references and sober, contemplative tone, elegies were frequently chosen to conclude contemporary collections.[40]

Most Romantic volumes with sophisticated arrangements, like *Lyrical Ballads* (1798) and Byron's *The Prisoner of Chillon, and Other Poems* (1816), depend for their meaning and structure on two framing poems. In such books, the choice of an opening almost always conditions the selection of a closing poem.[41] When the framing poems generate tensions and concerns explored by the other poems in the volume—as is again the case in *Lyrical Ballads* and *The Prisoner of Chillon* collection—a coherent perceptual "field" is created, within which the final poem takes on special significance. Thus, the questions raised in the "Ancient Mariner" are further explored throughout *Lyrical Ballads* and answered in "Tintern Abbey." So, too, "The Prisoner of Chillon" is best understood in terms of "Prometheus." Both poems concern protagonists who endure the almost unendurable pains of imprisonment and isolation that the volume defines as characteristic of the human condition. Yet by transforming Bonivard's chastened acceptance of suffering into triumphant defiance, Prometheus is able to create the "Victory" with which "Prometheus" and the volume end, resolving as well the madness and misery of "Darkness" and the encroaching chaos of "The Dream" in his assertion of the coherence and integrity of his own vision.

Nor should the importance of centerpieces be overlooked in volumes such as these. Placed twelfth amid twenty-three poems, "The Thorn" stands as a main structural node in *Lyrical Ballads*, bringing into sharp focus the central thematic concerns of the volume. Likewise, the intensely personal "To [Augusta]" is positioned at the middle of *The Prisoner of Chillon* collection, with Byron's own Promethean assertion: "They may torture, but shall not subdue me" (l. 23). In this way,

Byron is able to locate his volume thematically within the terms of his own misfortunes, mythologizing himself and personalizing his Prometheus so that the two can be seen as one in their suffering and in their final victory.

[V]

In collections such as *Lyrical Ballads* and *The Prisoner of Chillon*, one can see the heterogeneity and harmony that Coleridge defined as the principal qualities of an organic whole.[42] For, as was demonstrated in the previous chapter and will be shown at length in the following three, the major Romantic poets sought continually to create coherent volumes from seemingly disparate poems that harmonize on a sophisticated thematic level.[43] In his 1816 *Christabel; Kubla Khan, a Vision; The Pains of Sleep*, Coleridge himself joins three fragments concerning the visionary imagination and makes from them an entire volume dedicated to the world of dream and its polarities of vision and nightmare.

At the end of the preface to "Kubla Khan," Coleridge reveals his rationale for including "The Pains of Sleep": "As a contrast to this vision [i.e., "Kubla Khan"], I have annexed a fragment of a very different character, describing with equal fidelity the dream of pain and disease" (p. 54). The fragmentary nature of all the poems in the volume reinforces their connection with the dream and highlights the tenuous nature of visionary experience. Indeed, the well-known preface to "Kubla Khan," with its testimony to the fragility of vision, is preceded here by the preface to "Christabel," in which Coleridge apologizes for its fragmented condition, explaining: "But as, in my very first conception of the tale, I had the whole present to my mind, with the wholeness, no less than with the liveliness of a vision; I trust that I shall be able to embody in verse the three parts yet to come, in the course of the present year" (pp. v–vi). Like a dream, the volume argues, the imagination illuminates the mind with visions that, also like dreams, speedily fade away. In their wake they leave an all-too-vulnerable poet balanced precariously between vision and nightmare, ecstasy and despair.

Composed of only three poems, Coleridge's 1816 volume did not present him with problems of arrangement. That he was sensitive to such problems is evidenced by his strictures to Southey, who wanted to place "Christabel" as the opening poem of the *Annual Anthology* for 1799:

> In my last letter I said I would give you my reasons for thinking Christabel, *were* it finished and finished as spiritedly as it commences, yet still an improper opening Poem. My reason is—it cannot be expected to please all / Those who dislike it will deem it extravagant Ravings, & go on thro' the rest of the Collection with the feeling of Disgust. . . . It ought I think to be the last. The first ought, me judice, to be a poem in couplets, didactic or satirical—such a one as the lovers of genuine poetry would call sensible and entertaining. . . . *The great and master fault of the last anthology was the want of arrangement* [my italics].[44]

No doubt Coleridge's advice is prompted in part by his unhappy experience with the "Ancient Mariner" as the opening poem of *Lyrical Ballads* (1798).[45] Moreover, as Coleridge knew, through artful arrangement a book of miscellaneous poems could gain coherence and purpose. A random ordering, even of poems that harmonize thematically, fails to control the kind of impression the collection will make upon the reader and, more importantly, fails to shape its ultimate meaning. Radically different statements can be made not only by changing the juxtaposition of poems, but also, for example, by positioning a pessimistic work such as "Ode to Liberty" rather than a hopeful one such as "Prometheus Unbound" at the conclusion of a volume, or by placing a poem like "Lamia" instead of one like "The Eve of St. Agnes" at its beginning.

In well-structured volumes, epigraphs and dedicatory poems may be part of the framework established by the opening and closing poems, often serving as keys to the unity of the "field." For instance, in Robert Southey's 1797 *Poems*, which aspires to the same kind of organic unity characterizing the best Romantic volumes, an epigraph from Akenside focuses the themes of the whole:

> Goddess of the Lyre! with thee comes
> Majestic Truth: and where Truth deigns to come,
> Her sister Liberty will not be far.

Liberty and liberation are thematically central to a volume whose most prominent sections are entitled "The Triumph Of Woman," "On The Slave Trade," and "Botany Bay Eclogues." In fact, the opening poem of the collection is addressed to a reformer, Mary Wollstonecraft, who is pictured as wielding the "heaven-blest sword of Liberty" (p. 3), and the closing poem, "Hymn to the Penates," envisions the result of reform—the true liberty that springs from love:

> This is the state
> Shall bless the race redeemed of man, when Wealth
> And Power and all their hideous progeny
> Shall sink annihilate, and all mankind
> Live in the equal brotherhood of Love. (p. 220)

Developing Akenside's statement in the epigraph that Truth and Liberty are revealed in song, the final line of the "Hymn to the Penates," and hence the volume, proclaims Southey's relationship with "the pure song of Liberty and Truth." Here the echo of the epigraph not only underscores the thematic progression of the volume but provides it with structural closure as well.

"Hymn to the Penates" also culminates the theme of poet as wanderer, a theme beginning in the dedicatory sonnet where the poet is characterized as a "Pilgrim woebegone," whose wandering is both "Lonely" and "rugged." "Often at eve," he relates in the "Hymn to the Penates,"

> Amid my wandering I have seen far off
> The lonely light that spoke of comfort there,
> It told my heart of many a joy of home,
> And my poor heart was sad. (p. 218)

The speaker is but one of the many homeless figures in a volume that, through poems like the "Botany Bay Eclogues," "Mary," "The Widow," "The Soldier's Wife," and "On The Slave Trade," provides a gallery of outcasts from society. Hence, the importance of Southey's addressing the last poem of his volume to the Penates—"Household Gods" or "Domestic Deities" who at last fulfill his need for a "quiet haven" (pp. 204, 205, 218). Yet, "haven'd now / I think of those in the world's wilderness / Who wander on and find no home of rest / Till to the grave they go!" (pp. 218–19). Though it is filled with hope, the volume ends in anger and sadness, demanding from the Penates and from the poet's fellow beings that the world be made into a true and substantial home for all.

Southey's *Poems* gains added closure and integrity from the opening lines of the "Hymn to the Penates," which signal that poem's final position in the volume: "Yet one Song more! one high and solemn strain / Ere . . . / I hang the silent harp" (p. 203). Wordsworth and Coleridge likewise chose a "high and solemn strain" to end *Lyrical Ballads*, published a year after Southey's *Poems*, nor is this the only similarity between the two volumes.[46] For *Lyrical Ballads* also focuses upon the outcasts of society, also laments what man has made of man. Yet the subtlety with which Wordsworth and Coleridge treat the themes of homelessness and wandering in *Lyrical Ballads* goes far beyond Southey's mere social commentary to a vision of all human beings as perpetual wanderers, homeless within a world that refuses to provide any lasting havens. The comfortably "haven'd" poet appearing at the end of Southey's volume has no place in *Lyrical Ballads*, which ends with a poet courageously embracing his life as both wanderer and prophet.

Nevertheless, Southey's *Poems* is an instructive model. Although a minor collection, it shares the features shaping most major Romantic volumes: a strong framework that bonds thematically interactive poems, along with significant resonances in image and voice throughout the whole. Yet the qualitative differences in poetry and thought between *Poems* and *Lyrical Ballads* are telling. As with poetic structures of any kind, there is a wide gap in conceptual richness between first- and second-rate contextures—and hence in the kinds of unity to which they might aspire. That is to say, first, that poems in collections by the great Romantics tend to be complex and multifaceted in theme: there are more possible points of contact and interaction between them. Second, recognizing fully, in the words of Thomas McFarland, "the mutual dependence of that which is separated and that which is bound together," the major Romantics structured and, even, restructured their volumes in earnest.[47] They characteristically developed the "outer" structural energy in a collection of heterogeneous pieces so as to supplement and qualify the "inner" meaning of each. For these reasons alone, their collections are apt to possess a thematic coherence at once more substantial and more profound than those of their contemporaries.

"Remember," warns Coleridge, "that there is a difference between form as proceeding, and shape as superinduced; —the latter is either the death or the imprisonment of the thing;—the former is its self-witnessing and self-effected sphere of agency."[48] As a group of thinkers and makers, the major poets were more interested in open-ended, organic structures than in narrowly conceived, overdetermined ones. In *Lyrical Ballads* we are shown that the task of the poet-prophet is to challenge and educate humanity, to enlarge vision by breaking down the mind's tendency to see the world through the limiting frame of its own preconceptions. And the openness insisted upon in *Lyrical Ballads* receives its ultimate contextural expression in the open-ended visions fashioned in Keats's *Lamia* volume and Shelley's *Prometheus Unbound, with Other Poems*. The former ends in a fragment; the latter ends where, thematically, its first poem begins. Throughout both, poems condition each other's meaning so that no resolution in the book is left unquestioned. If anywhere, here—in the vital "self-witnessing and self-affecting" shape of these books—is the most distinctively high Romantic use of the volume.

Thematically rich, intricately unified collections like *Lyri-*

cal Ballads, with a Few Other Poems; *Lamia, Isabella, The Eve of St. Agnes, and Other Poems*; and *Prometheus Unbound, with Other Poems* epitomize Romantic contextural practices at their most sophisticated, representing achievements that few poetic volumes of any era have equaled. From diverse, sometimes contradictory poems, each book ultimately shapes a coherent "field," so that removed from *Lyrical Ballads* a work such as "The Idiot Boy" seems quite different and less substantial, as does "Fancy" from the *Lamia* volume, or "A Vision of the Sea" from *Prometheus Unbound.* Nowhere could we find better models to help us understand the artistry—as well as the meaning—Romantic poets invested in the shape of their books.

CHAPTER 3

The "Field" of *Lyrical Ballads* (1798)

The Ancient Mariner *grew and grew till it became too important for our first object . . . and we began to talk of a Volume.*

Wordsworth to Isabella Fenwick

We deem that . . . [Lyrical Ballads] *. . .* [*is*] *to a certain degree* one work, in kind tho' not in degree, *as an Ode is one work— & that our different poems are as stanzas,* good *relatively rather than absolutely.*

Coleridge to Joseph Cottle

CONTENTS.

Contents page of *Lyrical Ballads, with a Few Other Poems.*
Courtesy of Newberry Library, Chicago

[1]

Critical opinion about *Lyrical Ballads* (1798) is nowhere more divided than over the issue of its coherence as a collection.[1] Arguments for the unity of the volume must contend with three important objections voiced by critics. First, the financial need occasioned by Wordsworth and Coleridge's impending trip to Germany forced them to rush *Lyrical Ballads* through the press—resulting in a volume that "represents a considerable degree of compromise, expediency, and chance."[2] Second, doubts have arisen that a single plan was carefully adhered to during the creation of the volume, despite later statements made by each poet to the contrary.[3] And third, there is what John Jordan terms "the spread of the volume itself."[4]

Sufficient evidence exists, however, to counter these objections. Although *Lyrical Ballads* was in some ways a hasty production, it was produced by two formidable poets—both of whom, as we have seen, showed an unusual concern for the unity and ordering of their poetic works. Wordsworth's self-proclaimed distaste for miscellaneous poems "jumbled together at random" was matched by what Max Schulz calls Coleridge's "abiding concern for the design of a thing."[5] It is, in fact, hard to imagine that their lifelong care for the organization of their volumes did not manifest itself in 1798, however quickly *Lyrical Ballads* was assembled.[6] Indeed, while the poems were going through the press, Wordsworth traveled to Bristol several times to supervise the printing. On one of his last trips, he brought "Lines Written a Few Miles above Tintern Abbey, on Revisiting the Banks of the Wye during a Tour, July 13, 1798." And though often referred to as an afterthought to *Lyrical Ballads*, "Tintern Abbey" more probably stems from Wordsworth's sense that a fit conclusion was needed for the volume.[7]

In 1843, when Wordsworth told Isabella Fenwick that the "Ancient Mariner" was the seed from which the collection grew, he noted that *Lyrical Ballads* "was to consist as Mr. Coleridge has told the world, of Poems chiefly on natural subjects taken from common life but looked at, as much as might be, through an imaginative medium."[8] But Mr. Coleridge had, in fact, given a somewhat different set of particulars. The *Biographia* suggests that *Lyrical Ballads* was planned to consist of poetry of "two sorts," with each poet contributing only one type of poem.[9] The following passage is well known but worth quoting at length:

> . . . it was agreed, that my endeavours should be directed to persons and characters supernatural, or at least romantic; yet so as to transfer from our outward nature a human interest and a semblance of truth sufficient to procure for these shadows of imagination that willing suspension of disbelief for the moment, which constitutes poetic faith. Mr. Wordsworth, on the other hand, was to propose to himself as his object, to give the charm of novelty to things of every day, and to excite a feeling analogous to the supernatural, by awakening the mind's attention from the lethargy of custom, and directing it to the loveliness and the wonders of the world before us. (*BL*, 2:6)

Coleridge recounts here that, while he would link the extraordinary world with the ordinary, Wordsworth was to link the ordinary world with the extraordinary. From this a blending would result: the natural and supernatural worlds would become coextensive. Although the poems of *Lyrical Ballads* would be of "two sorts," they would exist as a vital imaginative body, presenting unity in multeity.

If true, much of what Coleridge suggests—as he himself notes in the *Biographia*—changed before *Lyrical Ballads* passed through the press. Neither poet seems to have worked according to any clear division of labor: Wordsworth wrote "Goody Blake and Harry Gill" and "The Thorn," which, as John Jordan has argued, "depend on a belief in the supernatural," even "if they have psychological explanations";[10] and Coleridge produced "The Nightingale," "The Foster-Mother's Tale," and "The Dungeon"—all very much centered in the natural world. Nor was there any discernible attempt to balance the number of contributions from each poet: Wordsworth wrote nineteen of the twenty-three poems in the collection. Such discrepancies, coupled with the difference between the recollections of the two poets, have led most critics to justifiable doubts that *Lyrical Ballads* was created from a precisely articulated aesthetic plan. Yet however divergent the comments later made by Wordsworth and Coleridge about the plan of the volume, it is clear from the Advertisement of 1798 and the preface of 1800 that both poets thought the volume had a purpose and a plan.

Thus, if "compromise, expediency, and chance" played a role in the formation of *Lyrical Ballads*, it is equally certain that the desire for a harmonized and unified collection played a role as well.[11] Coleridge seems to have just such a conception in mind when he tries to interest Cottle in publishing the 1798 edition by comparing the whole to an ode, with individual poems that "are as stanzas, good relatively rather than absolutely."[12] With his deft analogy, Coleridge shifts Cottle's attention away from what has been characterized in an earlier chapter as the "inner" meaning of the poems to their "outer" meaning as a group. Like the reader alert to what Coleridge called "that Impetuousity of Transition, and that Precipitation of Fancy and Feeling, which are the *essential* excellencies of the sublimer Ode" (*LC*, 1:289), Cottle is asked to see beyond the apparent incongruities of style and subject among the poems of *Lyrical Ballads* to their essential likeness.[13] As informed readers of the collection, we are similarly charged.

To be sure, Coleridge's comparison of *Lyrical Ballads* to an ode is both richly suggestive and somewhat limited. The "spread of the volume" indicates that there was probably no elaborate design for the positioning or even the selection of every poem. We should not expect, nor will we find, the sequentiality or coherence of a single long poem among the poems in the book. Yet, in its pairing of such poems as "Expostulation and Reply" with "The Tables Turned" and "Anecdote for Fathers" with "We Are Seven," in its use of "Ancient Mariner" and "Tintern Abbey" as framework poems and "The Thorn" as a centerpiece, in its thematically integrated though not always spatially juxtaposed clusters of poems, *Lyrical Ballads* does show signs of significant organization. Not only are local transitions made between a few sets of poems, but, as we shall see, a larger system of resonant effects operates throughout the volume.

Wordsworth and Coleridge further promoted the unity of *Lyrical Ballads* by publishing it anonymously, as the work of a single poet.[14] To consider the effectiveness of such a strategy we must unlearn most of what we know about the volume and see it through the eyes of a contemporary ignorant of its dual authorship. Such a reader has only the evidence of the volume to guide him, and this evidence is purposely misleading. Twice in the Advertisement, reference is made to the "author" of the volume. This fictive persona, apparently responsible for all of the poems in *Lyrical Ballads*, is the objective embodiment of a poetic friendship which Thomas McFarland aptly characterizes as "nothing less than a symbiosis, a development of attitude so dialogical and intertwined that in some instances not even the participants themselves could discern their respective contributions."[15]

Not until the preface of 1800 did Wordsworth disavow in public the existence of this fictive Coleridge-Wordsworth. Yet even there he states that Coleridge's poems would never have been joined to his own had not he believed that "the poems of my Friend would in a great measure have the same tendency as my own, and that, though there would be found a difference, there would be found no discordance in the colours of our style; as our opinions on the subject of poetry do almost entirely coincide" (Owen, pp. 153–54). From this almost entire coincidence of the two poets' opinions about poetry arose the amalgam "poet" of the Advertisement.

Stephen Parrish has shown that *Lyrical Ballads* is in many ways a dramatic work. The appreciative reader is tempted to look behind the scenes to discover the dramatist. This impulse is perhaps what prompts William Heath to comment that the placement of "Tintern Abbey" at the end of the volume "seems designed to answer that reader who asks, justifiably, what consciousness operates behind the voice singing in most of these ballads, and why he should attend to it."[16] As Heath implies, the poems of *Lyrical Ballads* reflect the unity of their "author's" poetic style and thoughts. To discover the shape of the world presented by the volume is to disclose the shape of his consciousness. In other words, each poem of the volume contributes to the larger perceptual "field" created by the collection as a whole.

If in both language and subject *Lyrical Ballads* (1798) sets an agenda for the well-known debate about poetry that Wordsworth joined more openly in 1800, at an even more fundamental level the volume is concerned with exploring the proper role of the poet himself. Paul Sheats has claimed that the narrators of both "Simon Lee" and "The Idiot Boy" function "in the same way as the pedlar."[17] However, no one has yet recognized the number of resemblances between the Pedlar, renamed the Wanderer in *The Excursion*, and the "author" of *Lyrical Ballads*—particularly in the breadth of their minds. The "author" of *Lyrical Ballads*, for instance, is capable of producing poetry ranging from the abstruse "Ancient Mariner" to the contemplative "Tintern Abbey" to the more folkish "Goody Blake and Harry Gill." Likewise, the narrator of *The Excursion* tells us that the Wanderer "often touched / Abstrusest matter, reasoning of the mind / Turned inward; or at my request would sing / Old songs, the product of his native hills" (*PW*, 1:64–67).[18]

Taught by nature to reach out to others with sympathy and love, the Wanderer is "an indulgent listener" to the "tongue / Of garrulous age; nor did the sick man's tale / To his fraternal sympathy addressed, / Obtain reluctant hearing" (*PW*, 1:417–20). Similarly taught by nature, the "author" of *Lyrical Ballads* also extends sympathy and understanding to "garrulous age" and the "sick man's tale." And just like the "author," the Wanderer is able to perceive those passions and feelings "Essential and eternal in the heart, / That mid the simpler forms of rural life, / Exist more simple in their elements, / And speak a plainer language" (*PW*, 1:344–47). No wonder Wordsworth writes in the preface to *The Excursion* that the character of the Wanderer is "chiefly an idea of what I fancied my own character might have become in his circumstances" (*PW*, 5:373).[19]

Yet though the Wanderer is endowed with the "vision and faculty divine," he "wants the accomplishment of verse" (*PW*, 1:79, 81). The "author" of *Lyrical Ballads*, on the other hand, is a poet whose own commitment to wandering leads him to encounter a world every bit as disturbing as the one surrounding the ruined cottage. His wandering is more costly, more heroic than that of the Wanderer because of his public effort as poet to confront both the closed minds of his fellow beings—ruled by what the Advertisement terms "pre-established codes of decision" (Owen, p. 3)—and a world in which radical loss seems the only certain principle. Through the figure of the "author," Wordsworth and Coleridge define the troubled consciousness that is the poet's lot in such a world while at the same time insisting upon the poet's public responsibilities. In fact, Coleridge's own understanding of the poet's necessary relationship to the public seems even to inform his remarks on the ode-like nature of *Lyrical Ballads*.

In the dedicatory letter of "Ode to the Departing Year" (1796), Coleridge writes to Thomas Poole, "You, I am sure, will not fail to recollect, that among the Ancients, the Bard and the Prophet were one and the same character" (*LC*, 1:289). As Coleridge knew, the ode from its inception had been used as a vehicle for prophetic utterance. Implied, therefore, in the very use of the form is the poet's obligation to articulate his vision to the public. A poet-prophet must see clearly not only the conditions of the world but also the consequences if these conditions remain unchanged. Public and hortatory, the poet's verse tends to survey the potentiality of the human mind, locating the imaginative possibilities of the mind as well as the forces arrayed against them.

Wordsworth, of course, shared Coleridge's concern for the public responsibilities of the poet.[20] In the prospectus to *The Recluse*, Wordsworth declares the human mind to be his "haunt" and the "main region" of his song. This is no less true of *Lyrical Ballads*, whose poems share a common focus on the mind's relationship to the world. Dialectical in nature, the "field" of the volume thematically juxtaposes alienation and communion, mystery and understanding, misery and joy, motion and stillness, homelessness and home.

In *Lyrical Ballads* as a whole, the mind is depicted as being easily cut off from both the outer world and its own inner resources—subject to imprisonment within the small circle of its own subjectivity, where all else lies shrouded in mystery. Perhaps this helps to explain why Wordsworth and Coleridge found the ballad so well suited to their purposes. Alun R. Jones suggests that Wordsworth found in the stark, unornamented form of the ballad a fit means of exploring "the elemental condition of mankind."[21] This is so. But Wordsworth also saw that the ballad is a form comfortable with mystery. Often at its heart are lacunae, informational gaps that leave the causes for events within the poem unexplained. We are never told, for example, why the king wants Sir Patrick Spens dead. Furthermore, the ballad is frequently structured as a mystery that unfolds through a series of questions and answers. Utilizing this characteristic of the genre, Wordsworth and Coleridge constructed a type of literary ballad in which mystery plays both a thematic and structural role. Wordsworth once told Barron Field: "The whole scope of my poetry . . . is to teach mankind that a primrose is something more than a primrose."[22] Likewise, many of the poems in *Lyrical Ballads* present a person, place, or thing that the reader discovers is more than it first appears to be. Each entity is the locus of a mystery into which the reader or auditor becomes initiated during the course of the narrative.

Questions play an important role in this initiatory process. They serve a structural function similar to the role they play in the traditional ballad and act as the bridge by which an isolated subjectivity attempts to connect with its world. Thus, often the mere formulation of the proper question has great significance. It can, for instance, bring on an unanticipated revelation, like the question the Wedding Guest poses to the Mariner: "Now wherefore stoppest me?" or Matthew's question in "Expostulation and Reply": "Why William, sit you thus alone, / And dream your time away?" It can also both elicit an explanation for the puzzling spectacle of a healthy, "full grown" man weeping on a public road and suggest the humanity of the questioner: "My friend / What ails you? wherefore weep you so?" ("Last of the Flock," ll. 15–16). Moreover, it can signal the inadequacy of a mind that insists upon rational explanations, like the question posed to little Edward in "Anecdote for Fathers": "Now, little Edward say why so; / My little Edward, tell me why" (ll. 37–38), or the question asked of the young girl in "We Are Seven": "I pray you tell / Sweet Maid, how this may be?" (ll. 27–28).[23] At other times in *Lyrical Ballads* a question is used by a narrator to draw attention to a mysterious circumstance that the ballad then explores. Such is the case at the beginning of "Goody Blake and Harry Gill"—"Oh! what's the matter? what's the matter? / What is't that ails young Harry Gill?" (ll. 1–2)—and the beginning of "The Idiot Boy"—"Why bustle thus about your door, / What means this bustle, Betty Foy?" (ll. 7–8).

Important questions abound in *Lyrical Ballads*. Almost always the questioner is somewhat changed by the act of questioning itself as well as by the answer. For questions are the proper responses for the characters of the volume to make to the mysterious otherness surrounding them. Questions not only help to plumb the depths of the mystery, but they also attempt to establish the kind of dialogue that is the first step toward reducing one's alien status in the world. Thematically, the questions raised by the opening "Ancient Mariner" resound throughout *Lyrical Ballads*, to be answered at last in "Tintern Abbey."[24]

Early in January 1797, Charles Lamb wrote a letter to Coleridge praising the "Ode to the Departing Year":

> Sincerely, I think your Ode one of the finest I have read. The opening is in the spirit of the sublimest allegory. . . . Now your concluding stanza is worthy of so fine an ode. The beginning was awakening & striking; the ending is soothing and solemn.—. Are you serious when you ask, whether you shall admit this *ode* [i.e., into *Poems* (1797)]? it would be . . . mere insanity to reject this.[25]

Lamb, of course, could not foresee that his appreciative comments about the "Ode to the Departing Year" would so well describe the volume his friend Coleridge was to help produce a little over a year later. If Wordsworth and Coleridge had consciously taken Lamb's criteria for the proper movement of an ode as a structuring principle, they could not have picked two better poems than "Ancient Mariner" and "Tintern Abbey" to open and close the volume. The first is indeed "awakening and striking," the second is "soothing and solemn." What better way to describe the movement of *Lyrical Ballads*? Acting as a framework, "Ancient Mariner" and "Tintern Abbey" contain the keys for understanding the unified "field" of the volume. Like Coleridge's "Ode to the Departing Year," *Lyrical Ballads* begins "in the spirit of the sublimest allegory"—with "Ancient Mariner."

[II]

From the start there was no doubt that "Ancient Mariner" would begin the volume. Sometime in late May 1798, Joseph Cottle visited the two poets at Alfoxden. He later recalled this visit in *Early Recollections: Chiefly Relating to the Late Samuel Taylor Coleridge* (1837):

> At this interview it was determined, that the volume should be published under the title of "Lyrical Ballads," on the terms stipulated in a former letter: that this volume should not contain the poem of "Salisbury Plain," but only an extract from it; that it should not contain the poem of "Peter Bell," but consist rather of sundry shorter poems, and, for the most part, of pieces more recently written. I had recommended two volumes, but one was fixed on, and that to be published anonymously. It was to be begun immediately and with the "Ancient Mariner;" which poem I brought with me to Bristol. (1:314–15)

Though Cottle's account of events concerning the printing and publication of *Lyrical Ballads* is often questionable, it is certain that he returned to Bristol with a copy of "Ancient Mariner" to be printed at the beginning of the volume. As a joint production of Wordsworth and Coleridge, "Ancient Mariner" is an especially fit poem to open a volume intended itself to be a joint production. Indeed, the extent to which "Ancient Mariner" develops concerns that preoccupy both poets is often overlooked by critics.

On 20 November 1797 Dorothy Wordsworth recorded the genesis of "Ancient Mariner" and the volume that would emerge from it: "The evening was dark and cloudy: we went eight miles, William and Coleridge employing themselves in laying the plan of a ballad, to be published with some pieces of William's" (*EY*, p. 94). Founded upon a dream related to Coleridge by his friend John Cruikshank, "Ancient Mariner" was plotted largely by Wordsworth, who not only suggested the nature of the mariner's crime and punishment as well as other minor details but also contributed lines to the poem. That such a plot would suggest itself to Wordsworth is unsurprising: his own *Adventures on Salisbury Plain*, a section of which appeared in *Lyrical Ballads* as "The Female Vagrant," contains a mariner who sins against community by committing murder and becomes a tormented wanderer as the result of his crime. Nor is it surprising that Coleridge was amenable to such a plot, since his mind was drawn to wanderers like Cain and the Wandering Jew and, as Jonathan Wordsworth points out, he "had been disproportionately impressed by *Adventures on Salisbury Plain*, read to him in the autumn of 1795."[26]

The figure of the Ancient Mariner had consequences, in turn, for other characters who appear in the poems of the 1798 and 1800 editions of *Lyrical Ballads*. "The Thorn," after all, is narrated by an ancient mariner who wanders the countryside with telescope in hand; and Leonard of "The Brothers" returns to his home to find his brother dead: with no home to anchor him, he goes on "shipboard, and is now / A Seaman, a grey-headed Mariner" (ll. 434–35). The power "Ancient Mariner" exerted over Wordsworth's imagination can also be seen in two rejected manuscript endings written in January or

March 1798 for *The Ruined Cottage* in which the narrator tells us, "I seem'd a better and a wiser man" and "I am a better and a wiser man."[27]

However, Wordsworth's most intense response to the concerns of "Ancient Mariner" is in the poems of *Lyrical Ballads* (1798) themselves. Perhaps because "Ancient Mariner" seems so different in style from the other poems of the volume, its importance as the opening poem of a joint volume has often been ignored. This is particularly troubling because, as we have seen, the two poets placed it decisively at the front of the collection and many of its concerns not only originate with Wordsworth himself but continued to interest him. Although "Peter Bell" is often recognized as Wordsworth's answer to "Ancient Mariner," the poems he included in *Lyrical Ballads* usually receive no such recognition. Only a closer look at "Ancient Mariner" itself will illuminate the nature of the seed from which the volume grew.[28]

"Ancient Mariner" is a subversive poem: its intent is to expose the world as we are accustomed to perceiving it as a fictive creation of "our own pre-established codes of decision." The convictions arising from such codes allow us to live at ease in an explainable world governed by causal relationships. However, they in no way help to account for the mystery that lurks just beneath the surface of this artificial construct. Like the Book of Job, "Ancient Mariner" announces the inadequacy of rational explanations for a mysterious universe.[29] Indeed, like Job's messengers, the Ancient Mariner alone escapes catastrophe to tell his story. The Wedding Guest, then, as auditor of this tale has an awakening analogous to that of Job, a man forced to discard a worldview no longer tenable—an awakening shared also by the reader.

The "Ancient Mariner" begins abruptly, with an immediate violation of causality. As mysteriously as he is later to leave ("The Marinere . . . / Is gone" [ll. 651, 653]), the Mariner appears at the scene of a wedding feast: "It is an ancyent Marinere, / And he stoppeth one of three" (ll. 1–2). Neither how the Mariner came to be there nor his reason for stopping this particular one of three is explained. Moreover, we are made acquainted not with his name but with his state of being: "It is an ancyent Marinere."[30] Indeed, we later learn that the Mariner's first exposition of his story is a response to the hermit's urgent question: "What manner man art thou?" (l. 610).

At the beginning of "Ancient Mariner," as in the beginning of many of the *Lyrical Ballads*, a character within the poem is confronted by a situation he is at a loss to explain. Invariably, he responds with a question that starts the dynamic process of the poem: "By thy long grey beard and thy glittering eye / Now wherefore stoppest me?" (ll. 3–4). Here, the poem begins with a demand for an explanation of motion arrested. The Wedding Guest requires to know why he has been stopped from attending the wedding feast. Fit ending for a comedy, a wedding feast is a microcosmic celebration of macrocosmic order. To participate in such a celebration in a world out of joint is to practice, wittingly or unwittingly, self-deception. This is no comic world, and the Wedding Guest's somewhat anxious and wishful attempt to transform what promises to be an ominous tale into a portion of the wedding festivities is as misguided as it is futile: "Nay, if thou'st got a laughsome tale, / Marinere! come with me" (ll. 11–12). The Mariner's tale is, of course, anything but "laughsome"; instead of wedding festivities, the Mariner has a quite different ceremony in mind. He is to preside over a divorce: the alienation of the Wedding Guest from the comfortable world in which he has lived for so long.

The Mariner's ceremony defines itself in opposition to the wedding feast. In contrast to the "merry din" of the feast, the Mariner insists upon a receptive stillness: "He holds him with his glittering eye— / The wedding guest stood still" (ll. 17–18). The Mariner's tale will progress only after the Wedding Guest has sat still upon a stone while the "Merry Mynstralsy" of the wedding party enters the hall. This stone functions as what Hartman would term an "omphalos," a solid center of reality that remains reassuringly firm while the Wedding Guest's rationally created world crumbles around him.

In a similar way, a stone is used as a site for silent receptivity in "Expostulation and Reply." There, William sits on an "old grey stone" for "the length of half a day" (l. 2), dreaming his time away.[31] The argument of this poem, which replaced "Ancient Mariner" as the opening poem in *Lyrical Ballads* (1800), is somewhat analogous to that of "Ancient Mariner." Matthew, an advocate of knowledge gained rationally through books, confronts his friend William, a man who scorns the limitations of such knowledge. William, instead, sees the world as filled with mystery and wonder, a "mighty sum / Of things for ever speaking" (ll. 25–26). Such a world can only be understood through acts of perception undistorted by any of the mind's "pre-established codes of decision." Through a "wise passiveness" the mind can open itself to a frameless encounter with its world, because

> The eye it cannot chuse but see,
> We cannot bid the ear be still;
> Our bodies feel, where'er they be,
> Against, or with our will.
> ("Expostulation and Reply," ll. 17–20)

Variations of these lines twice appear prominently in Coleridge's work. Once, in the *Biographia*, he speaks of the "wonders of the world," which the mind would be capable of perceiving "but for which, in consequence of the film of familiarity and selfish solicitude we have eyes, yet see not, ears that hear not, and hearts that neither feel nor understand" (*BL*, 2:5–6). The other variation of these lines is actually an anticipation of them: in "Ancient Mariner" we are told that "The wedding-guest sate on a stone, / He cannot chuse but hear" (ll. 21–22). Both times Coleridge also echoes a phrase that appears in a prophetic and apocalyptic context in the books of the New Testament, moving from Mark 8:18 to Acts 28:26–28, and finding its briefest statement in forceful repetitions throughout Revelation: "He that hath ears, let him hear."[32] This echo is especially appropriate as preface to the Mariner's story, which is to be revelatory for the Wedding Guest. Moreover, it is a subtle reminder of the joint necessity that compels both auditor and speaker in this poem. For if the Wedding Guest is compelled to listen, the Mariner, like many prophets, is compelled to reveal what he has experienced:

Forthwith this frame of mine was wrench'd
  With a woeful agony,
Which forc'd me to begin my tale
  And then it left me free. (ll. 611–14)

Indeed, the Mariner becomes imprisoned within the confines of his own experience, forced "at an uncertain hour" by "a woeful agony" to tell his "ghastly aventure" (ll. 615, 612, 618). A true obsessive-compulsive, he must relate his tale to a man who must, in turn, listen: "The moment that his face I see / I know the man that must hear me; / To him my tale I teach" (ll. 621–23).

Before he begins to "teach" his tale, however, the Mariner carefully prepares his student. And this preparation is itself enough to effect a transformation in the Wedding Guest. In the world of *Lyrical Ballads*, as in Wordsworth's "Intimations Ode," the child is the "best philosopher" because his mind has not yet been structured by "pre-established codes of decision" or blinded by custom to the mysterious world surrounding him. Thus, the narrator of "Anecdote for Fathers" can tell his little Edward: "my heart / For better lore would seldom yearn, / Could I but teach the hundreth part / Of what from thee I learn" (ll. 57–60).

As Keats defines it, "negative capability" is embodied by one who "is capable of being in uncertainties, Mysteries, doubts without any irritable reaching after fact & reason."[33] The children of *Lyrical Ballads* naturally have such a stance: they live comfortably in a mysterious world without requiring "fact & reason" to explain the mystery. Indeed, "fact & reason" are often meaningless to children, as the narrator of "We Are Seven" discovers. Only the adult who can become like a child and face his world with silent receptivity is capable of living in it comfortably. Such a man is William of "Expostulation and Reply," who can speak of a morning "When life was sweet I knew not why" (l. 14). The adults in the volume who cannot become like children are often obsessed by "fact & reason," like the narrators of "Anecdote for Fathers," "We Are Seven," and, especially, "The Thorn."

The Wedding Guest, however, is forced to straddle both of these worlds: he is an adult temporarily compelled to become like a child. His reduction to this childlike state of receptivity is the result of a purposeful strategy employed by the Mariner that "stops" the world of "fact & reason." In the Wedding Guest's arrested motion, then, is the beginning of his transformation: "The wedding guest stood still / And listens like a three year's child; / The Marinere hath his will" (ll. 18–20). The Mariner has thus started to "teach" his tale even before his narrative begins.

The framework surrounding the Mariner's tale—the movement from motion to motion arrested, then the return to motion that the Wedding Guest is to experience—is a repetition of the rhythm of the tale itself. Indeed, the world of the Mariner's tale is primarily experienced in terms of motion. There can be little doubt, of course, about what form that motion first takes: "Merrily did we drop / Below . . . below . . . / Below . . ." (ll. 26–28). The parallel voyages of the Wedding Guest and the Mariner both begin in a merriment that quickly changes into anguish as they drop below all structures into a world of dazzling strangeness.

As the Mariner's ship departs from the familiar world of "mine own countrée," its motion is under the crew's control: "The ship was cheer'd, the Harbour clear'd" (l. 25). However, this control is soon lost as the familiar world gives way to an elemental world of "Storm and Wind." Here, motion is random and violent: "A Wind and Tempest strong! / For days and weeks it play'd us freaks— / Like Chaff we drove along" (ll. 46–48). The ship thus journeys farther south than its crew had intended, voyaging through an alien land of "Mist and Snow" in which "Ne shapes of men ne beasts we ken" (l. 55). The alien nature of such a land challenges community: man becomes a stranger to himself and the world surrounding him. Significantly, the Mariner chooses this point in his narrative to interject twice to the Wedding Guest: "Listen, Stranger." For he is not only recounting the moment in which he began to recognize his own estrangement from the world, he is also forcing the Wedding Guest to see that all men, whether they recognize it or not, are similarly estranged. His killing of the albatross, then, becomes symbolic of his own mental condition.

The Mariner himself has no explanation for an act as random and as violent as the "Storm and Wind" that take control of the ship's movement. The crew, however, insists upon evaluating the murder of the albatross by rational criteria. Their attempt to establish a causal relationship between the killing of the albatross and subsequent weather conditions is not only foolhardy but also makes them accomplices in the Mariner's crime:

> Then all averr'd, I had kill'd the Bird
> That brought the fog and mist.
> 'Twas right, said they, such birds to slay
> That bring the fog and mist. (ll. 95–98)

Like Job's comforters, the crew members are ignorant of the true nature of their world. Invoking laws of causality to justify the Mariner's act, they each become more criminal than he.

There is an order that seems to function even in the mysterious regions of this elemental world. Paradoxically, it operates through love, yet it is capable of revenge. The spirit who "lov'd the bird that lov'd the man / Who shot him with his bow" (ll. 409–10) is to exact vengeance upon the Mariner and crew. He, however, is only a part of a larger organization of supernatural spirits who participate in a revenge that first expresses itself in terms of motion arrested. For, immediately attendant upon their complicity in the murder of the albatross, the crew becomes "the first that ever burst" into the "silent sea" of the Pacific. There, the motion of the ship ceases completely:

> Day after day, day after day,
> We stuck, ne breath ne motion,
> As idle as a painted Ship
> Upon a painted Ocean. (ll. 111–14)

Halted at the equator, at the very center of mystery the Mariner and crew experience the otherness of a world where there is an abundance of water but none to drink, where sea creatures are "slimy things" that "crawl with legs / Upon the Slimy sea" (ll. 121–22), and where "The Death-fires danc'd at night" (l. 124).

The Mariner, then, like William of "Expostulation and Reply" and the Wedding Guest, is stationed at an omphalos. Silence reigns here as well: "We could not speak no more than if / We had been choked with soot" (ll. 133–34). Forced into silent receptivity, the Mariner's mind focuses upon all that moves. His fixity is dramatically apparent in his description of the approaching "spectre-ship":

> I saw something in the Sky
>   No bigger than my fist;
> At first it seem'd a little speck
>   And then it seem'd a mist:
> It mov'd and mov'd, and took at last
>   A certain shape, I wist. (ll. 139–44)

The movement of the ship defies all human preconceptions about motion: "Withouten wind, withouten tide / She steddies with upright keel" (ll. 161–62). Propelled by other than natural means, the spectre-ship passes between the Mariner and the sun, momentarily presenting him with an image of his imprisonment within a phenomenal world whose mystery baffles the mind's attempts at understanding:

> And strait the Sun was fleck'd with bars
>   (Heaven's mother send us grace)
> As if thro' a dungeon grate he peer'd
>   With broad and burning face. (ll. 169–72)

If the sky appears as a dungeon grate, then the earth itself is a dungeon, presenting one with the options of the death-in-life of the prisoner or the possible life-in-death of the corpse. In the Mariner's world, however, even the power to choose between these states is not within human control. Instead, the fate of the Mariner and crew is decided by a deadly game of dice through which the Mariner is consigned to death-in-life, the crew to death.

With the "many men so beautiful" dead (l. 228), the Mariner is left alone in a completely alien world. His desperate attempt to reconnect himself with this world through prayer ends in a "wicked whisper" that makes his heart "as dry as dust" (l. 239). Trapped between an imprisoning sky and sea, the Mariner falls prey to an emotional paralysis lasting seven days. At this point the Mariner is a man stripped of all "preestablished codes of decision," whose world has shrunk to the small circle of "the curse in a dead man's eye" (l. 252). His only desire is to die.

But the profound stasis of a mind at the limit of contraction makes that mind sensitive to external motion. In "Expostulation and Reply" William asks Matthew, "Think you . . . / . . . / That nothing of itself will come, / But we must still be seeking?" (ll. 25, 27–28). By an enforced passivity, the Mariner gains what he could not get through prayer. External motion calls up internal motion: the Mariner is brought back to life by the "moving Moon" that "no where did abide" (ll. 255–56). As his eyes are led from the moon to the ocean illuminated by moonlight, the Mariner bursts out of his contracted world. For upon the water a new motion attracts his eyes: "I watch'd the water-snakes: / They mov'd in tracks of shining white" (ll. 265–66). Within the shadow of the ship, the water snakes move in dazzling beauty: "every track / Was a flash of golden fire" (ll. 272–73). This is a beauty to which the Mariner now responds:

> O happy living things! no tongue
> Their beauty might declare:
> A spring of love gusht from my heart,
> And I bless'd them unaware! (ll. 274–77)

A movement from without thus stimulates a movement from within. By an act of perception the Mariner is able to break open the closed circle of his tortured self-consciousness to embrace the mysterious beauty of the water snakes. This act of expansion is also an act of love that makes community possible. Ironically, the community he sought through prayer is available only in those still moments in which the self openly encounters its world, moments that are themselves necessary prerequisites for prayer. It is unsurprising then that the Mariner finds: "The self-same moment I could pray" (l. 280). Moreover, the albatross fastened to his neck by the crew falls off "like lead" into the sea. The dead weight of complete alienation has been removed from the Mariner. His episode of enforced stillness has ended with the full recognition of the meaning of community. Yet it is not without its ominous implications, for the Mariner's blessing of the water snakes is as essentially unmotivated as his killing of the albatross.

From motion arrested to motion. After a revitalizing sleep the Mariner awakes to find that he can once again move freely: "I mov'd and could not feel my limbs, / I was so light" (ll. 297–98). He also finds a world in motion:

> The upper air bursts into life,
>   And a hundred fire-flags sheen
> To and fro they are hurried about;
> And to and fro, and in and out
>   The stars dance on between. (ll. 305–9)

However, this world in motion turns out to be less than comforting as the ship, manned by walking corpses, begins its voyage home. Juxtaposed to the voluntary outward voyage is the unwilled motion of the ship's return. Clearly, the Mariner is once again in a strange and threatening world: "It had been strange, even in a dream / To have seen those dead men rise" (ll. 325–26). His moment of community with the water snakes is now demonically parodied in his "community" with the crew members: "We were a ghastly crew" (l. 332).

The movement made possible by the moment of stillness is also a movement away from that stillness. If the mind is for a moment at home in its world, it cannot long remain in that moment. This is, of course, the irony inherent in the Mariner's return to his "own countrée." For except in brief moments of community in the "Kirk" where "all together pray" (l. 639), the Mariner has no home. "The man hath penance done, / And penance more will do," says a spirit (ll. 413–14). Locked into what is paradoxically an endless purgatory, the Mariner is possessed by a vision of a moment of community in which he cannot remain. Here, there is no wedding between the mind and its world, only a furtive and endlessly frustrating romance. For beneath the comfortable home one fictively structures is a mysterious foundation whose sudden shifts are rationally inexplicable. Once exposed as the artificial product of "fact and reason," it collapses, leaving the mind alone and vulnerable in its ruin. Homeless, one becomes a wanderer searching for that moment of liberation in which the prison house of the world is transformed into a new and more substantial home. To become an "ancyent Marinere" is to live briefly in this home only to be left homeless once more, trapped in purgatory between the hell of a fictively created world and the heaven created by the mind's marriage to its world. To be an "ancyent Marinere" is to be obsessed by this experience, compelled endlessly to relive it through the course of endless wanderings.

From motion arrested to motion: ". . . and now the wedding-guest / Turn'd from the bridegroom's door" (ll. 653–54). The Wedding Guest's moment of enforced stillness has literally revealed a new heaven and a new earth to him. No longer able to celebrate the old order, his first movement is away from the "bridegroom's door." The Mariner's ceremony has been successfully performed. The Wedding Guest is now a "sadder and a wiser man" (l. 657); divorced from the comfortable world in which he lived, he exits the poem in that purgatorial mental state to which the Ancient Mariner gives his name.

The sublime allegory, to borrow Lamb's phrase, of "Ancient Mariner" and, ultimately, *Lyrical Ballads* itself, concerns, then, theodicy and the nature of life in purgatory. The mind's fundamental problem is that it is in motion seeking stillness, built upon a paradox that enables it to see and experience briefly a joy it can never fully realize. Thus the individual is imprisoned within a mysterious phenomenal world that points to the presence of an even more inexplicable noumenal world. For, as Coleridge later explains in "Dejection: An Ode," the noumenal world manifests itself in the phenomenal:

And thence flows all that charms or ear or sight,
  All melodies the echoes of that voice,
All colours a suffusion from that light. (ll. 73–75)

To hear the voice from which all voices arise, to see the light from which all colors derive, is to feel the joy of the moment of stillness. This is the ontological home for which all humanity longs. Forced from this home, the mind becomes alienated from its own world, obsessed by its alienation, and subject not only to its own foibles but also to the larger inconsistencies and cruelties of an unjust social order. As a volume, *Lyrical Ballads* asks if the existence of such a world can be justified—and, if so, from what stance can it be successfully confronted?

[III]

"I pass, like night, from land to land," the Ancient Mariner tells the Wedding Guest (l. 619). The darkness of the Mariner's night filters throughout *Lyrical Ballads*. Character after character discovers the inadequacy of a human society based upon sterile preconceptions and close-mindedness and is subsequently cast adrift in a type of death-in-life. Alienation of this kind is generally expressed in the volume by motion of two sorts: the cramped near-paralysis of the prisoner or the aimless wandering of the outcast.

Albert of "The Foster-Mother's Tale," the second poem of the volume, is both a prisoner and a wanderer.[34] During his youth, Albert's immense learning convinces him of the falsity of his society's codes of decision. His subsequent "heretical and lawless talk" (l. 55) causes him to be cast into a dungeon. Imprisoned by the forces of an old and sterile world, Albert fittingly escapes to the "new world" of America (l. 76), where he "all alone, set sail by moonlight / Up a great river . . . / And ne'er was heard of more" (ll. 78–80). What we know of the Albert of *Osorio* is irrelevant here. More to the point is his function in *Lyrical Ballads*, where, of all the many prisoners and wanderers, Albert is the only character really to escape from his world. The Foster-Mother tells Maria that it is supposed that Albert "lived and died among the savage men" (l. 81). Ironically, though, the men of the old world are more truly savages. The openness of a landscape in which one can set sail alone "Upon a great river, great as any sea" (l. 79) promises much in contrast to the "hole" into which Albert is cast by the civilized men of his society.

Yet Albert's wanderings in the new, unstructured world of America represent a type of liberation unavailable to the other characters of the volume. Maria properly characterizes his story as a "sweet tale / Such as would lull a listening child to sleep" (ll. 68–69). The true prisoners in the poem are Maria and the Foster-Mother, for whom there is no escape. Indeed, even the Female Vagrant, who attempts such an escape, can find no liberation in the wartorn America she visits as the wife of a soldier. That America is merely a new world structured upon the same life-denying principles of the old. Her tale, like that of most of the other characters in *Lyrical Ballads*, is anything but "sweet." For these characters are confronted by a world in which only the child or the idiot can feel completely at home.

The dungeon into which Albert is thrown in "The Foster-Mother's Tale" first objectifies in *Lyrical Ballads* the dungeon grate through which the sun seems to peer at the Ancient Mariner. But the dungeon grate materializes again in both "The Convict" (poem #22) and "The Dungeon" (poem #14). Indeed, the narrator of "The Convict" himself peers "through the glimmering grate, / That outcast of pity [to] behold" (ll. 11–12). In the extremity of his alienation, the Ancient Mariner's heart becomes as "dry as dust." And we are told that on the "woful day" when Martha Ray of "The Thorn" (poem #12) is abandoned by her lover, "A cruel, cruel fire . . . / Into her bones was sent: / It dried her body like a cinder / And almost turn'd her brain to tinder" (ll. 128–32). We are thus well prepared to understand the dire alienation of the convict, whose "bones are consumed, and his life-blood is dried, / With wishes the past to undo" (ll. 21–22). Estranged from even himself, in grief "self-consumed" (l. 29), the convict is also the "Poor victim" (l. 45) of a society that chooses to alienate him further by confining him to what in "The Dungeon" is called an "uncomforted / And friendless solitude" (ll. 12–13).

"Have I not reason to lament / What man has made of man?" (ll. 23–24), concludes the narrator of "Lines Written in Early Spring." This question serves as a fit preface to the group of poems that immediately follow it, consisting of "The Thorn," "The Last of the Flock," and "The Dungeon." Indeed, "The Dungeon" begins by indignantly echoing, "And this place our forefathers made for man!" (l. 1). As if he were not already vulnerable enough to the forces of an alien world that defeats his understanding, man insists on structuring society upon principles that violate community. "The Last of the Flock" (poem #13) and "The Complaint of the Forsaken Indian Woman" (poem #21), poems that border "The Dungeon" and "The Convict," respectively, examine other "outcasts of pity" imprisoned by the structures that people create for one another.

Both the Shepherd of "The Last of the Flock" and the Indian Woman of "The Complaint of the Forsaken Indian Woman" are forsaken by their society.[35] Refused aid from his parish in "a time of need" (l. 42), the Shepherd is forced to sell his sheep, one by one. For the Shepherd, however, each sale is prophetic of all that stands between himself and complete nakedness:[36]

> To see the end of all my gains,
> The pretty flock which I had reared
> With all my care and pains,
> To see it melt like snow away!
> For me it was a woeful day. (ll. 56–60)

Like the "woful day" on which Martha Ray is forever alienated from her world, this woeful day leaves the Shepherd permanently estranged from his surroundings: "No peace, no comfort could I find, / No ease, within doors or without, / . . . / Ofttimes I thought to run away" (ll. 75–76, 79). Obsessed by his loss, the Shepherd can find no further meaning in his family or in life itself: "And now I care not if we die, / And perish all of poverty" (ll. 39–40).

Such a mental contraction dooms the Shepherd to be the prisoner of his own closed mind, "a jarring and dissonant thing / Amid this general dance and minstrelsy" (ll. 25–26), as the succeeding poem, "The Dungeon," phrases it. And it is as such that the narrator of "The Last of the Flock" first encounters him: "I have not often seen / A healthy man, a man full grown / Weep in the public roads alone" (ll. 2–4). If, then, the Shepherd is a victim of his own failure of vision, this failure would not be possible without the existence of an economic system that first encourages him to value his life in terms of his property and then abandons him to face his losses unaided. In a society in which each member is taught to look after his own interests, the welfare of others is of little importance.

"The Complaint of the Forsaken Indian Woman" poignantly restates the theme of "The Last of the Flock." Here, a woman overcome by sickness is abandoned by her companions: "Alas! you might have dragged me on / Another day, a single one!" (ll. 21–22). Her child given to "A woman who was not thy mother" (l. 32), the forsaken Indian Woman is "For ever left alone" (l. 59). As an "outcast of pity," trapped within the double prison of the structures of her society and a diseased body, the Indian Woman expresses more than the Shepherd's mere indifference to life: "Before I see another day / Oh let my body die away!" (ll. 1–2). Her plight reveals that one can be betrayed by internal as well as external forces. For the body can become as great a prison as any created by man for man. Certainly this is the case with Simon Lee.

Like the Shepherd, Simon Lee is a victim of poverty; like the forsaken Indian Woman, he is also a victim of his own body; and like both, he faces unaided a source of immedicable pain. Once a man "so full of glee" (l. 18), Simon is trapped by the passage of time in much the same way as Matthew, another "man of glee" ("The Fountain," l. 20), who appears in *Lyrical Ballads* (1800). Both men suffer because they can no longer be what they once were. Though their losses through time have been great—Matthew survives his family and Simon is the "sole survivor" (l. 24) of the inhabitants of Ivor Hall—each "Mourns less for what age takes away / Than what it leaves behind" ("The Fountain," ll. 35–36). And for Simon Lee time has left poverty, an infirm body, and a haunting sense of the past. This helps to explain why Simon's spirit seems so imprisoned by his broken body, in marked contrast to the old man in "Old Man Travelling," whose "bending figure" (l. 5) is the home for a mind "by nature led / To peace so perfect" (ll. 12–13).

Troubled in mind and infirm of body, Simon, "the poorest of the poor" (l. 60), is forced to work, "though weak, / —The weakest in the village" (ll. 39–40). Alone, Simon Lee can do little to combat an assault from within and without that has inevitable results: "Few months of life has he in store, / . . . / For still, the more he works, the more / His poor old ancles swell" (ll. 65, 67–68). Thus, the substance of the tale "the gentle reader" is to find in "Simon Lee" concerns not only the "burthen weighty" of time but also, as in "The Last of the Flock" and "The Complaint," the way in which the alienation of one human being from another is ultimately fatal for each. In fact, *Lyrical Ballads* contains two striking examples of the suicidal state of mind responsible for this alienation.

Through the course of his alienation, the Ancient Mariner learns the importance of community. His departing words to the Wedding Guest memorably state this knowledge: "He prayeth best who loveth best, / All things both great and small" (ll. 647–48). To participate in a state of mind that would make aliens of other living things is to make oneself an alien, cut off completely from community. Although it is the third poem of the volume, "Lines Left upon a Seat in a Yew-tree" is the first written by Wordsworth, and it stands as his preliminary statement of the ethic of "Ancient Mariner." Contempt or disdain for others, as the youth in the "Yew-tree" discovers, is ultimately suicidal.

Because his talents are neglected by the world, the youth "with rash disdain" (l. 19) turns away from his fellow beings

"And with the food of pride sustained his soul / In solitude" (ll. 20–21). Just as Blake's Urizen is always pictured in circumscribed space, the similarly solipsistic youth of the "Yew-tree" sits surrounded by the yew tree he has "taught" to encircle him (l. 10). And as he sits, the youth gazes upon the barren rocks before him, in which he finds an "emblem of his own unfruitful life" (l. 29). The youth cannot long survive upon "the food of pride." He dies completely isolated, proof that "The man, whose eye / Is ever on himself, doth look on one, / The least of nature's works" (ll. 51–53). Rephrasing the Mariner's recognition of the importance of community, the narrator of the "Yew-tree" comments: "he, who feels contempt / For any living thing, hath faculties / Which he has never used" (ll. 48–50).

These faculties also remain unused by Harry Gill, a man who vows to take vengeance on "Old Goody Blake" because she takes sticks from his hedge for firewood "when her old bones . . . [are] cold and chill" (l. 62). The delight Harry Gill takes in seizing this poor woman is indicative of the coldness of his heart, a coldness that is soon to become his ontological condition. For in response to Goody Blake's prayer, "O may he never more be warm!" (l. 100), Harry turns away from her "icy-cold," and "all who see him say 'tis plain, / That, live as long as he may, / He never will be warm again" (ll. 118–20). Those in *Lyrical Ballads* who feel contempt for others live suicidal lives, self-exiled into the "icy-cold" imprisonment of their own solipsism.

On the other hand, those characters in the volume who attempt to love others are not usually successful. The Ancient Mariner's tale, testifying to the divorce between the mind and the world, begins a noncontiguous group of poems concerned with marriage but ending in radical divorce. If the Wedding Guest is prevented from celebrating the marriage of a bride who is "Red as a rose" (l. 38), it is because there is a force in his world that can turn this red into the scarlet associated with the abandoned Martha Ray. The abandoned brides and brides-to-be of the *Lyrical Ballads* find themselves lonely, desperate wanderers. Indeed, the Mariner's powerful lament for his isolation is to echo throughout the marriage group: "Alone, alone, all all alone / Alone on the wide wide Sea" (ll. 224–25). This striking repetition of the "al" sound is to reappear in "The Female Vagrant" (poem #5) with much the same effect.

The Female Vagrant suffers increasing degrees of isolation, beginning with her first estrangement from her society, when she and her father are evicted forcibly from their home: "All but the bed where his old body lay, / All, all was seized, and weeping side by side, / We sought a home where we uninjured might abide" (ll. 52–54). The Female Vagrant's alienation is marked, like the Mariner's, by an inability to pray: "I could not pray:—through tears that fell in showers, / Glimmer'd our dear-loved home, alas! no longer ours!" (ll. 62–63).[37] Left homeless, she speaks to her lover "of marriage and our marriage day" (l. 70). Yet even though they soon marry, marriage is only a temporary solution to the Female Vagrant's homelessness. Destitution shortly forces her family to America where "All perished—all, in one remorseless year, / Husband and children! . . . / . . . all perished" (ll. 131–33). With all ties to humanity severed, she returns to England with only one desire: to "shun the spot where man might come" (l. 171).

Yet the Female Vagrant, again like the Mariner, finds a still moment of joy at sea, where the "heavenly silence" that "did the waves invest" brings "a joy to . . . [her] despair" (ll. 142, 144). Even so, she is forced to recognize the painful contrast between this moment of joy and the constant despair that reawaits her on land:

> Some mighty gulph of separation past,
> I seemed transported to another world:—
> A thought resigned with pain, when from the mast
> The impatient mariner the sail unfurl'd,
> And whistling, called the wind that hardly curled
> The silent sea. (ll. 163–68)

The "impatient mariner" is part of a world that refuses to remain motionless. Forced from stillness by the inexorable movement of the ship homeward, the Female Vagrant feels just as inexorably doomed to homelessness: "From the sweet thoughts of home, / And from all hope I was forever hurled" (ll. 168–69). Indeed, she returns to her "own countrée" an alien, "homeless near a thousand homes" (l. 179). A prisoner of "that perpetual weight which on her spirit lay" (l. 270), she has been as the poem closes "Three years a wanderer" (l. 262) across the English countryside.

Whereas marriage is useless as a remedy for alienation, it sometimes serves as a cause. Such is the case with both the Mad Mother and Martha Ray. Originally from "far . . . over the main" (l. 4), the Mad Mother is literally an alien to her surroundings. And this alienation is compounded by her marriage: though the Mad Mother can tell her child, "I am thy father's wedded wife" (l. 72), she must also painfully admit, "Thy father cares not for my breast" (l. 61). Abandoned by her husband, the Mad Mother becomes a homeless wanderer with only her child between her faltering mind and the radical loneliness that leads to insanity: "She has a baby on her arm, / Or else she were alone" (ll. 5–6).

Martha Ray, however, has nothing to shield her from such loneliness; she is even suspected of murdering her newborn child. Because she is betrayed by "unthinking" Stephen Hill, Martha Ray's wedding day becomes the "woful day" when she is forever alienated from her world. Like the Mad Mother, Martha, it is said, "was with child, and she was mad" (l. 139) —yet "in her womb the infant wrought / About its mother's heart, and brought / Her senses back again" (ll. 150–52). Martha, of course, can gain no lasting comfort from her child, if she ever actually was pregnant and did indeed give birth. Instead, like the Ancient Mariner she becomes an obsessive-compulsive, moving perpetually between her hut and the mountaintop, who in her "exceeding pain" is heard endlessly to repeat: "Oh misery! oh misery! / O woe is me! oh misery!" (ll. 252–53).

The characters of the marriage group, like those in the cluster of poems about imprisonment, are isolated aliens in their world, obsessed by their losses, helpless before the mystery at the heart of existence. Nor does there seem to be a way for them to reconnect with others. If, as we have seen, questions are a necessary step to this end, often a character's most earnest questions are left unanswered. Indeed, the volume insists that unanswered questions are an inevitable condition of human life. For words themselves are powerless to bridge completely the gap between the mind and the surrounding world.

While defending his use of tautology to Isabella Fenwick, Wordsworth says:

> . . . now every man must know that an attempt is rarely made to communicate impassioned feelings without something of an accompanying consciousness of the inadequateness of our own powers, or the deficiencies of language. During such efforts there will be a craving in the mind, and as long as it is unsatisfied the Speaker will cling to the same words, or words of the same character. (Owen, p. 140)

The inadequacy of words paradoxically leads to the mind's obsession with these same words. In a similar way, the mind's inability to comprehend certain aspects of its world can lead to obsession with these aspects. Thus, repetition, another characteristic of the traditional ballad, is also used often in *Lyrical Ballads* to depict obsession. For instance, the narrator's inability in "Anecdote for Fathers" (poem #9) to understand young Edward's preference of Kilve to Liswyn farm results in his fixation on the same question: "And five times did I say to him, / Why? Edward, tell me why?" (ll. 47–48). Likewise, the narrator of "We Are Seven" (poem #10), unable to understand the young girl's view of death, is obsessed with the desire to make her understand the logic of his arithmetic. His many subtractions of two from seven end in this last futile repetition: "But they are dead; those two are dead! / Their spirits are in heaven!" (ll. 65–66). Mystery and obsession, then, are two related forces in *Lyrical Ballads*. It is therefore unsurprising that "The Thorn," the poem in the volume that deals most directly with mystery, is the poem most filled with the questions of its narrator and the obsessions of its characters.

"The Thorn," moreover, gathers together the thematic strands of the preceding poems, which, in addition to mystery and obsession, include alienation, homelessness, and human suffering. Placed twelfth of twenty-three poems, "The Thorn" is itself composed of twenty-three stanzas, and at its midpoint—thus at the very center of the book—is the stanza concerning Martha Ray's aborted marriage plans and her attendant madness.[38] Here the reader reaches the heart of the darkness within *Lyrical Ballads*.

[IV]

At its most fundamental level "The Thorn" is a poem concerned with epistemology. As a prisoner of one's own subjectivity, how can one know anything about the surrounding world? As Paul Sheats has remarked, the word "know" is the leitmotif of the narrator's discourse.[39] Clearly, the narrator of "The Thorn" is obsessed by his lack of verifiable knowledge about Martha Ray. Though he informs the reader, "I'll tell you every thing I know" (l. 105), his knowledge proves extremely limited: "No more I know, I wish I did" (l. 155). For Martha Ray is shrouded in mystery.

Literally an alien to his surroundings, the narrator encounters her, "When to this country first I came" (l. 183). It is appropriate that their first encounter occurs during a violent storm that baffles the narrator's senses: "'Twas mist and rain, and storm and rain, / . . . / And then the wind! in faith, it was / A wind full ten times over" (ll. 188, 190–91). Like the "Wind and Tempest strong" in "Ancient Mariner," this storm is a violent reminder to man that he lives in an elemental world over which he has only limited control. Driven to seek what he expects to be the shelter of a nearby crag, the narrator instead finds the "jagged crag" to be "A woman seated on the ground" (l. 198). This woman, completely exposed to the fury of the storm, is an image of unaccommodated humanity. Like the face of Moneta in *The Fall of Hyperion*, her face initiates the narrator into the central mystery of the world—human suffering:

> I did not speak—I saw her face,
> Her face it was enough for me;
> I turned about and heard her cry,
> "O misery! O misery!" (ll. 199–202)

From this point on the narrator is obsessed with discovering the reason for such suffering.

There is a comic element in the futile way the narrator attempts to come to terms with this mystery. His careful measurement of the pond and solicitation of hearsay evidence does seem, as Sheats remarks, to give him the manner of "an amateur detective reporting on a private inquest into a village mystery."[40] However, this comic element exists only because of the tragic inadequacy of empirical facts to explain a "village mystery" whose implications are universal. The narrator himself is only too aware of the inadequacy of his methods. Though an amateur detective, he is careful to make distinctions between hearsay evidence and evidence that he has gathered firsthand.[41] Hearsay evidence is useless to dispel the mystery:

> For what became of this poor child
> There's none that ever knew:
> And if a child was born or no,
> There's no one that could ever tell;
> And if 'twas born alive or dead,
> There's no one knows, as I have said . . .
> (ll. 157–62)

Yet the narrator's own empirical observations are just as useless. His only certainty is that Martha Ray can be found on a mountaintop lamenting at all hours of the day and night, seated between a muddy pond and a heap of moss that lie close to an aged thorn. This is the locus of mystery: "'But what's the thorn? and what's the pond? / 'And what's the hill of moss to her? / . . . / I cannot tell'" (ll. 210–11, 214).

The thorn, the pond, and the hill of moss are all parts of a phenomenal world that refuses to yield its secrets to man. Each acts as a symbol of mystery. Thus, the thorn is a convoluted "mass of knotted joints" (l. 8), suggesting the complex, unsolvable mystery surrounding Martha Ray. And the pond seems to all to conceal "The shadow of a babe" (l. 227) just below its surface. But especially interesting in this context is the "beauteous heap" (l. 36) of moss. For the world described in *Lyrical Ballads* is usually not evoked in terms of color. Besides green and an occasional blue, few colors appear in any of the poems. One notable exception to this is "Ancient Mariner," a poem emanating the colors of a mysterious phenomenal world capable of baffling man's senses. The only other exception lies near the center of the central poem of the volume. The beauteous heap of moss in "The Thorn" is the repository of all colors: "All lovely colours there you see, / All colours that were ever seen" (ll. 38–39). It is also the most tantalizing site in the poem. Though all the villagers agree that Martha Ray buried her baby beneath the mound of moss, their attempt to verify this assumption by digging up the baby's body results in the only supernatural occurrence in the poem reported without qualification by the narrator:

> But then the beauteous hill of moss
> Before their eyes began to stir;
> And for full fifty yards around,
> The grass it shook upon the ground. (ll. 236–39)

A symbol of the dazzling richness of the phenomenal world, the beauteous hill of moss refuses to allow human beings to pierce beneath its surface to discover what lies hidden below. Though prevented by the mound's movement from gaining certain knowledge, the villagers, in an echo of the Mariner's shipmates, still "aver" (l. 240) that the baby is buried there.[42] They thus disguise their inability to solve the mystery of their world with a false veneer of certainty that is as foolish and misguided as the attempt made by the Mariner's shipmates to explain their mysterious world through causality. The mentality responsible for the villagers' pretense at having solved the "village mystery" enables them to live comfortably in a world based upon as tenuous a foundation as that of the world originally inhabited by the Wedding Guest.

The narrator, however, is not content with such a cast of mind. His only certainty is that the mystery surrounding the suffering of a fellow human being cannot be solved by the empiricism with which he almost compulsively responds. He, like the Mariner, is obsessed by the nature of a world that defeats rational explanation. This obsession is responsible for his garrulousness, particularly the many questions and repetitions that fill his account. The "burthen of the mystery" lies as heavily on man as the heavy tufts of moss that strive to drag the thorn to the ground. Too often, his questions, like those asked by the narrator of "The Thorn," go unanswered:

> "And wherefore does she cry?—
> Oh wherefore? wherefore? tell me why
> Does she repeat that doleful cry?" (ll. 86–88)

[V]

The opening and central poems of *Lyrical Ballads* thus help to form the bulwark of a structure over which the dark night of the Mariner seems thematically to hold sway. Against this darkness, however, stand the credal poems of the volume, works emphasizing the plenitude available to a human mind responsive to all it encounters. To such a mind, both nature and others can be a source of joy. By "stopping" the world it fictively creates and opening itself to its surroundings, the mind, however briefly, can even redeem the night world it inhabits.

Stopping the world requires the kind of silence that fills the night world of the first credal poem, "The Nightingale" (poem #4): "All is still, / A balmy night!" (ll. 7–8). Such a stillness permits man to open himself "to the influxes / Of shapes and sounds and shifting elements / Surrendering his whole spirit" (ll. 27–29). The surrender of his "whole spirit" requires man to abandon his mental defenses against mystery. Only then does he find that within mystery itself is a source of joy from which he has been willfully cut off. For the night contains the song of the nightingale as well as the plaintive cries of Martha Ray.

Fittingly, the locus of the nightingale—about which the narrator says, "never elsewhere in one place I knew / So many Nightingales" (ll. 55–56)—is an abandoned grove, where the structures man once imposed on the world have been burst: "This grove is wild with tangling underwood, / And the trim walks are broken up, and grass, / Thin grass and king-cups grow within the paths" (ll. 52–54). There, the nightingale's song speaks of a world filled with reciprocity and love. Not only do the nightingales "answer and provoke each other's songs" (l. 58), but these songs themselves are lovingly attuned to the motion of their surroundings. A receptive watcher can see "Many a Nightingale perch giddily / On blosmy twig still swinging from the breeze, / And to that motion tune his wanton song" (ll. 83–85).

In connection with Wordsworth's poetry, Roger Murray has remarked upon the presence of "that speechless, imageless moment of pure feeling, that prelude or postlude to communion that occupies the pauses of the poem, its silences."[43] Such a moment, as evidenced by both "Ancient Mariner" and "The Nightingale," occurs in Coleridge's poems as well. Here, the "gentle maid" of the grove, the archetype in the poem of human receptivity,

> oft, a moment's space,
> What time the moon was lost behind a cloud,
> Hath heard a pause of silence: till the Moon
> Emerging, hath awaken'd earth and sky
> With one sensation, and those wakeful Birds
> Have all burst forth in choral minstrelsy,

As if one quick and sudden Gale had swept
An hundred airy harps! (ll. 75–82)

For the duration of this hallowing, this moment of joyful communion prepared for by stillness, there is a blending in which all distinctions between self and otherness vanish.

Wordsworth wrote to Walter Savage Landor of his liking for poetry "where things are lost in each other, and limits vanish, and aspirations are raised."[44] Certainly his poetry is filled with these moments; *Lyrical Ballads* (1800) contains this notable example, which was later published as part of the fifth book of *The Prelude*:

And, when it chanced
That pauses of deep silence mock'd his skill,
Then, sometimes, in that silence, while he hung
Listening, a gentle shock of mild surprize
Has carried far into his heart the voice
Of mountain torrents, or the visible scene
Would enter unawares into his mind
With all its solemn imagery, its rocks,
Its woods, and that uncertain heaven, receiv'd
Into the bosom of the steady lake.
("There Was a Boy," ll. 16–25)

In a fragment that de Selincourt conjectures was written between the summer of 1798 and February 1800 and, quite probably, rejected from *The Prelude*, Wordsworth speaks

Of that false secondary power by which
In weakness we create distinctions, then
Believe that (*all*)[*sic*] our puny boundaries are things
Which we perceive and not which we have made.[45]

The consciousness resulting from the mind's need to structure its world rationally, "Not only is not worthy to be deemed / Our being, to be prized as what we are, / But is the very littleness of life."[46]

The mind is only truly in touch with being when it breaks

through all barriers of subjectivity and rationally created structures in moments of framelessness

> In which all beings live with god, are lost
> In god and nature, existing in one mighty whole,
> As indistinguishable as the cloudless east
> At noon is from the cloudless west when all
> The hemisphere is one cerulean blue.[47]

This is why William of "The Tables Turned" insists that "Our meddling intellect / Mis-shapes the beauteous forms of things" (ll. 26–27). If man instead approaches his world with the openness of "a heart / That watches and receives" (ll. 31–32), he can learn "more of man; / Of moral evil and of good" (ll. 22–23) from a single impulse from a vernal wood than from all the wisdom recorded in the "barren leaves" (l. 30) of books. Or as the writer of "Lines Written at a Small Distance" tells his sister, "One moment now may give us more / Than fifty years of reason" (ll. 25–26).

By the limited response of a measured and measuring mind we impose the shackles of "joyless forms" ("Lines," l. 17) upon time. We, however, through silent receptivity can transform the dead and joyless forms of time into joyful "hour[s] of feeling" ("Lines," l. 24). Time is then part of a "living Calendar" ("Lines," l. 18), experienced in terms of an all-encompassing motion, a "blessed power that rolls / About, below, above" ("Lines," ll. 33–34). Like the nightingale, the mind can attune itself to this motion, framing from it the measure of a soul that "shall be tuned to love" ("Lines," l. 36). The resultant harmony becomes, like the nightingale's song, both the answer to and the cause of other songs, stealing from "heart to heart" and moving "From earth to man, from man to earth" in a universal birth of love ("Lines," ll. 22, 23).

In the midst of these hallowed moments of reciprocity and community, one is truly at home in the world. Perhaps this is why, after invoking such a moment, the narrator of "The Nightingale" turns his thoughts homeward: "And now for our dear homes" (l. 90). The thought of home, in turn, provokes the narrator to think of his child, whose as yet unstructured mind allows him the peace provided by a moment of stillness: "And he beholds the moon, and hush'd at once / Suspends his sobs, and laughs most silently" (ll. 102–3). As a link to these moments of joy and community, the nightingale's song provides such an effective defense against darkness, "That should you close your eyes, you might almost / Forget it was not day!" (ll. 63–64). The narrator is therefore determined that his son shall "grow up / Familiar with these songs, that with the night / He may associate Joy!" (ll. 107–9). Even in the midst of darkness, then, his son will find a home.

However, most of the characters of *Lyrical Ballads*, as we have seen, find this a home in which they cannot long dwell. If in nature "there is nothing melancholy" ("Nightingale," l. 15), that is because melancholy originates in human consciousness. And it is the mind that conditions our perception of nature, not the other way around. Indeed, like the "night-wandering Man" (l. 16) cited in "The Nightingale" who responds to the nightingale's song with melancholy, the poet of "Lines Written in Early Spring" finds that the "thousand blended notes" (l. 1) sounded throughout the grove in which he sits bring "sad thoughts to the mind" (l. 4). Here, nature is again filled with reciprocal and joyous motion: "The budding twigs spread out their fan, / To catch the breezy air" (ll. 17–18), and the "least motion" (l. 15) made by birds in their play "seem'd a thrill of pleasure" (l. 16). Human nature, however, is only a brief visitor in this world: "To her fair works did nature link / The human soul that through me ran" (ll. 5–6).

The natural world and the human soul are distinct, and the knowledge that the mind not only creates but actively fosters this separation makes even these brief moments of marriage seem more concerned with divorce. No wonder the poet of "Lines Written in Early Spring" cannot prevent himself from responding to the harmony of his surroundings with a dissonant lament about "What man has made of man" (l. 8). In a disconcerting way, the credal lyrics seem to reach conclusions about the human condition similar to those reached by "Ancient Mariner." Even the daylight world summons thoughts about the night.

Of all the "night-wandering" inhabitants of the world presented by *Lyrical Ballads*, only the Idiot Boy (in poem #16) has a permanent home. Unburdened by a rationally structured consciousness as well as unimprisoned by his own subjectivity, the Idiot Boy possesses the openness of a mind incapable of imposing frames upon the world. Thus Betty Foy's repeated pleas for her son to come home again from his night-journey are a sign of her ignorant love. For wherever Johnny goes he is at home. And to be at home in *Lyrical Ballads* is to feel joy: "For joy he cannot hold the bridle, / For joy his head and heels are idle, / He's idle all for very joy" (ll. 84–86).

The essence of his condition is revealed in Johnny's answer to his mother's loving request: "Tell us Johnny, do, / Where all this long night you have been, / What you have heard, what you have seen" (ll. 448–50). Silently wandering through the long night from "eight o'clock till five" (l. 456), Johnny perceives that the "cocks did crow to-whoo, to-whoo / And the sun did shine so cold" (ll. 460–61). By his conversion of the owl's song and the moon into a cock crow and the sun, the Idiot Boy has triumphantly turned night into day. This is indeed his "glory" (l. 462). As Wordsworth explained to John Wilson, "I have often applied to Idiots, in my own mind, that sublime expression of scripture that, *their life is hidden with God*" (*EY*, p. 357). Perhaps the key word here is "hidden." The idiot is in touch permanently with a realm most men find only in their childhood, or, like the Mariner, regain only to lose again.[48] Chief among this last group is the poet.

Immediately following a poem centrally concerned with an idiot's response to the night is "Lines Written at Evening," a poem focused on a poet's response to the gathering "evening darkness" (l. 39). This poet sees the peacefulness of the silently flowing Thames at evening as deceptive: "Such views the youthful bard allure" (l. 9). No longer a "youthful bard" himself, the poet cannot forget the night that lies beyond the evening's moment of stillness: ". . . let him [the youthful bard] nurse his fond deceit, / And what if he must die in sorrow!"

(ll. 13–14). Yet the moment itself is so enchanting he cannot resist asking that the Thames glide silently,

> Thy quiet soul on all bestowing,
> 'Till all our minds for ever flow,
> As thy deep waters are now flowing.
>
> Vain Thought! (ll. 22–25)

A moment cannot last "for ever," and even if it could, people seem resistant to opening their minds to stillness. Small wonder, then, that he considers his request to the Thames to be a vain thought.

A poet, caught between a vision of a suffering humanity and a vision of possible community and joy, can easily give way to despair and, like the figure of Collins invoked in "Lines Written at Evening," "find no refuge from distress, / But in the milder grief of pity" (ll. 31–32). Balanced precariously between the paradisal naiveté of the youthful bard's day and the hellish distress of the aged poet's night is the purgatorial evening of the poet of "Lines Written at Evening," who despite his knowledge is still a lover of silence: "How calm! how still! the only sound, / The dripping of the oar suspended!" (ll. 37–38). For in the stillness of the gently gliding Thames can be seen the vital "image of a poet's heart" (l. 27), "bright," "solemn," and "serene" (l. 28).

[VI]

"The beginning was awakening & striking; the ending is soothing and solemn." Just as they all found their beginning in "Ancient Mariner," all roads of inquiry in *Lyrical Ballads* lead to the "soothing and solemn" conclusion provided by "Tintern Abbey." The two poems stand as seed and fruit; between them is a maturation that progresses through the exhaustive exploration of the human condition accomplished in the volume's other poems. Much of the seed, however, can still be found in the fruit: both examine the nature of a mysterious phenomenal world in which the mind seems imprisoned; both contain moments of stillness during which a person ceases to be an alien in this world; and both detail the suffering of individuals who, after having experienced these moments, are forced to live outside of them.[49]

Fundamentally, then, "Ancient Mariner" and "Tintern Abbey," like the poems they hold in tension between them, are concerned with radical loss. The "Ancient Mariner" provides no strategy for dealing successfully with the loss it depicts. In its world, mystery, alienation, and obsession seem to triumph over people who are so befuddled that most do not even recognize the nature of their predicament. Yet the "Ancient Mariner" differs from "Tintern Abbey" as night from day. Opposed to the Mariner's bleak night is the midsummer's day of the speaker of "Tintern Abbey." This is not to say that "Tintern Abbey" ignores the questions posed by "Ancient Mariner." On the contrary, only its dearly bought comprehensiveness allows "Tintern Abbey" its affirmations. For it is a poem whose vision accounts for the length of both "five summers" (l. 1) and "five long winters" (l. 2) in the life of its speaker.

Like the Mariner returning to his "own countrée," the speaker of "Tintern Abbey" returns to the Wye valley "after many wanderings" (l. 157). From motion to motion arrested: "The day is come when I again repose / Here . . ." (ll. 9–10). In the stillness of the Wye valley, the wanderer can once again repose—this time, however, to evaluate the moment of stillness itself. This moment seemingly allows man "with an eye made quiet by the power / Of harmony, and the deep power of joy" (ll. 48–49) to "see into the life of things" (l. 50). The "burthen of the mystery" (l. 39) is thus lightened temporarily. Here, however, complexities multiply.

It is by now a critical commonplace that the speaker of "Tintern Abbey" qualifies his assertions both about the cause and the efficacy of such moments. He, unlike many of the people in *Lyrical Ballads*, recognizes the inadequacy of attempting to impose causal relationships upon this "unintelligible world" (l. 41). Important qualifications, like "such, perhaps, / As may have had no trivial influence / On . . ." (ll. 32–

34) and "Nor less, I trust / To them I may have owed another gift . . ." (ll. 36–37) accompany what would otherwise be powerful assertions about these moments. Moreover, even in the moment of stillness people cannot be still completely; instead they are "laid asleep / In body" (ll. 46–47), "the breath of this corporeal frame, / And even the motion of our human blood / Almost suspended" (ll. 44–46). The motion of the blood, of course, can only be "almost suspended." We are always in motion and must awake from a sleep from which ultimately we gain merely temporary solace. In such sleep are rays of comforting light amidst a disconcerting darkness. But one's eyes must adjust to darkness before one can make headway through it. Such an adjustment allows one, like the old man in "Old Man Travelling," to move not "with pain, but . . . / With thought" (ll. 6–7). "Tintern Abbey" and the entire volume itself ask that this adjustment be made.

The poet of "Lines Written at Evening" voices his doubt about the power of the silently flowing Thames to induce profound and lasting change with a regretful "Vain thought!" Yet he still turns for solace to a river in which he finds the "image of a poet's heart." In a similar way, the speaker of "Tintern Abbey" regretfully entertains doubts about the power of the Wye: "If this / Be but a vain belief . . ." (ll. 50–51). These doubts, however, are countered by his realization of the number of times his thoughts have turned to the memory of the Wye for comfort against encroaching darkness:

> . . . yet, oh! how oft
> In darkness, and amid the many shapes
> Of joyless day-light . . .
> . . . .
> How oft, in spirit, have I turned to thee
> O sylvan Wye! Thou wanderer through the woods,
> How often has my spirit turned to thee!
> (ll. 51–53, 56–58)

The speaker of "Tintern Abbey" also turns to a river for comfort—but to the Wye, not the silent Thames. For, like most of the inhabitants of *Lyrical Ballads*, like the speaker of "Tintern

Abbey" himself, the Wye is a "wanderer through the woods." If one cannot live in stillness, if there is no place in which one can permanently repose or no moment in whose infinite extension one can find a home, then one's only reasonable alternative is to embrace motion and willingly become a wanderer. That the speaker's spirit has turned all along to a fellow wanderer for comfort against darkness proves that he has already begun this embrace. If the deep-flowing waters of the Thames provide an image of a poet's heart, the wandering of the Wye provides an image of his mind.

To embrace motion is to recognize its presence in time as well as space and to accept the inevitable loss it brings. Gone in the adult is the framelessness with which a youth's mind participates in constant community with its world: "That time is past, / And all its aching joys are now no more" (ll. 84–85). This loss is great. Maintaining mental equilibrium in its wake requires an almost heroic act of mind to locate in the speaker's present condition something that might serve as a sufficient counterweight: "Not for this / Faint I, nor murmur: other gifts / Have followed, for such loss, I would believe, / Abundant recompence" (ll. 86–89). As his "I would believe" implies, there is an act of will involved in the daring assertion he is about to make. For the speaker attempts to establish the consequences of radical loss as more than compensating for the loss itself. If nature can no longer be experienced as his "all in all" (l. 76), it can instead speak to him, as it had to the poet of "Lines Written in Early Spring," of humanity.

Moreover, nature can speak to him of "A motion and a spirit, that impels / All thinking things, all objects of all thought, / And rolls through all things" (ll. 101–3). Through such speech it can give one a "sense sublime" (l. 96) of his participation in a community overlooked even in childhood. As the vital principle operant in all things, motion is the basis of that community. However, the only way to find a home in this kind of community is by accepting the perpetual homelessness imposed by constant motion. And constant motion also necessitates the constant loss of which the "still, sad music of humanity" (l. 92) is expressive. In his perception of the meaning of this music, in his ability to recognize in "nature and the language of the sense" the community of and necessity for motion, the speaker finds, paradoxically, an anchor: "The anchor of my purest thoughts, the nurse, / The guide, the guardian of my heart, and soul / Of all my moral being" (ll. 110–12).[50]

Here is indeed abundant recompense for loss. No longer "all in all," nature is still much. For it can both teach us to embrace wandering and provide us with moments of silent joy to help offset the suffering of homelessness within the hellish world that we have made for each other, so that "neither evil tongues, / Rash judgments, nor the sneers of selfish men, / Nor greetings where no kindness is, nor all / The dreary intercourse of daily life, / Shall e'er prevail against us" (ll. 129–33). Further, as both the stimulus and product of "all the mighty world / Of eye and ear, both what they half-create, / And what perceive" (ll. 106–8), nature draws us into an encounter in which we learn the value of bursting through the confining bonds of selfhood.

The act of perception itself is thus a moral lesson concerning the value of overcoming otherness. In this way nature leads man back to man. More than this, nature cannot do. For nature is part of a larger mystery whose "burthen" it helps to lighten but can do nothing to remove. The only hearts that nature "betrays" are those who cannot truly love it because they perceive it to be either more or less than it is. One who loves nature, however, knows that it can help the mind to face the darkness of this world, but, more important, understands that nature's greatest lesson is that humanity not only can but must help itself.

Motion implies motionlessness. Thus to embrace motion fully requires the courage to face death, the ultimate loss time forces upon human beings:

> Nor, perchance,
> If I should be, where I can no more hear
> Thy voice, nor catch from thy wild eyes these gleams
> Of past existence, wilt thou then forget

> That on the banks of this delightful stream
> We stood together; . . . (ll. 147–52)

Like the nightingale, the mind can respond to motion with reciprocal motion. To the motion of time it responds with memory.[51] If time necessitates loss, memory can create a storehouse of comforting images to help one cope with loss, a storehouse that becomes the only real home a wanderer ever has: "thy mind / Shall be a mansion for all lovely forms, / Thy memory be as a dwelling-place / For all sweet sounds and harmonies" (ll. 140–43).

Chief among these harmonies are the "exhortations" the speaker now addresses to his sister, for they proceed from love—humanity's most effective response to loss. Like the song of the nightingale, "that with the night" can help the mind "to associate Joy," the speaker of "Tintern Abbey" hopes that his exhortations will help give his sister joy in the midst of darkness: "Oh! then / If solitude, or fear, or pain, or grief, / Should be thy portion, with what healing thoughts / Of tender joy wilt thou remember me, / And these my exhortations!" (ll. 143–47). If human beings are alienated from the world by forces beyond their control, then they must do all within their control to combat this alienation. Only love can heal the wounds caused by alienation and loss: it is the force that breaks down the artificial barriers the mind creates between itself and all that surrounds it. The joy felt within the moment of stillness is thus love; and though the stillness cannot last, love can.

Therefore, as the speaker and his sister stand together on the banks of a stream that speaks to them of wandering and all the subsequent losses to which they will be subject, he, in his most heroic gesture, can assert the power of love to stand as abundant recompense for all loss:[52]

> That after many wanderings, many years
> Of absence, these steep woods and lofty cliffs,
> And this green pastoral landscape, were to me
> More dear, both for themselves, and for thy sake.
> (ll. 157–60)

"Tintern Abbey" and the other credal poems of *Lyrical Ballads* suggest that human beings must ultimately learn their values from the high points of their own imaginative and moral experience—and retain such experiences throughout life as a means of nurture and renewal.

[VII]

The "field" of *Lyrical Ballads*, then, is polarized between its beginning in otherness, "It is an ancyent Marinere," and the love expressed in its final words, "for thy sake." Both "Ancient Mariner" and "Tintern Abbey" are told to single auditors, with the intention of educating these listeners to the true nature of their world. However, the Mariner speaks compulsively to a man he addresses as "Stranger." His tale is of a night of which the Wedding Guest is at first unaware, and then by which he is overwhelmed. "Tintern Abbey," on the other hand, is a voluntary and courageous confrontation with darkness, addressed to a "dear, dear Friend," with the intention of helping this loved one find a stance from which to encounter night successfully. Opposing the Mariner's involuntary wandering is the speaker's embrace of wandering. The Mariner, to quote "Tintern Abbey" out of context, is "more like a man / Flying from something that he dreads, than one / Who sought the thing he loved" (ll. 71–73). Ultimately, however, more is risked by the man who seeks the thing he loves. For, as we have seen, the Mariner is locked into a Blakean limit of contraction: he cannot fall below the purgatory in which he lives, though he must endlessly suffer its condition. But the speaker of "Tintern Abbey" lives in a more tenuously based purgatory: by voluntarily embracing the darkness of the human condition within an inexplicable world, he suffers the possibility of falling into the hell of a deep despair. Yet only in this way can he fashion the "exhortations" that give him value as a poet. Only by entering freely into night can he hope to emerge into day.[53]

The characters of *Lyrical Ballads* have no means for determining theodicy: the ways of God are part of a mystery far beyond their comprehension. In their world human beings must justify their own existence. They must create the values by which they live. That is why the "poet" of the volume has so much at stake. For, ultimately, the ability of Wordsworth-Coleridge to see the disastrous consequences of man's continued inhumanity to man is responsible for the human and humane poetry of the collection. As a whole, *Lyrical Ballads* exposes those like the Mariner's shipmates, who first convict him and then become accomplices in his crime; those like the townspeople in "The Thorn," who, without any grounds for certainty, decide the question of Martha Ray's guilt; those responsible for the building of dungeons and the imprisonment of their fellow human beings within them; all those whose "pre-established codes of decision" result in rash and heartless judgments that condemn others to live in isolation, poverty, and misery without the consolation of sympathy, aid, or love.

Like the many moments of stillness it contains, the unified field of *Lyrical Ballads* "stops" the world for its readers. If successful, it will release them back into motion both sadder and wiser. But theirs will be the solemn sadness of those who have recognized their predicament, embraced their wandering state, and opened their hearts to their fellows. The result of this openness is community with all that is human: "human passions, human characters, and human incidents" (Advertisement, p. 3). From this comes love and understanding—the basis for an earth made heaven.

CHAPTER 4

"Lamia" Progressing

Keats's 1820 Volume

It is my intention to wait a few years before I publish any minor poems—and then I hope to have a volume of some worth—and which those people will realish [sic] *who cannot bear the burthen of a long poem.*

Keats to George and Georgiana Keats

That which is creative must create itself.

Keats to J. A. Hessey

CONTENTS.

Contents page of Keats's *Lamia* volume.
Courtesy of Library of Congress,
Special Collections Division

[1]

After the failure of *Endymion*, Keats—as he later put it—decided "to use more finesse with the Public."[1] In 1820 he would substitute for the often tedious form of the long poem a group of shorter poems that, read together, would be epic in scope but not burden the reader. This time he would indeed use more finesse—and produce "a volume of some worth."

Keats had already seen the kind of coherent statement he could make by grouping poems in his 1817 volume. There, as Jack Stillinger has remarked, nearly every poem is related to "the question of whether he can and should be a poet."[2] As important a question in this early collection is what type of poet Keats ought to be. Beginning Keats's project of self-discovery, *Poems* opens by observing that "Glory and loveliness have passed away."[3] But they have passed, in part, because they no longer suffice. The mind is now unable to respond with unequivocal delight to a world promising natural plenitude, for it has learned that process underlies the foundations of that world, and that whatever is given will be taken away. Fittingly, then, in the concluding poem of the 1817 collection, "Sleep and Poetry," Keats dedicates himself to becoming a poet of the "agonies, the strife / Of human hearts" (ll. 124–25). Only such a poet can possibly accommodate human beings to the loss that is at the center of human experience. The *Lamia* volume records Keats's attempts at this accommodation.

In a letter to his sister Fanny, written late in December 1819, Keats confides: "I have been very busy . . . preparing some Poems to come out in the Sp[r]ing" (*LK*, 2:237). Before the *Lamia* collection was actually published in early July 1820, Keats's health had declined dramatically. Yet despite his illness, evidence suggests that, with the possible exception of "Hyperion," Keats oversaw the printing of the collection.[4] In all likelihood, his editor Taylor and Taylor's literary adviser Woodhouse guided Keats in selecting and arranging the poems. These two freely altered the printer's copy of the 1820 volume, suggesting small textual changes that Keats in several cases accepted gratefully.[5] There is little reason to suppose that this collaboration did not extend to the organization of the collection itself, especially given Taylor's interest in such matters. Without evidence to the contrary, however, we ought to assume that the final contextural decisions—like the textual ones—were left to Keats himself. Indeed, Jack Stillinger has found that in the production of the *Lamia* collection, as in his other volumes, "Keats was allowed to have his way in things that mattered to him."[6]

Still, we might with good reason question whether Keats wanted "Hyperion" to appear in the collection. The Advertisement to the volume openly claims that he did not: "If any apology be thought necessary for the appearance of the unfinished poem of HYPERION, the publishers beg to state that they alone are responsible, as it was printed at their particular request, and contrary to the wish of the author" (*Poems*, p. 736). Yet, in reaction to the defensive, embarrassed tone of the Advertisement, Keats crossed it out entirely in a copy presented to Burridge Davenport, disowning it as "none of my doing—I w[as] ill at the time."[7] Moreover, Woodhouse's earlier draft of the Advertisement implies that, regardless of who first thought to include "Hyperion," Keats later acquiesced in the choice: "The Publishers have however prevailed upon him [i.e., Keats] to allow of its [i.e., "Hyperion"] ⟨being printed in⟩ . . . this volume."[8] Two trial layouts in Woodhouse's notebook for the title page of the book—one without "Hyperion," the other listing "Hyperion" as the second poem—further suggest that Keats not only may have consented to admit "Hyperion," but may even have decided on its placement (*somebody* moved it from the second place to the last).[9]

More important, finally, than whether Keats assembled the *Lamia* volume alone or jointly with his editors is that it does show sophisticated organization. In general, its thirteen poems are grouped by genre: the three opening romances are followed by clusters of three odes, four rondeaus, and two odes—with the fragment "Hyperion" concluding the whole. Within these groups, poems are positioned without reference to their chronological order of composition. For instance, although it was almost certainly written before the "Ode to a

Nightingale" and the "Ode to a Grecian Urn," the "Ode to Psyche" is placed after both; conversely, "Lamia" is the first of the romances, though the last composed. Such positionings, along with the placement of the five odes into two separate groups rather than a single generic block, suggest that the order of the poems is itself important.[10]

In fact, as the reader moves sequentially from the opening "Lamia" to the concluding "Hyperion," he discovers a complex system of verbal echoes, transitional links, and thematic progressions through which each poem revises the meaning of its predecessor. Stanley Fish has shrewdly observed that "one can analyze an effect without worrying whether it was produced accidentally or on purpose," although, as Fish somewhat ruefully concedes, "I always find myself worrying in just this way."[11] Whereas it is, perhaps, impossible to prove that Keats consciously organized the *Lamia* volume as a progressive and self-revising structure, it can be shown that such a reading is consonant with Keats's own view of the poetic process and the actual movement of the poems themselves.

Five months before the publication of the collection, Keats wrote to Fanny Brawne that "it will be a nice idle amusement to hunt after a motto for my Book which I will have if lucky enough to hit a fit one" (*LK*, 2:277). If pursued, his search must have been futile: the volume appeared without a motto or preface provided by its author. Ironically, had he remembered, Keats could have plundered one of his own letters for an apt motto: "That which is creative," he had written to J. A. Hessey, "must create itself" (*LK*, 1:374). Stuart Sperry has noted Keats's "insistence on the integrity of the creative process and the life of the work, that the poem must to a large degree evolve its own values and implications as it proceeded, that it must discover its own significance and create its own conclusions."[12] Assembled, the *Lamia* poems began to evolve their own implications and conclusions. Nor need Keats have initially planned it so: as he once told Haydon, "things which [I] do half at Random are afterwards confirmed by my judgment in a dozen features of Propriety" (*LK*, 1:142).

In August 1819, when all of the poems to appear in the *La-*

mia volume had been completed except "To Autumn," Keats wrote Reynolds: "the best sort of Poetry—that is all I care for, all I live for" (*LK*, 2:147). A comment earlier in the same letter provides a clue to the sort of poetry that helped shape Keats's aspirations: "the Paradise Lost becomes a greater wonder" (*LK*, 2:146). In *Paradise Lost* Keats found the epitome of epic style and scope. He annotates his copy of the poem: "the Genius of Milton, more particularly in respect to its span in immensity, calculated him by a sort of birthright, for such an 'argument' as the paradise lost."[13] Milton's "span in immensity" was particularly attractive to a poet who criticized his contemporaries because "each . . . like an Elector of Hanover governs his petty state, & knows how many straws are swept daily from the Causeways in all his dominions & has a continual itching that all the Housewives should have their coppers well scoured: the antients were Emperors of vast Provinces, they had only heard of the remote ones and scarcely cared to visit them" (*LK*, 1:224).

To be an "Emperor of vast Provinces" is to be like the Elizabethan poets and Milton, capable of ranging through the entire imaginative spectrum—from a lark with fancy to the concrete richness of the vision in "To Autumn" to the abstract "Hyperion." The variety of genres and styles in the *Lamia* collection is thus purposeful: Keats is not only exploring the possibilities of poetic form, but he is also locating himself within poetic tradition. "Why should we be owls," he asks Reynolds, "when we can be Eagles?" (*LK*, 1:224).

Keats's letters show that Milton was very much in his thoughts during the summer of 1819. But so, as always, was Shakespeare. In August he writes to Bailey, "Shakespeare and the paradise Lost every day become greater wonders to me—I look upon fine Phrases like a Lover" (*LK*, 2:139). It has long been recognized that the council scenes of *Paradise Lost* and *Troilus and Cressida* coalesced in Keats's mind as he wrote the second book of "Hyperion." However, the extent to which Shakespeare's play influenced Keats's vision, particularly in the *Lamia* poems, has for just as long been overlooked.[14]

Not only did Keats know *Troilus and Cressida* thoroughly,

but, according to Caroline Spurgeon, there is "no doubt that he was reading and re-reading the play" in the spring and summer of 1820, while the *Lamia* volume was being prepared for publication.[15] Keats found in this reading a play that, perhaps above all else, concerns enchantment. "Let thy song be love," Helen tells Pandarus in *Troilus and Cressida*, adding, "This love will undo us all. / O Cupid, Cupid, Cupid!" (3.1.102–3).[16] Keats's 1820 volume begins with three long poems about pairs of lovers, each, in a different way, "undone" by love. Just as *Troilus and Cressida* broadens from its microcosmic examination of its lovers' relationships to a depiction of the world gone awry, so, in the examination of the relationships between its lovers, does the *Lamia* volume begin to depict a world with which human beings and their unrealizable desires are forever at odds.

Through the course of his love for Cressida, Troilus learns the danger of enchantment: the mind can seduce itself by shaping the world into the image of its own desires. The world it then views is one of wish fulfillment, the realm of romance. Here is a powerful source of intoxication. Such a world even threatens death because it provides a fulfillment so complete, a "sweetness so sharp," that the mind may be unable to bear its own pleasure.[17] Although Troilus experiences briefly the delights of this "sweet" world, he soon discovers that reality everywhere resists his efforts to temper it to a finer tone. "Why should I war without the walls of Troy / That find such cruel battle here within" (1.1.2–3), Troilus had asked when forsaking the public world for the private. At his own cost he ignores Cressida's warning that "to be wise and love / Exceeds man's might; that dwells with gods above" (3.2.148–49). Ultimately, as a victim of his mind's own seduction of itself, a disenchanted Troilus turns from a worthless love back to a worthless war, lost in the middle of an absurd conflict between the "cruel battle" without and within.

Troilus and Cressida illustrates the need for an ironic perspective that can prevent the mind from succumbing to enchantment. However, this perspective, as evidenced by Thersites, is not sufficient: it frees the mind from enchantment without rededicating it to anything else. Ironic detachment needs to be transcended by an embrace of the world's sad realities, even, as Hector sees, if it is at the expense of one's own martyrdom. But can the mind sustain this painful embrace? Keats's *Lamia* volume traces these same concerns and, finally, asks a similar question. Dramatized in the movement from poem to poem is Keats's own effort to discover the powers and limitations of both poetry and the imagination and to create a poetic adequate for exploring the "agonies, the strife / Of human hearts."

[II]

In the concluding speech of *Troilus and Cressida*, Pandarus cynically sums up a world in which every person seems solely concerned with gathering as much "honey" as possible:

> Full merrily the humble-bee doth sing,
> Till he hath lost his honey and his sting;
> And being once subdued in armèd tail,
> Sweet honey and sweet notes together fail.
> (5.10.41–44)

A life devoted to the gathering of honey contains the seeds of its own undoing: "sweet honey and sweet notes" inevitably fail.[18] Harold Bloom remarks that all "romance, literary and human, is founded upon enchantment."[19] And the result of that enchantment is often death. In "Isabella," Keats, using imagery similar to that of *Troilus*, provides the credo for the three romances beginning the *Lamia* volume:

> But, for the general award of love,
> The little sweet doth kill much bitterness;
> Though Dido silent is in under-grove,
> And Isabella's was a great distress,
> Though young Lorenzo in warm Indian clove
> Was not embalm'd, this truth is not the less—

Even bees, the little almsmen of spring-bowers,
Know there is richest juice in poison-flowers.
(ll. 97–104)

All of Keats's mortal lovers discover the cost of drinking from "poison-flowers"; "Lamia" begins the lesson in enchantment.

"Lamia," itself, commences with a search for honey: Hermes is in desperate pursuit of a "sweet nymph," who will eventually yield to the burning god "her honey to the lees" (1:31, 143). The "ever-smitten" (1:7) Hermes is perpetually enchanted, always desiring and always fulfilling desire, never and ever satiated. An avatar of the erotic turned in upon itself, Hermes becomes the god of enchantment. And Crete, "the idyllic mythological home of Venus,"[20] is a fit setting for him.

Crete is a world of pure erotic power. In Keats's vision, love and the imagination are closely akin. Each springs from the erotic energy necessary to embrace an object outside of the self. Certainly Keats saw in the self-annihilating, or "identity-destroying," power of the imagination an analog to love. However, both love and the imagination can fall victims to enchantment. Then love becomes mere autoeroticism, imagination mere fancy, both solipsistic. The danger is clear. Both powers can act to cut individuals off from the world, unless, of course, they are gods, whose worlds are the sum of their desires. A mortal mind can attempt to absorb a single object seen as a completion of itself only to find instead a phantom of its own projection. Lycius, and even, Lamia succumb to this fatal enchantment.

Keats's "Pleasure Thermometer" in *Endymion* is a scale of imaginative encounters of increasing intensity, climaxing in the annihilation of self marked by the love that gives one a "fellowship with essence" (1:779). In "Lamia," erotic energy becomes attenuated into a lust measured by degrees of erotic heat. And Hermes burns. As he leaves heaven, "bent warm on amorous theft" (1:8), a "celestial heat / Burnt from his winged heels to either ear" (1:22–23). "Now it is more noble to sit like Jove tha[n] to fly like Mercury," Keats writes to Reynolds, "let us not therefore go hurrying about . . . collecting honey-bee like, . . . but let us open our leaves like a flower and be passive and receptive—budding patiently under the eye of Apollo" (1:232). A mind consumed by its own heat cuts itself off from imaginative experience. Thus Lamia has seen Hermes in the intensity of his lust, "Among the Gods, upon Olympus old, / The only sad one" because he did "not hear / The soft, lute-finger'd Muses chaunting clear, / Nor even Apollo when he sang alone" (1:71–74). Significantly, the narrator here calls Hermes "the star of Lethe" (1:81), playing ironically with Hermes's role as psychopomp. Oblivious to all imaginative experience, deaf to Apollo's song, Hermes is the mind en route to Lethe—mental death. He is not to travel this route alone.

When Hermes first encounters Lamia he discovers in her the embodiment of Crete's erotic power. Lamia is pure erotic potentiality waiting to be released into the world. She thus comprehends the full range of erotic possibilities, including an imagination capable of casting itself throughout the cosmos; "where she will'd, her spirit went" (1:205). Within the coils of her "serpent prison-house," this imaginative energy turns upon itself, creating a form in constant flux—"a gordian shape of dazzling hue"—changing in appearance with each breath she takes (1:203, 47). Lamia's imaginative power, however, has given her a vision of a Corinthian youth for whom she falls into a "swooning love" (1:219). As a victim of this enchantment, she greets Hermes with a voice that comes "as through bubbling honey, for Love's sake" (1:65). Lamia desires a "sweet body" (1:39), which—travestying the imaginative mind's desire to encounter "the agonies, the strife / Of human hearts"—would be "fit for life, / And love, and pleasure, and the ruddy strife / Of hearts and lips" (1:39–41). Here, she and Hermes can be of mutual assistance.

By Lamia's power Hermes's "sweet nymph" has been kept invisible, safe from "the love-glances of unlovely eyes" (1:102). As Lamia breathes so does she change appearance, and in the potency of her very breath is the power to give the "charmed God" (1:112) sight of his nymph. In exchange for his promise to give her a woman's form, Lamia breathes upon Hermes's eyes, as he sinks on "half-shut feathers" (1:123) in ecstatic expectation. Hermes, however, is caught off guard temporarily by the sudden appearance of the image of his desire: "One warm flush'd moment, hovering, it might seem / Dash'd by the wood-nymph's beauty, so he burn'd" (1:129–30). But he quickly remembers his vow to Lamia and, at the peak of his "burning," turns to the "swoon'd serpent" (1:132), herself ecstatically expectant, putting "to proof the lythe Caducean charm" (1:133) that begins Lamia's transformation.

Two elements are important to this transformation: Hermes's caduceus and his heat. Keats knew from Lemprière that the powers of Apollo and Hermes met in the form of a coiled serpent: Hermes received the caduceus from Apollo in exchange for his gift of the lyre. If the lyre is the fanciful voice of enchantment tuned into an instrument of the imagination, the caduceus is an instrument of imaginative potency misdirected to merely erotic ends. As such, it channels Hermes's heat into Lamia's serpent body. The warmth of Hermes's lust causes his sweet nymph, who at first is "self-folding like a flower" (1:138), to bloom and surrender "her honey to the lees."

In Lamia this heat ignites a reaction of volcanic intensity. Indeed, the extent to which this is specifically a volcanic reaction has been overlooked. Lamia's eyes,

> Hot, glaz'd, and wide, with lid-lashes all sear,
> Flash'd phosphor and sharp sparks, without one cooling
> tear.
> The colours all inflam'd throughout her train,
> She writh'd about, convuls'd with scarlet pain:
> A deep volcanian yellow took the place
> Of all her milder-mooned body's grace;
> And, as the lava ravishes the mead,
> Spoilt all her silver mail, and golden brede;
> Made gloom of all her frecklings, streaks and bars,
> Eclips'd her crescents, and lick'd up her stars . . .
> (1:151–60)

In an article on Shelley's use of volcanic imagery, G. M. Matthews notes that areas of volcanic fallout are famous for their extreme fertility and beauty.[21] The volcano, then, is both a destructive and creative agent: attendant upon its fiery devastation is lush beauty. Lamia, herself, the scene of volcanic activity, is to become a "full-born beauty new and exquisite" (1:172). When her serpent body is "melted" away (1:166), the last of it to disappear is her shining crown, the outward form of her desire. As it vanishes, Lamia begins her reincarnation first as a voice, expressing desire: "her new voice luting soft, / Cried, 'Lycius! gentle Lycius!' " (1:167–68). Between this "luting soft" and Lamia's final shriek lie the major tensions of the poem.

"Lycius is seduced," writes Garrett Stewart, "by the music and conjuration, the sound and sight, of his own dreamy 'phantasy' sexually projected."[22] Lamia is indeed Lycius's dreamy "phantasy" sexually projected. Although her beauty is great, more important to her seduction of Lycius is her voice. Initially, it is her words themselves with which he falls in love: "For so delicious were the words she sung, / It seem'd he had lov'd them a whole summer long" (1:249–50). Like Hermes's voice promising her transformation—which, "warm" and "psalterian," "ravish'd" (1:114–115) Lamia—Lamia's voice so completely ravishes Lycius that his existence becomes dependent upon its continuance:

> "So sweetly to these ravish'd ears of mine
> Came thy sweet greeting, that if thou should fade
> Thy memory will waste me to a shade:—
> For pity do not melt!" (1:268–71)

Ironically, of course, it is Lamia's "melting" that has allowed her to assume her present form. Just as ironically, it is her further melting that will result in Lycius's death.

Lamia's voice, then, becomes the foundation upon which their romance and, ultimately, Lycius's life itself rest. Yet its "amorous promise" (1:288) provides a tenuous foundation at best. An enchanted Lycius awakes from a swoon, provoked by Lamia's coy pretense of leaving him, into the world created by Lamia's "song of love": "And as he from one trance was wakening / Into another, she began to sing, / . . . A song of love, too sweet for earthly lyres" (1:296–97, 299). Each of her words entices Lycius "on / To unperplex'd delight and pleasure" (1:326–27), to become, in short, an inhabitant of a world whose limits are contained wholly within the "palace of sweet sin" (2:31). Lamia creates in Corinth a palace that is itself a product of her song: "A haunting music, sole perhaps and lone / Supportress of the faery-roof, made moan / Throughout . . ." (2:122–24). For Lycius, Lamia becomes the creature of her own song, the embodiment of its "amorous promise."

Opposed to the enchanted world of Lamia's song is the "fearful roar" of Cupid's wings buzzing above her chamber door and the "noisy world" (2:13, 33) of Corinth. The angry buzzing of the wings of Cupid, who "has jealous grown of so complete a pair" (2:12), foreshadows disaster to a relationship predicated entirely upon its own self-sufficiency. To desire more than can be provided within the "golden bourn" (2:32) of the palace is to shatter the spell upon which it is based: "a moment's thought is passion's passing bell" (2:39). However, the "almost forsworn" claims of the "noisy world" make themselves heard in a "thrill / Of trumpets" that reclaims Lycius's ears from Lamia's song and, combining with Cupid's ominous buzzing, leaves "a thought a buzzing in his head" (2:33, 27–28, 29). A "mad pompousness" (2:114) enters Lycius's head: in a grand wedding feast he will attempt to marry his private world to the public. Such a marriage is impossible; Lycius's attempt to reconcile a Corinth in which all "Mutter'd" (1:353) with the music of Lamia's palace is as futile as it is misguided. Ultimately it is suicidal.

Objectifying the "noise" of Corinth, emerging from the "murmurous vestibule" of the palace on the day of the wedding feast, is the voice of Apollonius, "Gruff with contempt" (2:163, 292). Apollonius's reductive logic is impervious to Lamia's enchantment. He thus seems to Lycius "The ghost of folly haunting my sweet dreams" (1:377). Apollonius is, in fact, intent upon exposing these "sweet dreams" as the product of a serpent's song. In the process, this song is to fail utterly. When she is first questioned by Lycius about her fear of Apollonius, Lamia's music falters, her words become "blind and blank" (2:102).

Contrasting with Lamia's song is the harsh, ironic laughter of a man who sees through her enchantment. Just as Apollonius's "patient thought" began to "thaw / And solve and melt" the "knotty problem" of Lamia's true nature (2:161–62, 160), his piercing eyes begin to "melt [Lamia] into a shade" at the wedding feast (2:238). As Lycius presses her hand, he feels it suddenly grow hot with "all the pains / Of an unnatural heat" (2:252–53). Lamia "withers" (2:290) as a result of this heat; her "stately music no more breathes" (2:263), replaced instead by a "deadly silence" (2:266), which is broken only when Apollonius loudly denounces her to the assembled Corinthians: " 'A Serpent!' echoed he; no sooner said, / Than with a frightful scream she vanished" (2:305–6). "For pity do not melt!" Lycius had pleaded with Lamia. But now, her enchanting song reduced to a "frightful scream," Lamia melts away, ending Lycius's abortive wedding feast with a divorce so final that he cannot survive its terms. His arms "empty of delight" (2:307), Lycius dies a victim of his own urge to marry his private world to the public, his marriage robe becoming his funeral shroud.

Ironies are everywhere apparent in "Lamia." The three main characters all labor under their own misconceptions and limitations. Lamia is the imagination undoing itself, a victim of its own power to conjure up images of desire so powerful that they become self-consuming. To satisfy her desire Lamia takes form from Hermes, limiting herself in the process to a power of mere enchantment. Her ability to "unperplex bliss from its neighbor pain" (1:192) belies the very process through which she is incarnated. While it offers a world in which the "most ambiguous atoms" of "specious chaos" (1:195) are rearranged into coherent form, it also falsifies very real complexities.

Lamia becomes the author of a fiction, creating a romance world that she cohabits with Lycius. She is thus both victimizer and victim, so entrammeled in her own fiction that, when it is exposed as such by Apollonius, she can no longer exist. Lycius, too, is both victimizer and victim, enchanter and enchanted. Unable to forsake his "secret bowers" (2:149) or the world of Corinth, he stakes both his own life and Lamia's on a misguided attempt to wed the two worlds. And Apollonius, Lycius's self-professed protector, enjoys the mental satisfaction of his reductive truth at the cost of his pupil's life. Intent on preventing Lycius from being made "a serpent's prey" (2:298), he makes Lycius his own prey. All three have justifiable motives for their actions: Lamia loves Lycius and apparently intends him no harm, Lycius refuses to forsake a public for a completely private world, and Apollonius desires to save his former pupil from enchantment. All three become murderers. The world refuses to correspond to their simplistically wishful images of it. In the baffling world "Lamia" presents, the dreams of gods are real, those of human beings self-destroying.

Keats, however, locks the poem into an even more baffling dialectic. Pitted against each other are the "rainbow-sided" (1:54) Lamia and the rainbow-destroying Apollonius (2:231–38). It seems as though one can only choose between enchantment and "cold philosophy" (2:230). One either becomes involved in the world and succumbs to it, or one becomes a detached ironist like Thersites or Apollonius, whose harsh laughter is as much at his own expense as at that of others. The imaginative and rational powers battle each other to a deadly standoff in "Lamia." By refusing to take sides, by presenting a dilemma with no possible solutions, Keats himself becomes an ironist. Judging from his letters, it was a role in which he reveled: "I have been reading over a part of a short poem I have composed lately call'd 'Lamia'—and I am certain there is that sort of fire in it which must take hold of people in some way—give them either pleasant or unpleasant sensation. What they want is a sensation of some sort" (*LK*, 2:189).

"Lamia" is a poem intended to produce a "sensation of some sort." As such, it refuses to provide the terms by which it can be evaluated: nowhere can a center of meaning be located in the poem.[23] Perhaps Stuart Sperry is right to say that in "a number of respects *Lamia* is a work written by a poet against his better self."[24] The witty and detached style of "Lamia" allows Keats to remain aloof from the questions he raises, and in a sense, to abdicate poetic responsibility to meaning, while at the same time deliberately enticing the reader to take a position. Ultimately, the poem's final meaning is its refusal to mean. In its enticement and then frustration of its reader, "Lamia" itself becomes a demon of enchantment, a demon that the rest of the volume attempts to exorcise. This process begins in "Isabella," a work in many ways antithetical to "Lamia."

Both "Lamia" and "Isabella" are imaginatively reconstituted narratives. Each is the product of its narrator's self-conscious encounter with a literary text. Thus, the passage from Burton's *Anatomy of Melancholy* upon which "Lamia" is based follows the poem in the 1820 volume and the narrator of "Isabella" often refers to his source, claiming that his poem is intended to honor Boccaccio and "greet" his "gone spirit" (l. 158). Moreover, each narrative is based upon a work depicting devastating loss, where love ends in death. Significant is the way each narrator faces this loss. Whereas the narrator of "Lamia" is ironic and detached from his narrative, the narrator of "Isabella" is sympathetic and involved. That the narrator of "Lamia" has devised a strategy, albeit self-defeating, for facing loss results in his cynicism. That the narrator of "Isabella" can devise no such strategy results in his pathos.

While wishing fervently for the "gentleness of old Romance" (l. 387), the narrator of "Isabella" is fascinated by a far more complex reality that presents him with the mysteries of the "yawning tomb" (l. 386). His many repetitions and digressions signal his own inability to confront successfully the "wormy circumstance" of his tale (l. 385). For the misery he depicts, he knows no remedy. In contrast, the narrator of "Lamia" can be glib about what he perceives to be the inevitable destruction of love in the world:

> Love in a hut, with water and a crust,
> Is—Love, forgive us!—cinders, ashes, dust;

> Love in a palace is perhaps at last
> More grievous torment than a hermit's fast. (2:1–4)

This same perception is a source of great pain to the narrator of "Isabella." His narrative is to begin with the hopefulness of spring and end in the bleakness of approaching winter, detailing the fatal effects of enchantment.

Like Lamia and Lycius, Isabella and Lorenzo are mutually enchanted by the sight and sound of each other:

> He might not in house, field, or garden stir,
> But her full shape would all his seeing fill;
> And his continual voice was pleasanter
> To her, than noise of trees or hidden rill. (ll. 11–14)

Their enchantment is expressed in imagery by now familiar. Lorenzo's reluctance to breathe "love's tune" and confess his feelings for Isabel, for instance, allows "Honeyless days and days" to pass (ll. 30, 32). Further, his passion for Isabel is experienced in terms of heat: "Love! thou art leading me from wintry cold, / Lady! thou leadest me to summer clime" (ll. 65–66). As with Hermes, this heat causes his lover to open receptively like a flower. Lorenzo then becomes like a bee, gathering honey from the "sweet Isabella" (l. 33): "I must taste the blossoms that unfold / In its ripe warmth this gracious morning time" (ll. 67–68). As a result of this tasting, Isabel returns to her chamber singing "of delicious love and honey'd dart" (l. 78). Also like Lamia and Lycius, the lovers meet in "secret bowers": "Close in a bower of hyacinth and musk, / Unknown of any, free from whispering tale" (ll. 85–86). Their love, too, is predicated upon the existence of a private world that conflicts with the public.

If Hermes appears as the god of enchantment in "Lamia," he appears by proxy in "Isabella," precipitating a similar tragedy. For Lemprière notes that Hermes is also the god of merchants and commerce. As represented by Isabella's brothers, the public world of commercial interest puts an end to her love. This is a world productive of "ledger-men" (l. 137), whose only interest is self-interest. To such men it is a "crime"

(l. 172) punishable by death that "the servant of their trade designs, / Should in their sister's love be blithe and glad" (ll. 165–66) when they intend her instead to marry a rich nobleman. Ambushed in the forest, Lorenzo becomes their helpless victim: "There in that forest did his great love cease" (l. 218). But Isabella proves to be an even greater victim.

At the exact center of the poem, in its only enjambed stanzas, "Isabella" announces its central concern: how "sweet Isabel / By gradual decay from beauty fell, / Because Lorenzo came not" (ll. 255–57). "She weeps alone for pleasures not to be," the narrator tells us (l. 233). "And she had died in drowsy ignorance, / But for a thing more deadly dark than all" (ll. 265–66). At the beginning of their love Isabel and Lorenzo "to each other dream" (l. 8). Isabella's dream of the dead Lorenzo is thus a continued product of their love. It is also revelatory for Isabel, educating her out of "drowsy ignorance" into a dreadful new knowledge.

Lorenzo's lament to Isabella, the "soft lute" gone from "his lorn voice" (ll. 278, 279), is reminiscent of many characters in *Lyrical Ballads*: "I am a shadow now, alas! alas! / Upon the skirts of human-nature dwelling / Alone: I chant alone the holy mass . . ." (ll. 305–7). Unlike those characters, of course, Lorenzo is dead, reduced like Lamia into an "aching ghost" (2:294). His explanation to Isabella of his murder and continued love for her climaxes in his parting "Adieu!" (l. 321). Lamia's playful "Adieu!" (1:286) to Lycius is enough to make him swoon. Lorenzo's final parting to Isabella, however, awakens her: "It made sad Isabella's eyelids ache, / And in the dawn she started up awake" (ll. 327–28) with a new understanding of her world:

> "Ha! ha!" said she, "I knew not this hard life,
>   I thought the worst was simple misery;
> I thought some Fate with pleasure or with strife
>   Portion'd us—happy days, or else to die . . ."
>
> (ll. 329–32)

Isabella had lived in a world of romance, where bliss and pain remain unperplexed. She learns, however, that the mind can experience worse than "simple misery" and yet live. "[T]hou has school'd my infancy," she tells Lorenzo's departed ghost. "I'll visit thee for this, and kiss thine eyes" (ll. 334–35). Attendant upon the collapse of one world is madness in the next. "What feverous hectic flame / Burns in thee, child?" asks her nurse (ll. 348–49). The "feverous hectic flame" of her own unrealizable desires consumes Isabella. Her new schooling has given her a picture of a world that her mind cannot accommodate. Instead, it contracts to the small circle of the garden-pot into which she places Lorenzo's head beneath a basil plant:

> And she forgot the stars, the moon, and sun,
> And she forgot the blue above the trees,
> And she forgot the dells where waters run,
> And she forgot the chilly autumn breeze;
> She had no knowledge when the day was done,
> And the new morn she saw not: but in peace
> Hung over her sweet basil evermore,
> And moisten'd it with tears unto the core. (ll. 417–24)

Nurtured by both Isabella's tears and Lorenzo's "fast mouldering head" (l. 430), this "sweet basil" becomes the only fruitful issue of their love, the final meeting ground of the two lovers.[25] As such, it obsesses Isabella. To remove this last vestige of her romance world, as her brothers do, is to remove the only foundation upon which Isabella's mind can rest; it is, ultimately, to kill her. In a voice now ominously "lorn" (l. 492), like that of the dead Lorenzo, Isabella endlessly laments her last and cruelest loss: "O cruelty, / To steal my basil-pot away from me" (ll. 503–4). Isabella becomes the victim of a world in which constant loss is unavoidable. The mind can either attempt to endure such a world or retreat further into its own fantasies. Undone by her own fictions, Isabella dies voicing her desire: "And so she pined, and so she died forlorn, / Imploring for her basil to the last" (ll. 497–98).

Jack Stillinger's comparison of "Isabella" to a lyrical ballad is in many ways just.[26] In its consideration of human suffering, in the obsession of its protagonist, and in the repetitions of both its protagonist and narrator, "Isabella" resembles many lyrical ballads, particularly "The Thorn."[27] Yet perhaps an equally valid comparison can be made to the first book of *The Excursion.* There, Margaret, her eye ever "busy in the distance, shaping things / That made her heart beat quick" (1:881–82), is a victim of her own self-consuming desire for her lost husband.[28] Though knowing that "what I seek I cannot find" (1:766), she cannot refrain from stopping passing strangers to ask countlessly the "same sad question" (1:900), much like Isabella asking perpetually for her basil. Margaret finally dies, undone by her own love, forgetting all but what the world has denied her. The narrator reacts to her story with the "impotence of grief" (1:924). But Wordsworth's speaker has the consolation of Christianity to counterbalance the misery he describes; the narrator of "Isabella" has no such comfort. He is left in the impotence of his own grief, helplessly lamenting the fatal effects of enchantment:

> O Melancholy, turn thine eyes away!
>   O Music, Music breathe despondingly!
> O Echo, Echo, on some other day,
>   From isles Lethean, sigh to us—O sigh!
> Spirits of grief, sing not your "Well-a-way!"
>   For Isabel, sweet Isabel, will die . . . (ll. 481–86)

In a letter to Woodhouse, Keats dissociated himself from the narrator's pathos in "Isabella," declaring, "in my dramatic capacity I enter fully into the feeling: but in Propria Persona I should be apt to quiz it myself" (*LK*, 2:174). The pathos of the narrator of "Isabella" is no more satisfactory than the cynicism of the narrator of "Lamia." The two extremes needed to be synthesized in a voice, which could be sympathetic yet wary, from a narrator whose ability to depict a moment of fulfillment is predicated upon his knowledge of the fleetingness of that moment. In his "dramatic capacity," Keats produces such a narrator in "The Eve of St. Agnes."

Like the two preceding poems, "The Eve of St. Agnes" is about enchantment, but unlike the two previous narrators this narrator does not re-create a narrative whose burden he is unable to bear successfully. Rather, he is engaged in a fiction of his own devising that allows him a self-aware playfulness: he can for a time "wish away" (l. 41) a world hostile to his romance because he knows that his poem must inevitably return to that world. Ultimately, "The Eve of St. Agnes" is a romance whose concern is the limitations of romance. The innocent world of young love it depicts survives only through frequent strategic manipulations: within the narrator's larger fiction are the fictions of his two protagonists.

The occasion of St. Agnes's Eve provides the strategies for both Madeline and Porphyro to realize their desires. Once again in the volume, the public world aligns itself against two lovers. Her love for Porphyro thwarted by the animosity between their families, Madeline retreats from a public to a private world, seeking fulfillment of her desires in the dreams of St. Agnes's Eve. These dreams promise "visions of delight" (l. 47) in which young virgins who observe the proper ceremonies might "soft adorings from their loves receive / Upon the honey'd middle of the night" (ll. 48–49). Madeline can thus attempt to better reality; without the cost of her virginity she can enjoy all the delights of "the honey'd middle of the night." No wonder, then, that she sighs "for Agnes' dreams, the sweetest of the year" (l. 63). Madeline is enchanted by a fantasy of her own projection; by observing the rites of St. Agnes's Eve, she is to play "the conjuror" (l. 124) and attempt to call up and enjoy fully the image of her desire. Just as the enchanted Hermes is oblivious to Apollo's song, Madeline, as she passes through the mansion to her bedroom, is so "[f]ull of this whim" (l. 55) that she scarcely hears the "music, yearning like a god in pain" (l. 56).[29] "Hoodwink'd with faery fancy" (l. 70), Madeline is "amort" (l. 70) to all but "the bliss to be before to-morrow morn" (l. 72).

When informed by Angela of Madeline's intent, the enchanted Porphyro, with "heart on fire / For Madeline" (ll. 75–76), concocts a "stratagem" of his own (l. 139). For the "burning Porphyro" is part of a reality excluded from the "enchantments cold" of St. Agnes's Eve (ll. 159, 134). Within her dreams Madeline is "Blissfully haven'd both from joy and pain" (l. 240); she has entered a world whose privacy exceeds even that of the secret bowers shared by the other lovers in the volume. And if sexual receptivity is indicated in the volume by the opening of a flower, Madeline's solipsistic state is described in terms of a flower closing: "As though a rose should shut, and be a bud again" (l. 243). Porphyro attempts to counter this "cold" enchantment with rites as elaborate as those followed by Madeline to achieve her dreams. Images of light and heat attend his effort to make a bower out of Madeline's "chilly room" (l. 275) by first preparing a feast as exotic as that Lamia prepares for her wedding. Like Lamia's, this is also an untasted feast. Its "perfume light" (l. 275) is unable to rouse Madeline from "a midnight charm / Impossible to melt as iced stream" (ll. 282–83). To release "St. Agnes' charmed maid" from such a chill "steadfast spell" (ll. 192, 287), Porphyro finally resorts to what in the volume has proven to be the most potent charm of all—a lover's song.

Opposing "all the noise" (l. 261) present in the world of the mansion, Porphyro takes up Madeline's "hollow lute" (l. 289) deep in "the retired quiet of the night" (l. 274) and, almost overmastered by desire, sings a song appropriately entitled "La Belle Dame Sans Merci." Through his song Porphyro is able to create the bower he seeks. Madeline is thawed, recalled from the icy reaches of her desire to an enchanted middle ground between desire and reality. She must first, however, accept the "painful change" between the Porphyro of her dreams and the Porphyro who now appears "pallid, chill, and drear" (ll. 300, 311). Significantly, it is the difference in not only Porphyro's appearance but his voice that distresses her:

"but even now
Thy voice was at sweet tremble in mine ear,
Made tuneable with every sweetest vow;
. . . .
Give me that voice again, my Porphyro,
Those looks immortal, those complainings dear!"
(ll. 307–9, 312–13)

Yet Madeline's own "voluptuous accents" (l. 317) signal her acceptance of the Porphyro she beholds in her half-dreaming state. These same "voluptuous accents" heat Porphyro into almost unbearable desire. While Madeline descends from the heights of her dream, Porphyro rises to meet her descent—"Ethereal" and "flush'd" (l. 318), "Beyond a mortal man impassion'd far" (l. 316). Porphyro is thus "melted" (l. 320) into Madeline's dream. The two lovers unite in a "Solution sweet" (l. 322) in which desire accommodates reality by not only transforming but being transformed by it.

Attendant upon their union, however, is the setting of St. Agnes's moon. St. Agnes's dreams are only, as Michael Ragusis reminds us, for virgins.[30] Madeline has been forced to pay the price of her desires. Reality will have its due from the "sweet dreamer" (l. 334): the end of her dreaming is to end dreaming for her. If for a moment the lovers can forget the wintry world, that moment has ended. "'Tis dark" (ll. 325, 327), the narrator twice insists. The dark, stormy world surrounding the lovers threatens the survival of their love. "Like phantoms" (l. 362) they "glide" out of the mansion through the storm, bent far "o'er the southern moors" (l. 351), vanishing abruptly from the world of the poem.

"And they are gone: aye, ages long ago / These lovers fled into the storm" (ll. 370–71). Madeline and Porphyro cannot, and do not, stay to confront their world. The possibilities for fulfilled desire that they represent are instead apotheosized out of the world presented by the poem into a nebulous world beyond the storm. The lovers' triumph in "The Eve of St. Agnes" is thus ultimately also their defeat. Like the previous lovers of the volume, they find no way to connect their private desires with public reality. Love in the world is formidably beset by darkness and mental death, and Madeline and Porphyro's escape is reminiscent of Albert's in the "Foster-Mother's Tale" of *Lyrical Ballads*. For available to them is a possibility from which the other characters in the volume, as well as the narrator himself, are quite cut off. As the lovers recede in time and immediacy from the narrator—"gone . . . ages long ago"—he is left contemplating a world devoid of enchantment, where the "be-nightmar'd" (l. 375) Baron and his warrior guests hold sway, and where the Beadsman and Angela succumb to deaths that complete the logic of their life-denying lives. The consequence of enchantment is invariably disenchantment. That the narrator can willingly return to the world he has temporarily wished away allows him the joy of participating fully in his fiction. That he must return to this world, his fiction being subject to the limits of all fiction, leaves him trapped between a paradisal vision of fulfilled desire and a hellish reality.

"This love will undo us all." The three romances beginning Keats's 1820 volume show that, at best, romance and the enchantment necessary for romance, both literary and human, offer a temporary respite from reality, a type of wish-fulfilling imaginative play. At worst they undo the mind.[31] While it is certain that the mind must desire in order to survive, it is just as certain that, all too often, the desiring mind engages a world produced by its own wishful distortions, the perverted projection of an imagination self-seduced into mere fancy, a love self-projected into mere lust. From such fictions result madness and death.

The world presented by the volume seems knowable only by transposing the physics of Newton's Third Law of Thermodynamics into psychic terms: for every motion of the mind the world responds with an equal and opposite motion. The more the mind desires, the more it will be frustrated; the more it seeks pleasure, the more it will be given pain; the more it retreats into its own fictions, the more it will be destroyed by reality. The self-revising form of the volume assumes in the opening group of romances three different stances to confront this frightening dialectic, ranging from the ironic detachment of "Lamia" to the helpless sympathy of "Isabella" to the self-conscious play of "The Eve of St. Agnes." All are inadequate, though the narrator of "The Eve of St. Agnes," with his understanding of the limitations of his own fiction, seems most successful. His poem begins to illustrate what the volume next begins to consider—that the poet himself must become the meeting ground of the conflicting worlds opposed by the desiring mind and resistant reality; his breast, their battleground.

[III]

"My heart aches," begins the poet of the "Ode to a Nightingale," the first of three odes grouped together in the 1820 collection. "Ode to a Nightingale" marks the first generic change in the dramatic movement of the volume. Like most dramas, the *Lamia* volume has its soliloquies: the larger scope of narrative poetry gives way to the more focused concerns of the ode; a multiplicity of voices gives way to a single voice—that of the "sole self" of the poet ("Ode to a Nightingale," l. 72). To confront the disconcerting dialectic emerging from the narratives is the ode, a form founded upon dialectic. "I must take my stand upon some vantage ground and begin to fight" (*LK*, 2:113), Keats wrote in the spring of 1819, approximately at the same time he was composing these odes. This statement applies clearly to his poetry as well as to his life. For in the "Ode to a Nightingale," "Ode on a Grecian Urn," and "Ode to Psyche," Keats begins in earnest to take such a stand. The narrator who evades the import of the questions he raises in "Lamia" is at a far remove from the poet of the odes, who takes his place upon a vantage ground where every thought is felt upon his pulse. In the odes Keats is to isolate and examine in closer detail the questions raised in the narratives about the nature of desire, enchantment, and the imagination—all centering around the question of the poet's proper relationship to poetry and to his world.

The "Ode to a Nightingale" is another poem about enchantment. Its context in the volume only serves to emphasize Morris Dickstein's perception that "Keats associates the song of the nightingale with the poetry of romance."[32] In many ways the "Ode to a Nightingale" is the sum of the romances that precede it. Once again it is a singing voice that is the agent of enchantment. The nightingale, like Lamia, becomes the embodiment of its voice for the listener. And like Lycius, the poet projects all that he desires upon that voice. "Love, thou art leading me to summer clime," an enchanted Lorenzo tells Isabella. The voice of the nightingale, singing "of summer in full-throated ease" (l. 10), leads the poet to discover, like Lorenzo, the death awaiting the mind's voyage into a premature summer.

Such a death is presaged at the beginning of the poet's experience of the nightingale's song. At the height of his enchantment, Porphyro tells the still sleeping Madeline, "Open thine eyes . . . / Or I shall drowse beside thee, so my soul doth ache" (ll. 278–79). The aching heart and "drowsy numbness" (l. 1) felt by the poet of the "Ode to a Nightingale" is akin to that experienced by Porphyro.[33] He is quite literally "too happy" (l. 6) in the enchantment of the nightingale's song. Troilus, whirled around by an "imaginary relish so sweet that it enchants" his sense, fears that death will be the consequence of his experiencing "some joy too fine, / Too subtle, potent, tuned too sharp in sweetness / For the capacity of my ruder powers" (3.2.21–24). Similarly, Hermes, "the star of Lethe," is the god of an enchantment whose very potency leads to mental death. Toward such a death the enchanted happiness of the poet leads his mind, "as though of hemlock I had drunk, / Or emptied some dull opiate to the drains / One minute past, and Lethe-wards had sunk" (ll. 2–4).

Unlike the completely oblivious Hermes, however, the poet is not totally consumed by enchantment. If his imagination has been turned in upon itself, fancifully creating in the nightingale a symbol of a world that is the ontological equivalent of the romance's bower, it is also still attuned to another voice. Against the song of the nightingale is the groaning voice of humanity. To enter into the enchanted world of the nightingale's song is wishfully to leave a world "where men sit and hear each other groan" (l. 24); it is to "fade away into the forest dim" (l. 20), quite forgetting the imperatives of a world "Where but to think is to be full of sorrow / And leaden-eyed despairs" (ll. 27–28). Keats's muse is thus the daughter of oblivion as he enters, on the "viewless wings of Poesy" (l. 33), the dark bower of the nightingale's domain. Ominously, these "viewless wings," like Lamia's "viewless servants" (2:136), are in the service of a mind dominated by its own fanciful desires.[34]

It is by now a critical commonplace to note the analogy between Keats's description of the nightingale's realm and a passage from Milton's invocation to the third book of *Paradise Lost*:

> Then feed on thoughts, that voluntary move
> Harmonious numbers; as the wakeful Bird
> Sings darkling, and in shadiest Covert hid
> Tunes her nocturnal Note.[35]

The irony of this analogy, however, has long gone unnoticed. Left in darkness, deprived of his sight, Milton can assert triumphantly that his increased inner vision more than compensates for his loss. But, as books 11 and 12 of *Paradise Lost* demonstrate, Milton's inner eyes will not avert themselves from a world in which humanity groans. Unlike the Keats who follows the voice of the nightingale into a secret bower of the mind, Milton follows the "Voice divine" (7:2) of Urania, which leads him to a vision of hell as well as heaven.

In his appeal to Urania in book 7 of *Paradise Lost*, Milton asks that he be permitted such range, that with "safety" Urania guide him from "Empyreal Air" back down to his "Native Element" and not leave him "forlorn" (7:15, 14, 16, 20). The nightingale finally leaves Keats forlorn because it cannot permit him comparable range: it can provide no vision of the hell of human misery, nor can it secure the passage of his mind from the heaven of its song back down to his "Native Element." Rather than offering greater vision, the "embalmed darkness" of the nightingale's domain offers tunnel-vision, replacing the "leaden-eyed despairs" of thought with "each sweet" provided by the "seasonable month" (ll. 43, 28, 43, 44) of May.

The mind's flight to this "embalmed darkness" becomes a half-willing embrace of its own demise: wishfulness all too easily becomes death-wishfulness. The urge to die an "easeful Death" (l. 52) at the height of his enchantment inevitably results from Keats's attempt to resist disenchantment, to prolong at all cost the moment in which he possesses a world responsive to his desires. Yet no matter how "rich" (l. 55) such a death seems, it would also cut him off permanently from the nightingale's song: "Still wouldst thou sing, and I have ears in vain— / To thy high requiem become a sod" (ll. 59–60). Because the poet now sees the oblivion lurking at the heart of his enchantment, he can perceive the nightingale's undying song as funereal, as a "high requiem" that would continue to be sung over his own dead body.

In one of his last letters to Charles Brown, Keats writes: "I wish for death every day and night . . . , and then I wish death away, for death would destroy even those pains which are better than nothing. . . . [D]eath is the great divorcer for ever" (*LK*, 2:345). "To cease upon the midnight with no pain" (l. 56) is also to "destroy even those pains which are better than nothing" (*LK*, 2:345). Finally, the thought of his own death and his participation in the continuous flux of hungry human generations divorces Keats from a nightingale that is "not born for death" (l. 61). The nightingale instead is the deathless voice of enchantment forever haunting humanity, audible to Keats just as it was in "ancient days" and "fairy lands forlorn" (ll. 64, 70).

The secret bower created by the nightingale's song cannot survive a moment's thought: "Forlorn! the very word is like a bell / To toll me back from thee to my sole self!" (ll. 71–72). As with Lamia's palace, to venture beyond its boundaries is to destroy its fanciful creation: "Adieu! the fancy cannot cheat so well / As she is fam'd to do, deceiving elf" (ll. 73–74). First perceived as a song of summer, the nightingale's song becomes next a "high requiem" and finally a "plaintive anthem" (l. 75), "buried deep / In the next valley-glades" (ll. 77–78). When Lamia's "stately music no more breathes," Lycius dies. And Isabella, her enchantment over, dies "forlorn." That the speaker remains to contemplate the loss of the nightingale's song is a measure of his own imaginative vitality. If, for a time, his imagination allows itself to be enchanted into mere fancy, it soon rejects the limits thereby imposed upon it. In the same letter to Brown quoted above, Keats writes: "Is there another Life? Shall I awake and find all this a dream? There must be we cannot be created for this kind of suffering" (*LK*, 2:346). In the "Ode to a Nightingale," as in the preceding romances, the mind finds itself trapped between an imagined world of fulfilled desires and a world filled with human suffering, between an enchanted song and a groan.

Since the "Ode to a Nightingale" follows three romances, much is compressed into its opening three words. All of the aching hearts in the preceding poems are thereby recalled; in fact, the poem itself seems for a moment to be concerned with love and erotic tensions. Through this juxtaposition the volume keeps alive the erotic tensions of the romances while focusing specifically on the problems of the poetic imagination—once again emphasizing that love and the imagination are both erotic powers, the means by which the mind embraces openly its world. Moreover, "Ode to a Nightingale" is the first poem of the volume to center its attention upon the poet himself, the voice behind the narratives. The poem's dialectical progression works out the terms by which an invocation to a muse becomes the means of discovering the muse's own insufficiency. Made explicit in the "high requiem" of the nightingale's song is what has been implicit in the volume all along—that a poetic based upon enchantment, and the escape afforded by enchantment, is, ultimately, a poetic of death. Also made explicit in the poem is the poet's own battle with enchantment, his fight to resist the powers of his own fiction.

Whereas the "Ode to a Nightingale" is the first poem in the *Lamia* volume to be concerned primarily with the poet, the "Ode on a Grecian Urn," the succeeding poem, is the first to concern primarily art itself. Because both activities are dependent on the imagination, the mind can be waylaid by the act of interpretation as easily as by the act of creation. Like the narrators of the first two poems in the volume, the poet of the "Ode on a Grecian Urn" imaginatively reconstitutes a work of art, creating in the process his own work. In the silence of the urn is an enchantment as potent as that of the nightingale's song.

The opening of the "Ode on a Grecian Urn" again asserts the connection between the imagination and eros. The poem itself details the terms by which a work of art can seduce the imagination. Keats's perception of the urn as a "still unravish'd bride" (l. 1) prompts Stuart Sperry to comment: "The sexual metaphor is central to the wit and logic of the poem, for it suggests that vital penetration of imagination necessary to bring any object into the fullness of aesthetic apprehension."[36] However, if the poet's imagination is once more seduced out of the confines of his "sole self," it is a more cautious poet who allows his mind to enter and reconstitute the "flowery tale" expressed so "sweetly" by the urn (l. 4). The "Ode on a Grecian Urn" begins with the kind of wariness of enchantment that is missing from the "Ode to a Nightingale" until its end.[37]

Like the nightingale's song, the silent urn invites the poet's mind into a world unresistant to desire. "Heard melodies are sweet, but those unheard / Are sweeter . . ." (l. 11). While the nightingale sings of summer, the silent urn depicts an eternal spring, where trees cannot ever shed their leaves, where love is "For ever warm and still to be enjoy'd, / For ever panting, and for ever young" (ll. 26–27). In the romances of the *Lamia* collection, the vulnerability of a mind in love is always apparent. Madeline begs Porphyro: "Oh leave me not in this eternal woe, / For if thou diest, my love, I know not where to go" (ll. 314–15); Lorenzo asks Isabella: "Ah! what if I should lose thee, when so fain / I am to stifle all the heavy sorrow / Of a poor three hours' absence?" (ll. 203–5); and Lycius tells Lamia: "if thou should'st fade / Thy memory will waste me to a shade" (ll. 269–70). Keats himself wrote to Brown about Fanny Brawne: "I eternally see her figure eternally vanishing" (*LK*, 2:345). To desire is to be vulnerable to loss everywhere except in the "Sylvan" realm of the urn, where the object of desire "cannot fade" (ll. 3, 19). "Things won are done, joy's soul lies in the doing" (1.2.273), says Cressida. The urn portrays a frozen world of being, where things are never lost because they are never won. Paradoxically, the more the mind empathizes with the urn—that is, the more it enters a world that denies loss—the more the necessity for loss is reaffirmed. Opposed to the tantalizing silence of the urn, which would tease the mind out of thought, is the thoughtful voice of the poet. And this voice cannot forget the exigencies of its own condition.

Critics often comment that the poet's imagination can never exhaust the possibilities for interpretation presented by the urn.[38] However, there is also a way in which the urn cannot exhaust his imagination. Like the "golden bourn" of Lamia's palace and the nightingale's song, the urn can only continue to enchant a mind content to remain within its confines. When the poet's imagination is led to picture a scene not itself on the urn, the forever silent town he envisions ends his enchantment. The eternal silence of that eternally desolate town counters the enchanting silence of the urn. The scene the poet's imagination provides concerns loss; he supplies unconsciously what the urn omits. If the urn can lead the mind into a world where "Beauty is truth, truth beauty" (l. 49), the mind finally demands a more rigorous beauty, a more profound truth, in the acceptance of loss.

"Rigor of beauty is the quest," writes William Carlos Williams at the beginning of *Paterson*. The "Ode on a Grecian Urn" marks both an end and a new beginning to the quest dramatized in the *Lamia* volume for an art that is both beautiful and true. For it discovers that the type of art the urn represents is of only limited value to humanity; while this art temporarily comforts by providing visions of a world without loss, it ultimately reminds one of one's exclusion from such a world. The urn is thus both a "friend to man" and a "Cold Pastoral" (ll. 48, 45). "I must take my stand upon some vantage point and begin to fight." What is needed is a type of art resistant to enchantment, an art in which the mind halts its retreat from the world and confronts suffering and loss. In "A

Servant to Servants," Robert Frost writes that the "best way out is always through." The "Ode to Psyche" begins Keats's journey "through."

The first steps on the way "through" lead Keats to the bower of Psyche and Cupid. There, "fainting with surprise" (l. 8), he receives a vision of the first avatars of successful love in the volume. Moreover, in Psyche he finds the representative of a mind whose desire is fulfilled only through intense suffering. Kenneth Allott notes that "Psyche . . . has known in her own person—as no true Olympian could ever know—suffering and seemingly hopeless longing. She is . . . a late and more sophisticated personification of human nature subjected to an inevitable and cruel process of growing up and growing old."[39] Here is a divinity worthy of worship. Indeed, Keats's first sight of Psyche asleep beside Eros has all the force of an apocalyptic revelation: his swoon, rather than being one of the volume's many falls into enchantment, is symbolic of his assumption of the role of poet-prophet. "I see, and sing, by my own eyes inspired" (l. 43)—the song and heat of the volume's lovers are replaced by the arduous song and "heat" of Psyche's newfound "pale-mouth'd prophet" (l. 49).

Presenting the mind with a model for endurance through suffering and fulfillment through loss, Psyche's union with Eros is to be celebrated in and by the imagination. Such a celebration calls for a realigning of mental powers. To be Psyche's prophet requires building "a fane / In some untrodden region" (ll. 50–51) of the mind. Her worship demands that the mind open itself to accept the "pleasant pain" of "new grown" thoughts (l. 52), that it face the consequences of disenchantment. Gone is the attempt to unperplex bliss from its neighbor pain; gone too is the attempt to retreat inward, both having been replaced by the "wreath'd trellis of a working brain" that promises only the questionable amount of "soft delight / That shadowy thought can win" (ll. 60, 64–65).

Harold Bloom reminds us that in *The Excursion* Wordsworth invokes a muse greater than Milton's, "For I must tread on shadowy ground." Bloom is right to think that this "shadowy ground" is "the haunt of Keats's 'shadowy thought,' and its place is the 'Mind of Man.' "[40] Keats's new determination to explore the mind's relationship to the world, to enlarge his own consciousness under Psyche's aegis, makes her a muse characterized by radical openness above all things. Fittingly, then, Keats keeps a "rosy sanctuary" (l. 59) at the center of the sublime terrain of the uncharted regions of his mind, whose ever-open casement will allow Eros free and constant access to Psyche. He thus recovers what had been lost through enchantment—the true erotic possibilities of a love and an imagination turned outward in an open encounter with the world.

The "Ode to Psyche" celebrates the imagination's ability to appoint its own deities and become the arbiter of all human values. As the last of the initial group of odes in the volume, it culminates their search for an authentic stance toward the world, an authentic poetic. However, the "Ode to Psyche" only marks a beginning, and a hesitant beginning at that. If the imagination is to mediate the mind's encounter with a world of process and loss, it has also proven itself vulnerable to enchantment. Psyche's "rosy sanctuary" will be dressed "With all the gardener Fancy e'er could feign" (l. 62); and as the word "feign" indicates, fancy is not only capable of creating but also of falsifying, or enchanting. At the exact center of a volume estimating the cost of enchantment, seventh among its thirteen poems, is a poem concerned with the power of enchantment—"Fancy."

[IV]

"Fancy" is the first of four poems in the volume to which Keats referred as "specimens of a sort of rondeau which I think I shall become partial to—because you have one idea amplified with greater ease and more delight and freedom than in the sonnet" (*LK*, 2:26). Usually given scant critical attention, these "rondeaus" take on a greater significance by their position in the *Lamia* volume. There, they form a climax, a turning point begun at the "Ode to Psyche." The mind, contracted to the realm of the "sole self" in the odes, begins to reengage its world along the lines projected by "Psyche," but not before examining the limit of that contraction in "Fancy."

"Oh, sweet Fancy! let her loose; / Every thing is spoilt by use," writes Keats in "Fancy" (ll. 67–68).[41] Discontent with a world where "Pleasure never is at home" (l. 2), the mind succumbs to its power to improve upon reality. "Hoodwink'd with faery fancy," Madeline dreams of a Porphyro capable of satisfying all of her desires. Similarly, for one who cannot find a face he "would meet in every place" (l. 74), "winged Fancy" is able to produce "a mistress to thy mind" (ll. 79, 80). Breaking fancy's "prison-string" (l. 91) would, however, allow the mind to collapse into a solipsistic, self-consuming enchantment. "Fancy," writes Stuart Ende, "emerges as a self-sufficient power of mind, the autonomous and self-sufficient quality that enables mind to exist apart from outward circumstance . . . and even to defy it."[42]

In a letter to George and Georgiana, Keats follows his copy of "Fancy" with the quotation below from Hazlitt's comments on Godwin's *St. Leon*, a study of a mind collapsed into solipsism:

> He [Hazlitt] says of St. Leon, "He is a limb torn from Society. . . . The faces of Men pass before him as in a speculum; but he is attached to them by no common tie of sympathy or suffering. He is thrown back into himself and his own thoughts. . . . *His is the solitude of the Soul, not of woods, or trees, or mountains*—but the desert of society—the waste and oblivi[on] of the heart. He is himself alone. His existence is purely intellectual, and is therefore intolerable to one who has felt the rapture of affection, or the anguish of woe." (*LK*, 2:24–25)

Although Keats quotes this passage ostensibly to give the Georges a specimen of Hazlitt's "usual abrupt manner, and fiery laconicism" (*LK*, 2:24), his association of these remarks with "Fancy" is fascinating. Even more fascinating is the Hazlitt discussion Keats goes on to quote, distinguishing between the more fanciful art of Walter Scott and the imaginative art of

Godwin, which ends with the following evaluation of Godwin's work:[43]

> There is little knowledge of the world, little variety, neither an eye for the picturesque, nor a talent for the humorous in Caleb Williams, for instance, but you cannot doubt for a moment of the force of the conception. The impression made upon the reader is the exact measure of the authors genius. For the effect both in Caleb Williams and St. Leon, is entirely made out . . . by intense and patient study of the human heart, and by an imagination projecting itself into certain situations, and capable of working up its imaginary feelings to the height of reality. (*LK*, 2:25)

"This appears to me quite correct" (*LK*, 2:25), declares Keats, who himself had pledged to become a chronicler of "the agonies, the strife / Of human hearts." He then comments, "[N]ow I will copy the other Poem—it is on the double immortality of Poets" (*LK*, 2:25), and he transcribes "Bards of Passion," a poem celebrating the imagination's power to study the human heart and mind. In the *Lamia* volume, perhaps the most important transition is the movement from "Fancy" to "Bards of Passion." Fancy is in this way contrasted with imagination, solipsism with empathy and understanding, and the enchanted dreamer and the poet are finally made distinct.

Although fancy promises delights that will never cloy, they are also insubstantial and illusory. In contrast, the "never cloying" pleasures of which "Bards of Passion" speaks (l. 28) result from the poetic imagination's attempt to console and teach humanity. In return for the knowledge they have left behind on earth in their poetry, poets gain a heaven

> Where the nightingale doth sing
> Not a senseless, tranced thing,
> But divine melodious truth;
> Philosophic numbers smooth;
> Tales and golden histories
> Of heaven and its mysteries (ll. 17–22)

No longer an agent of enchantment, the nightingale has become, like Urania, a "Voice divine," a true muse singing to the poets of "heaven and its mysteries." The eternal delight they enjoy is thus constant enlightenment, a never-ending knowledge progressing toward an understanding of an infinite universe. More important for Keats, these "Double-lived" (l. 4) poets have gained heaven because of their concern for humanity:

> Here, your earth-born souls still speak
> To mortals, of their little week;
> Of their sorrows and delights;
> Of their passion and their spites;
> Of their glory and their shame;
> What does strengthen and what maim. (ll. 29–34)

Speaking to humanity of human joys and sorrows—of "What doth strengthen and what maim"—such poetry and such poets deserve to be celebrated, for they provide the only true link between earth and heaven: "the souls ye left behind you / Teach us, here, the way to find you" (ll. 25–26). To turn from "Fancy" to "Bards" is thus to accept poetic responsibility and begin the project outlined in the "Ode to Psyche" by expanding out of the contracted world of the sole self. In a letter to Bailey, Keats writes that "Fancy is the Sails [of Poetry], and Imagination the Rudder" (*LK*, 1:170). "Bards" marks the volume's subjection of fancy to the imagination's control. The two rondeaus that follow show a new kind of playfulness—fancy subjected to the free play of the imagination—reversing the reduction of imagination begun in "Lamia."

Though playful, "Lines on the Mermaid Tavern" and "Robin Hood" result from a serious search for a type of poetry adequate to teach the contemporary world. The two poems first appear in a letter to Reynolds in which Keats writes:

> It may be said that we ought to read our Contemporaries. that Wordsworth &c should have their due from us. but for the sake of a few fine imaginative or domestic passages, are we to be bullied into a certain Philosophy en-

> gendered in the whims of an Egotist. . . . I don't mean to deny Wordsworth's grandeur & Hunt's merit, but I mean to say we need not be teazed with grandeur & merit—when we can have them uncontaminated & unobtrusive. Let us have the old Poets, & robin Hood. (*LK*, 1:223, 224–25)

Written, as Keats goes on to say, in "the Spirit of Outlawry" (*LK*, 1:225), "Lines on the Mermaid Tavern" and "Robin Hood" spurn contemporary poetry for the larger, more heroic vision of the past: "Why should we be owls, when we can be Eagles?" But if Keats celebrates the poetic grandeur of the Elizabethans, those "Emperors of vast Provinces," and the moral heroism of Robin Hood, he also recognizes that "All are gone away and past!" ("Robin Hood," l. 37). Though he can locate himself within a tradition of vision, Keats must still define the shape that tradition is to take in the contemporary world.

One of the most daring juxtapositions of the volume comes at the end of "Robin Hood," where the celebration of a past heroism heralds the beginning of a new heroism. Immediately following the last two lines of "Robin Hood"—"Though their days have hurried by / Let us two a burden try"—is "To Autumn." "Robin Hood" is addressed "To a Friend," John Hamilton Reynolds, and the "burden" in which Reynolds is invited to join is thus the creation of a new kind of poetry with all of the imaginative vitality of the old, the kind of poetry represented by "To Autumn."

The four rondeaus as a group, then, move from fancy to imagination. They concern the creation of a poetry true to both poetic tradition and the complexities of the contemporary world. In their commitment to a poetry that is public, educative, and morally courageous, they make the necessary transition from Keats's vow to become Psyche's prophet to his prophecy—"To Autumn," the "Ode on Melancholy," and "Hyperion."

[V]

"To Autumn" is about a moment of imaginative grace. The third poem from the end of the volume, it balances by antithesis "The Eve of St. Agnes," the third poem of the volume. For, like "The Eve of St. Agnes," the moment of fulfillment "To Autumn" depicts is possible only because the poem allows for the fleetingness of that moment. Not only is the autumn it hymns the transitional season between the fertility of summer and the bareness of winter, but, as numerous critics have remarked, the poem itself moves from early to late autumn, from morning to evening, from life to death, from fulfillment to loss. Thus, unlike "The Eve of St. Agnes," "To Autumn" is a poem that confronts, rather than retreats from, a world of process and loss: its vision is the product of a mind on its way "through." As such, it defines itself against all of the other poems in the volume about enchantment, particularly "Fancy."

In "Fancy" the fulfillment of the mind's desires is examined in terms of seasonal imagery:

> Summer's joys are spoilt by use,
> And the enjoying of the spring
> Fades as does its blossoming;
> Autumn's red-lipp'd fruitage too,
> Blushing through the mist and dew,
> Cloys with tasting . . . (ll. 10–15)

No single season can satisfy a fanciful mind, ever hungry for what it lacks. Consequently, such a mind gains its fulfillment in the heart of winter, when fancy can better the reality of any of the seasons by presenting them all simultaneously:

> She will bring, in spite of frost,
> Beauties that the earth hath lost;
> She will bring thee, all together,
> All delights of summer weather;
> All the buds and bells of May,
> From dewy sward or thorny spray;

All the heaped autumn's wealth,
With a still, mysterious stealth . . . (ll. 29–36)

By mixing these "three fit wines in a cup" (l. 38), fancy can offer all that the mind desires. To "quaff" (l. 39) this mixture is to experience an illusory moment of intense fulfillment, during which the mind experiences simultaneously the songs of autumn and spring:

thou shalt hear
Distant harvest-carols clear;
Rustle of the reaped corn;
Sweet birds antheming the morn:
And, in the same moment—hark!
'Tis the early April lark,
Or the rooks, with busy caw,
Foraging for sticks and straw. (ll. 39–46)

"To Autumn," however, resolutely resists such enchantment, insisting instead on what Keats has elsewhere called "the real of beauty."[44] The poem's triumph is that it can accommodate the songs of autumn without the assurances contained within the songs of spring: "Where are the songs of spring? Ay, where are they? / Think not of them, thou hast thy music too" (ll. 23–24). Composed of the "wailful choir" of mourning gnats (l. 27), the loud bleating of "full-grown lambs" (l. 30), the singing of hedge-crickets, the whistling of robins, and the twittering of "gathering swallows" (l. 33), the music of autumn is the rich, bittersweet melody of a world in flux. That "To Autumn" is able to sustain the burden of its own music is much. And if the gathering swallows at the end of the poem herald the coming of the wintry bleakness attendant upon autumn's ripe fulfillment, the "Ode on Melancholy" insists that the mind not retreat before such a prospect.

"No, no, go not to Lethe," admonishes the "Ode on Melancholy" in its opening line. As their placement in the volume indicates, "To Autumn" and the "Ode on Melancholy" are companion poems.[45] Each deliberately refuses to follow the "star of Lethe" into enchantment. Psyche, not Hermes, is the divinity presiding over these poems. Whereas "To Autumn" shows the vision surpassing enchantment that disenchantment can purchase, the "Ode on Melancholy" begins to estimate the cost of that purchase. For the mind that willfully refuses oblivion gains instead anguish, the "wakeful anguish" (l. 10) of a soul that knows that Joy's hand "is ever at his lips / Bidding adieu" (ll. 22–23).

"One begins with 'Joy,' the abstract concept," says Stuart Sperry, "and works toward the informing gesture, the 'adieu' (the theatrical, slightly affected word that occurs in each of the odes of the spring)."[46] As we have seen, this "adieu" is present in the romances as well as in the odes. Implied in every greeting of the mind with the object of its desire is parting: "I eternally see her figure eternally vanishing," Keats wrote of Fanny Brawne. Recalling a prominent metaphor in the volume, the "Ode to Melancholy" recognizes that "aching Pleasure nigh" turns "to poison while the bee-mouth sips" (ll. 23–24). "What is the price of Experience?" Blake asks in *The Four Zoas*, answering: "it is bought with the price of all that a man hath." That the mind is willing to pay this price for those pains that are better than the nothing of oblivion testifies to its courage. That it can continue to bear the pains of disenchantment without breaking, however, is far from certain. For he who bursts "Joy's grape against his palate fine; / . . . shall taste the sadness" of Melancholy's might, "And be among her cloudy trophies hung" (ll. 28–30). "To Autumn" and the "Ode on Melancholy" force the volume's most compelling question: Can the mind sustain the burdens of disenchantment and loss?

[VI]

With both disenchantment and loss, "Hyperion," the final poem of the volume, begins. For unlike Hermes and his fellow gods in "Lamia," Saturn and the Titans discover that their dreams are not real, nor do their pleasures "smoothly pass / . . . in a long immortal dream" ("Lamia," 1:127–28). The implications of that "shadowy thought" of which the "Ode to Psyche" speaks begin to be made clear in the figures of a despairing Saturn, who sits deep within the "shady sadness of a vale" (1:1), contemplating his loss of power, and a Hyperion who finds himself confronting within his own palace of light "darkness, death and darkness. / Even here . . . / The shady visions come to domineer" (1:242–44).

The Titans thus gain the knowledge of a world "Where but to think is to be full of sorrow / And leaden-eyed despairs." Such knowledge humanizes them: Thea presses her hand "upon that aching spot / Where beats the human heart, as if just there, / Though an immortal, she felt cruel pain" (1:42–44). Coelus tells Hyperion:

> Now I behold in you fear, hope, and wrath;
> Actions of rage and passion; even as
> I see them, on the mortal world beneath,
> In men who die. (1:332–35)

"This is the grief, O Son!," Coelus goes on to say. "Sad sign of ruin, sudden dismay, and fall!" (1:335–36). Even the "supreme God" Saturn is "At war with all the frailty of grief, / Of rage, of fear, . . . / . . . but most of all despair" (2:92, 93–95). For no logically explicable reason, a hungry generation of new gods is treading the old down; Saturn himself cannot discover the "reason why . . . [the Titans] should be thus [fallen]: / No, nowhere can unriddle, though I search, / And pore on Nature's universal scroll / Even to swooning . . ." (2:149–52). Like the human characters of the volume, the Titans are the victims of a universe whose mysteries are hidden even from its oldest powers. Indeed, Coelus calls Hyperion the "Son of Mysteries / All unrevealed even to the powers / Which met at thy creating" (1:310–12). The burden of an unfathomable universe, responsible for process and loss, thus lies as heavily on the Titans as on humanity.

Although there is no apparent rational cause for the Titans to fall, it is easy to see why they are not sufficient to stand. For the Titans are the "early Gods" of an "infant world" (1:51, 26) in which beauty seemed to be truth. As such they are able only to conceive of exercising power in terms of creating and perpetuating beauty. Saturn, therefore, laments that he is "buried from all god-like exercise" (1:107)

> Of influence benign on planets pale,
> Of admonitions to the winds and seas,
> Of peaceful sway above man's harvesting,
> And all those acts which Deity supreme
> Doth ease its heart of love in. (1:108–12)

Compared with a God who in Revelation promises to make "all things new" (21:5), Saturn's promise that upon his return to power "there shall be / Beautiful things made new" (1:131–32) demonstrates vividly his limitations. These same limitations make Saturn and the Titans, as proved by their council, powerless either to understand or remedy their fallen condition.

Oceanus, claiming that he has "wandered to eternal truth" (2:187), is the first to speak at the Titans' council. But the "eternal truth" he has discovered is only an extension of the Titans' underlying assumptions about the universe: all is guided by a principle of beauty. "[F]or 'tis the eternal law," says Oceanus, "That first in beauty should be first in might" (2:228–29).[47] His attempt to provide a rational and benevolent framework for an unknowable universe is misguided. For like Lamia, Oceanus disparts the "most ambiguous atoms" of "specious chaos" into coherent form. Like Lamia, too, he falsifies very real complexities. With the delusive knowledge that "We fall by course of Nature's law" (2:181), Oceanus bids Saturn and the Titans "to bear all naked truths, / And to envisage circumstance, all calm" (2:203–4). He would have them respond to process with stoic resignation, to loss with quietism. Sadly, only Clymene and Enceladus are able to answer Oceanus, she with the pathetic recognition that "all my knowledge is that joy is gone" (2:253), he with blind wrath. Neither they nor any of the Titans are able to provide a remedy for their condition. The Titans find themselves the gods of an "infant world" progressed into maturity, where their power to create "beautiful things" is no longer sufficient. Needed now is the ability "to bear all naked truths," the ability to confront successfully process, loss, and an inexplicable universe. Needed now is the imaginative vitality of Apollo and the younger gods. Recognizing this, Mnemosyne leaves her fellow Titans, traveling to Delos to educate the young Apollo into "naked truth."

Just as the island of Crete is the initial setting of the volume, the island of Delos is the last. And if Crete is the scene of imaginative contraction, Delos is the scene of imaginative expansion. There, Apollo already plays a music filled with "joy and grief" (2:289), containing, as Clymene tells the Titans, "A living death" in "each gush of sounds" (2:281). This music of warring contraries overpowers Clymene, ranging far beyond the limited scope of the most limited Titan. Though Apollo's music is yet in its infancy, its power springs from his "aching ignorance" (3:107), his own painful confrontation with "shadowy thought": "For me, dark, dark, / And painful vile oblivion seals my eyes" (3:86–87). Here, the "Ode to a Nightingale" is recalled. For unlike the poet who seeks escape from flux in the oblivion of the nightingale's "embalmed darkness," Apollo yearns to know about the continual passing of "hungry generations." The process by which the poet sinks "Lethe-wards," "as though of hemlock I had drunk," is reversed as Apollo is deified by the knowledge he gains from Mnemosyne, "as if some blithe wine / Or bright elixir peerless I had drunk" (3:118–19).

Like the Milton of *Paradise Lost* alluded to in the "Ode to a Nightingale," Apollo refuses to avert his eyes from a suffering humanity; indeed, his description of what he perceives in Mnemosyne's face is a condensed version of books 11 and 12 of *Paradise Lost.* However, if "Knowledge enormous" (3:113) deifies Apollo, "it is impossible to know," as Keats writes to Reynolds, "how far knowledge will console us for . . . the ill 'that flesh is heir to' " (*LK*, 1:277–78). Apollo's transformation into a god is accompanied by all of the fierce pain of Lamia's opposing transformation into a woman: "Soon wild commotions shook him, and made flush / All the immortal fairness of his limbs; / Most like the struggle at the gate of death" (3:124–26).

The knowledge of the past that will center Apollo mentally in the painful realm of the present exacts the anguish spoken of in the "Ode to Melancholy": "so Young Apollo anguish'd" (3:130). At stake in Apollo's confrontation with a universe knowable only through loss is whether the mind can sustain such an encounter. Geoffrey Hartman suggests that " 'Hyperion' [breaks off] when 'bearing' becomes 'overbearing,' when maturing, instead of strengthening the prophetic or foreseeing character, leads to an overload destructive of it."[48] This may well be so; for the "Hyperion" appearing in the *Lamia* collection does not close the description of Apollo's struggle with the triumphant conclusion still preserved in manuscript: "he was the God!" Instead the poem breaks off abruptly in mid-sentence, with Apollo's anguished shriek followed by the inconclusive conclusion of two rows of asterisks. Ominously, "Hyperion," like "Lamia," ends in a horrifying shriek. The most important question posed by the volume is thus left unanswered. Keats wrote to Bailey that "nothing in this world is proveable" (*LK*, 1:242). The skeptical position he takes in this letter is provided for the *Lamia* volume by the open-ended form of its final poem. "Hyperion" throws open for questioning any possibilities proposed by the volume for bearing "naked truth."[49]

[VII]

"That which is creative must create itself." "Hyperion" concludes the self-revising consideration of poetry that takes place in Keats's 1820 volume. The "hierarchy it ["Hyperion"] describes is largely a poetic or aesthetic one," says Sperry, who also asserts, quite correctly, that Keats in "Hyperion" surveys and rejects "the chief poetic attitudes of his day, from stoicism (one of the less appealing aspects of *The Excursion*) to the stormy desolation of a poem like *Childe Harold*."[50] It is true that in the Titans' inability to accommodate loss Keats was criticizing the failure of contemporary poetry to make this same accommodation. Yet in "Hyperion" he was similarly criticizing many of the previous poems of the *Lamia* volume. If, for instance, Oceanus's stoic resignation could be found in the Wordsworth of *The Excursion*, and Enceladus's fiery gloom could be found in the Byron of *Childe Harold*, Clymene's helpless pathos could be found in the Keats of "Isabella." "Hyperion," and hence the volume itself, rejects all poetry that is unable to confront honestly and courageously the complexities of a world resistant to human desire.

The subject of the first sentence of the *Lamia* volume is Hermes, the last Apollo; between these two brother deities lie the major tensions of the collection. The movement from the god of enchantment to the god of poetry is a progression from evasion to confrontation, from fancy to imagination, from solipsism to community, from romance to epic. "Faith in the power of poetry to express the profoundest kind of truth is the necessary condition of all Romantic attempts at epic," writes Karl Kroeber.[51] Such faith motivates not only "Hyperion," but the entire *Lamia* volume. In its progressive movement from poem to poem, the 1820 collection becomes an aggregate greater than the sum of its poems—a drama of poetic discovery truly epic in scope.

Beginning with the Drydenesque "Lamia" and ending with the Miltonic "Hyperion," the volume places Keats decisively in a line of poetic vision descending from the Elizabethans and Milton. And Milton, as he had taught Wordsworth before him, taught Keats that to gain an earth made heaven, the mind must first encounter hell. Indeed, with the publication of this volume, Keats realized his ambition to become a poet of "the agonies, the strife / Of human hearts." The *Lamia* volume addresses the loss at the center of human existence from every possible perspective, placing hope, finally, in the ability of the mind—and its creation, poetry—to endure what Oceanus terms in "Hyperion" "the pain of truth" (2:202).

Through the rigor of the quest dramatized in the whole, Keats's 1820 collection possesses a more austere beauty, a more profound truth than that offered by the Grecian urn. The skepticism with which the book ends is far from the cynicism with which it begins: throughout, Keats seems to advance in understanding, poise, and a kind of knowledge gained even in bafflement. When read in the order of the volume rather than chronologically, the *Lamia* poems present a poet who is forced to live in the painful realm of his own negative capability, not one who is gradually reconciled to process. If Keats is then ultimately responsible for the arrangement of the final poems, the open-endedness of the volume—with its abrupt ending in Apollo's shriek—ought to caution critics who see Keats's maturation as synonymous with his acceptance of the natural world.[52]

"I see by little and little more of what is to be done, should I ever be able to do it," Keats had written to Haydon (*LK*, 2:32). Uncertain of the mind's resources, unsure if it could pay the price of Experience, sure only that it must, Keats's *Lamia* poems collectively leave their most important question as a question. If the way to life is through death, as Apollo discovers, if "the best way out is always through," can the mind endure the way through?

CHAPTER 5

"Sphere within Sphere"

Interrelations in Shelley's *Prometheus Unbound* Volume

[Shelley was] [a]lways conscientious about the compatibility of the poems to be included in each of his published or projected collections.

Earl Wasserman

If I had intended to publish "Julian and Maddalo" with my name, yet I would not print it with "Prometheus." It would not harmonize.

Shelley to Charles Ollier

CONTENTS.

Contents page of *Prometheus Unbound, with Other Poems.*
Courtesy of Library of Congress, Special Collections Division

[1]

"I ought to say that I send you poems in a few posts to print at the end of 'Prometheus' better fitted for that purpose than any in your possession," Shelley informed his publisher Charles Ollier in May 1820.[1] The following July, he added two more poems to the volume, one of which—the "Ode to Liberty"—was to provide a fit conclusion to the whole. Nor should we be surprised, given Shelley's penchant for organizing his collections,[2] that he chose carefully the nine poems to be printed with "Prometheus Unbound," a work he owned as "the best thing I ever wrote" (*LS*, 2:164). Critics have subsequently confirmed the wisdom of Shelley's choices: almost every other poem in the volume has been discussed in terms of "Prometheus Unbound" and several poems have been considered in light of one another. Yet the collection as a whole has never been discussed at length as an integral unit.[3]

Although heterogeneous in genre and style, the *Prometheus Unbound* volume is in theme and imagery a complexly interrelated contexture, both reflecting and refining what Newman Ivey White has called "the intense unity of Shelley's artistic purpose in 1819 and 1820."[4] Shelley selected an epigraph for the 1820 collection that suggests the nature of its thematic unity: "Audisne Haec Amphiarae, Sub Terram Abdite?" ("Do you hear this, Amphiarus, hidden away under the earth?") He found this line from Aeschylus's lost *Epigoni* in Cicero's *Tusculan Disputations*, where it is addressed by Cleanthes to Zeno, the dead founder of Stoicism. Disgusted because Dionysius cannot endure physical suffering stoically, Cleanthes contemptuously remarks his contemporary world's inability to stand up to life. Earl Wasserman has noted that when Shelley copied this line into his notebook, he entitled it "To the Ghost of Aeschylus," thereby turning Aeschylus's own words against him, just as Shelley's "Prometheus Unbound" turns Aeschylus's tragic treatment of the Prometheus myth into comedy by depicting a Prometheus who endures pain and eventually triumphs over the tyrant Jove.[5] Yet Wasserman fails to see the full extent of Shelley's response to Aeschylus because he, like most Shelley scholars, overlooks the fact that the epigraph appears not with "Prometheus Unbound" alone, but on the title page to the entire collection.

Arrogant epigraphs, as Shelley knew, were common to Renaissance epics. Stuart Curran has argued that, after Shelley's failures with *Queen Mab* and *The Revolt of Islam*, he gave up the epic form to create instead a canon that is epic in pretension, presenting through a multiplicity of generic approaches a truer and more comprehensive epic vision.[6] Curran's insight reinforces what the epigraph implies: that by juxtaposing a number of harmonizing but heterogeneous poems within a single encompassing structure, Shelley created a volume that was itself epic in pretension.

In the very comprehensiveness of that volume is the key to Shelley's answer to Aeschylus. For Aeschylus's vision needed correction in two major ways. First, Prometheus must endure and triumph rather than capitulate to Jove: "I was averse from a catastrophe so feeble as that of reconciling the Champion with the Oppressor of mankind," Shelley wrote in the preface to the poem.[7] But this is merely to create the comedy of "Prometheus Unbound" as a contrary to Aeschylus's tragedy. To the resolved and limited form of Aeschylus's drama Shelley opposed the more open-ended and expansive vision of a poetic volume that recognized the conditional nature of any of its resolutions. Demogorgon's final warning in "Prometheus Unbound" that—though regained—paradise may well be lost again, is given dramatic immediacy and thematic power by the remaining poems in the collection.

Indeed, the "harmonizing" poems examine not only the conditions of a world in which the Promethean paradise has been lost, but also the stance from which the poet must confront that world. Within the *Prometheus Unbound* volume, "being" depends upon perceiving: the world is actively structured by the mind. And words structure the mind. As the narrator of the "Ode to the West Wind" reveals by comparing his own words to "Ashes and sparks" (l. 67), language is the real Promethean fire stolen from heaven. Asia confirms the power of this Promethean gift, stating that Prometheus gave humanity speech and "speech created thought, / Which is the measure of the Universe" (2.4.72–73). Asia's pun on "measure" suggests that language can take the imaginative form of music, expressing and creating a harmonious universe, or it can be a limited and limiting agent—a liberating song or a miscreative curse.

The power of words to structure reality allows Demogorgon in "Prometheus Unbound" to provide humanity with "spells" capable of restoring paradise and permits Shelley to attempt in the "Ode to the West Wind" to initiate apocalypse through the "incantation" of his verse (l. 65). Yet, however incantatory, poetic texts can have no power if they are not read and understood. The *Prometheus Unbound* poems are rather self-consciously crafted as scripts for readers who, in the act of reading itself, release whatever power is stored within. By reconstituting these texts, internalizing their rhythms and words, their promptings and cues, readers restructure their own minds.[8]

With so much depending on the reader, Shelley could not overlook the possibility—even the likelihood—that his poems might be misread or ignored. "I am told that the magazines, etc. blaspheme me at a great rate," he wrote Peacock, enclosing the final two poems of the volume for the press. "I wonder why I write verses for nobody reads them. It is a kind of disorder, for which the regular practitioners prescribe what is called a torrent of abuse" (*LS*, 2:213). Poems such as "Ode to the West Wind," "To a Sky-Lark," and the "Ode to Liberty" depict the dilemma of a poet who knows the urgency of his vision but feels painfully uncertain about the ultimate power of his words. As the epigraph to *Prometheus Unbound* certainly suggests, the true Promethean figure to emerge from the volume is the poet himself, who is prepared not only to accept and endure but to embrace suffering in order to educate—hence liberate—humanity from its own mental chains.

Most of the poems in the *Prometheus Unbound* volume concern, to some extent, liberty and liberation. Together they show that liberty, for the individual, is the freeing of all that is best in the mind—love and imagination—from the repressive and solipsistic forces of selfhood.[9] For society, liberty is the religious, moral, and political freedom from the tyrannical forces of Church and State. Once liberated, the imagination creates the humanized world of its perception: through love the mind and the world are both utterly transformed, joined harmoniously in complete relationship. As we shall see, in the 1820 volume, psychological states are expressed in terms of natural imagery: liberation—an awakening from mental death—is metaphorically conceived as the rising sun or advent of spring. Conversely, the curse uttered by Prometheus binds the soul and blights nature, precipitating the onset of winter. The "winged seeds" of spring, we are told in the "Ode to the West Wind," "lie cold and low" in their "dark wintry bed," "[e]ach like a corpse within its grave" (ll. 7, 8). Characteristically, then, the poet attempts to stir "an unawakened Earth" ("West Wind," l. 68)—more specifically, to summon up the sleeping deity whose return will end winter. Demogorgon, at the beginning of "Prometheus Unbound," as elsewhere throughout the volume, yet "Sleeps a voice unspoken" (2.1.191). Somehow, the poet must contrive to rouse that dormant power into speech.[10]

In a world where seeing and saying are tantamount to "being" and "becoming," power resides with those who control the grounds of discourse: poetics become politicized; poets, true—if unacknowledged—legislators. At stake for each poet is whose agenda will prevail. Noting that the Amphiarus of the epigraph was a half-hearted rebel against Zeus who finally becomes the thunder god's pious prophet, Harold Bloom concludes that " 'Amphiarus' can be read as a multiplicity of orthodox poets." Bloom then shrewdly wonders if Shelley had classed "the Lake poets as well as Aeschylus within that multiplicity."[11] While Shelley respected Wordsworth, Coleridge, and Southey as former Zeus-defiers, he no doubt felt that poetry needed rescuing from the pieties now issuing with such regularity from their pens. In a sense, his 1820 volume is intended as a reproof to all those who would allow the prophetic potentiality of poetic discourse to become servile or domesticated—a tool for tyranny.

Yet Shelley was just as concerned in the 1820 volume that poetry not embody mere defiance or despair. Charles E. Robinson offers an intriguing hypothesis about the purpose of Shelley's epigraph: "the address to Aeschylus/Dionysius under the name of Amphiarus is also and perhaps even more so an address to Byron/Dionysius." Remarking that "Byron knew the story of Dionysius's apostasy and had already likened himself to Dionysius under different circumstances," Robinson surmises that Shelley's epigraph announced to Byron "that his renegade philosophy was being challenged" by "Prometheus Unbound."[12] It would seem, however, that Shelley's entire volume challenges Byron's "renegade philosophy." Late in August 1818, Shelley joined Byron in Venice, where the two spent long hours discussing poetry and English politics. Apparently, their discussions served as the immediate catalyst for the poems in the 1820 collection.

When Shelley began "Prometheus Unbound," just days after leaving Byron in Venice, he doubtless had his friend's earlier "Prometheus" in mind, just as, in composing "Ode to Liberty," he was thinking of *Childe Harold IV*, which Byron had read to him in Venice and from which Shelley culled the epigraph for the poem. At Venice Shelley had also read Byron's "Ode on Venice," where, as in *Childe Harold IV*, he found Byron advocating a cyclical theory of history that dooms humanity to endless frustration:

> There is no hope for nations!—Search the page
> Of many thousand years—the daily scene,
> The flow and ebb of each recurring age,
> The everlasting *to be* which *hath been*,
> Hath taught us . . . little! . . .
> For 'tis our nature strikes us down.[13]

The future, "the everlasting *to be* which *hath been*," merely and endlessly repeats the past. The inability of human beings to arise triumphantly from the cycles of historical repetition is a function of their own limitations, "For 'tis our nature strikes us down." Ominously, we are unable to achieve mastery over a world of our own creation, whose complexities prove so baffling that all attempts to reform it are self-defeating. For, somehow, one's fate is beyond one's control, and one can do little more than react to a world gone wrong, hoping only to salvage oneself and the integrity of one's vision from its ruins. A symbol of human fate, Venice, though a city "the Earth may thank" for "The name of Freedom," is now "clothed in chains" (ll. 117, 120, 118).

The reading of a poem that so clearly serves as a historical equivalent to Byron's mythopoeic "Prometheus" may well have brought this earlier poem, with its chained protagonist, to Shelley's mind. For in the bound Prometheus, a victim of "The rock, the vulture, and the chain" (l. 7), Byron found "a symbol and a sign / To Mortals of their fate and force" (ll. 45–46), an avatar of the mind opposing its own "funereal destiny" as an "equal to all woes" (ll. 50, 54). As a teacher of humanity, then, Byron's Prometheus gives "A mighty lesson" (l. 44) in the art of defiance. But this defiance is predicated upon the presupposition that the mind is doomed perpetually to "wretchedness" (l. 51) and can do no more than remain unchanged. To adopt such a position is to abdicate not only the will but the hope for change; ultimately, it is to lay the groundwork for an inevitably "sad unallied existence" (l. 52). Byron's Promethean mind thus pronounces against itself a curse whose issue is an unending misery from which death is the only refuge. Victory costs not less than everything for the mind only capable of being "Triumphant where it dares defy, / And making Death a Victory" (ll. 58–59). Byron's Prometheus not only remains bound at the end of the poem, but his triumph is that he remains so. Such self-defeating constancy did not go without comment from Shelley.

Within two months of completing "Prometheus," Byron received a letter from Shelley admonishing him to "be persuaded with Coleridge that 'Hope is a most awful duty, the nurse of all other virtues.' I assure you that it will not depart, if it be not rudely banished from such a one as you" (*LS*, 1:504). Two years later, in the midst of composing "Prometheus Unbound," Shelley was still reacting to what he saw as Byron's hopelessness. In a letter to Peacock concerning *Childe Harold*

IV, he abhorred the poem's "expressions of contempt & desperation" (*LS*, 2:58). Shelley's 1820 collection was designed to transform "contempt & desperation" into pity and hope, defiance and hatred into forgiveness and love. Only in such a way could poetry retain the liberating power of language.[14]

Shelley's own doubts about the efficacy of human will and the regenerative powers of imagination and love were more often expressed in his private lyrics than in the poems he selected for publication. Yet the kinds of questions Byron raised could only be answered by one who could show that he was no easy optimist, one who recognized just how difficult any true change in the human condition would be. Thus, the nine accompanying poems work largely to destabilize the victorious ending of "Prometheus Unbound." Only by going on to question the hope it first proposes does the 1820 collection validate it.

Although there are significant positionings and juxtapositions in the *Prometheus Unbound* volume, the connections between the poems are not limited by physical contiguity or sequential progression.[15] Instead, with its interacting sets of themes and imagery, the *Prometheus Unbound* collection needs to be understood synchronically as a whole, even though, unlike the two other Romantic volumes we have examined in detail, it is dominated by a single poem. Since all of the major themes and tropes of the volume are introduced and most fully elaborated in the title poem, we must first examine "Prometheus Unbound" at length—even at the risk of temporarily losing sight of the other poems.

[II]

In contrast to Byron's poem in which Prometheus remains bound, unchangeable, and doomed to a self-made "sad unallied existence," Shelley's "Prometheus Unbound" announces the major themes of the 1820 volume: liberty, transformation, and the relationship established between the mind and its world through love. In "Prometheus Unbound" we are shown that once the mind ceases to return hate for hate, once it withdraws the curse it has called down upon itself by doubting its own power to re-create the world through love, a new and paradisal world is formed. Demogorgon, the potential power latent in every relationship, is released into this new world, where all things are mutually attracted and harmonized.[16] Attendant upon liberation, then, is transformation and relationship. Though each of the three is an aspect of the other, liberation is the primary concern of Act 1, transformation of Acts 2 and 3, and relationship of Act 4.[17]

Subtitled a "Lyrical Drama," another name for opera, "Prometheus Unbound" probes the limits of language as song, converting a dirge-like curse into a choral ode of joy sung by spirits whose words will refashion the universe: "our singing shall build / In the Void's loose field / A world for the Spirit of Wisdom to wield" (4.153–55). As the product and hypostasis of a liberated imagination, "Language is a perpetual Orphic song, / Which rules with Daedal harmony a throng / Of thoughts and forms, which else senseless and shapeless were" (4.415–17). Providing meaning and shape for an otherwise chaotic universe, words become agents of transformation, the deifiers of the human spirit: "And music lifted up the listening spirit / Until it walked, exempt from mortal care / Godlike, o'er the clear billows of sweet sound" (2.4.77–79).

The transforming power of words, however, can barbarize as well as deify, destroy as well as create. The burden of the drama's first act is, in fact, for Prometheus to liberate himself from the tyranny of his own words. In Shelley's *Julian and Maddalo*, Julian understands that "it is our will / That thus enchains us to permitted ill" (ll. 170–71). And it is Prometheus's will as expressed in the words of his curse that enchains both himself and mankind: "All that thou canst inflict," he tells Jupiter, "I bid thee do" (1.263). The curse is thus the surrender of the despairing mind to its own darkest powers, "those foul shapes, abhorred by God and man— / Which under many a name and many a form / Strange, savage, ghastly, dark and execrable / Were Jupiter, the tyrant of the world" (3.4.180–83).

From its perspective in the renovated universe of Act 4, the Earth rejoices at the dethroning of a

> Sceptered Curse,
> Who all our green and azure Universe
> Threatendst to muffle round with black destruction . . .
> Until . . .
> My sea-like forests, every blade and blossom,
> Which finds a grave or cradle in my bosom
> Were stamped by thy strong hate into a lifeless mire . . .
> (4.338–40, 344, 347–49)

The ironic context for this "Sceptered Curse," the word as active agent of destruction, is the "curse" (24:6) in Isaiah, where "The land shall be utterly emptied and utterly spoiled: for the Lord hath spoken this word" (24:3). In "Prometheus Unbound" it is not the will of a wrathful thunderer, the creator of man, which curses the earth to destruction, but the will of man, the creator of that wrathful thunderer, which does so.

The Prometheus who begins Shelley's drama "eyeless in hate" (1.9), a victim of his own curse, is all but identical to his Byronic predecessor—except that he is capable of change.[18] On this change hinges the transformation of the universe. Made wise by his suffering, Shelley's Prometheus gives a new meaning to Manfred's equation of sorrow with knowledge; to him sorrow is knowledge, and knowledge is the basis of liberty: "I hate no more, / As then ere misery made me wise" (1.57–58). His effort to recall the words of a curse so powerful that they write themselves "as on a scroll" (1.261) into the form of their speaker is an attempt to rewrite that scroll, to reform man. However, Prometheus discovers that he can do no more than withdraw his words—"Were these my words, O Parent? . . . / It doth repent me . . ." (1.302, 303). The *tabula rasa* so created needs to be filled by the regenerative word of love, the "transforming presence" of Asia (1.832). "In the world unknown," we are told, "Sleeps a voice unspoken" (2.1.190–91). Only Asia, the "Life of Life" (2.5.48), can stir and make speak the as yet unspoken words in which Demogorgon's power resides.

Love thus awakens relationships. But hope and the refusal to hate must first awaken love. In his curse Prometheus has told Jupiter: "O'er all things but thyself I gave thee power, / And my own will" (1.273–74). Sensing in the revocation of this curse his own overthrow, Jupiter sends Mercury and the Furies to attempt a coup: the usurpation of Prometheus's will. Though the Furies torment him with a vision of a humanity consumed by its own evil, Prometheus refuses to accede to Mercury's demand that he "Let the will kneel within" his heart (1.378) and acknowledge Jove's supremacy. His determination not to speak "that fatal word, / The death-seal of mankind's captivity" (1.396–97), not to utter the final life-denying "no" of despair that would make Jove secure eternally, results finally in a word that is the beginning of all affirmations in the drama: the "Follow" that prompts Asia's and Panthea's quest of Demogorgon. Moreover, it frees Panthea to join Asia and make that quest possible.

Critics have variously explained the function and origin of Panthea and Ione. Some of these explanations center around etymological studies of their names; many concern their link with Asia, considering the three sisters in terms of differing sets of mythological triple goddesses; almost all, though, agree with Carlos Baker's contention that "Shelley intended them [the Oceanides] to represent in mounting order [i.e., Ione, Panthea, and Asia], degrees of love and perceptiveness within the human mind."[19] However, no critic has yet mentioned that through Panthea and Ione Shelley shows that the sleeping potentiality of relationship, though all but absent from the world, yet retains some kinetic manifestation.

In the bond between the two Oceanides who sit beneath the suffering Titan, attempting to console both him and each other, is a power that will grow exponentially throughout the drama, until, in Act 4, they sit together watching not Prometheus in torment but the joyful integration of a universe where all things are interrelated through love. Since they are the seedlings of this larger growth, the only pair still capable of relationship in the wake of the Promethean curse, it is logical not only that we should see the regenerated world of

Act 4 primarily through their eyes, but that they should narrate the appearance of the orbs of the earth and the moon, the major symbols of relationship in the play. Perhaps most logical of all is that, as agents of relationship, the sisters are necessary to mediate between a bound Prometheus and a distant, still separated Asia, whose "transforming presence . . . would fade / If it were not mingled" with his (1.832–33).

Yet, though equal in affection, Panthea and Ione, as Baker suggests, are not equal in awareness or imagination. Panthea has the empathic power to interpenetrate completely all of those she loves. Indeed, her ability to love so fully creates in her the constant presence of the beloved. Thus Panthea describes to Asia the recent past, when "young Ione's soft and milky arms" were "Locked then as now behind my dark moist hair" (2.1.46–47).[20] And just as Panthea is with Ione "then as now," she is also continuously with Prometheus. Asia therefore sees that Panthea wears "The shadow of that soul by which I live" [i.e., Prometheus] (2.1.31).

In a dream that she relates to Asia, Panthea describes how Prometheus, apotheosized into a power like the "morning sun" (2.1.77), burned upon her until she "felt / His presence flow and mingle through my blood / Till it became his life, and his grew mine / And I was thus absorbed" (2.1.79–82). The significance of this dream is great. First, it works as a parallel to Jove's description of his rape of Thetis:

> Thetis, bright image of Eternity!—
> When thou didst cry, "Insufferable might!
> God! spare me! I sustain not the quick flames,
> The penetrating presence; all my being,
> Like him whom the Numidian seps did thaw
> Into a dew with poison, is dissolved,
> Sinking through its foundations . . ."
> (3.1.36–42)

Panthea's absorption is thus contrasted with Thetis's dissolution, Jove's sexual tyranny with Prometheus's love.

Psychologically, Jupiter's rape of Thetis can be seen as an attempt to pervert the mind's capacity for true sexuality, to destroy its ability to engage in relationship. If successful, Jove would have produced a "fatal Child" able to "trample out the spark" in the human mind (3.1.19, 24), making his reign secure by extinguishing in humanity Prometheus's gift of fire. Indeed, this "fatal Child" would be the incarnation of the "fatal word" that Prometheus has refused to speak, the denial of the mind's ability to love. However, instead of producing a fatal child, Jupiter's rape of Thetis is barren of issue—the Demogorgon who appears at the tyrant's throne announces himself to Jove as being only "thy child, as thou wert Saturn's child, / Mightier than thee" (3.1.54–55).[21] Mightier than Jupiter, Demogorgon is the child of another—his birth as an active force can be traced to Panthea's dream of Prometheus.

Just as Prometheus's curse writes itself on the features of the Phantasm of Jupiter "as on a scroll," Panthea's dream of Prometheus inscribes his image on her mind. Asia thus asks Panthea to "lift / Thine eyes that I may read his [i.e., Prometheus's] written soul" (2.1.109–10). But, in order to see the Prometheus lying beyond the "inmost depths" of Panthea's eyes (2.1.119), Asia must rekindle her own long dormant potentiality for relationship. Then she finds in Panthea's eyes more than her own reflection: "the deep blue, boundless Heaven / Contracted to two circles underneath / Their long, fine lashes—dark, far, measureless,— / Orb within orb, and line through line inwoven" (2.1.114–17). The Asia who finds infinity rather than a mirror in her sister's eyes is like a Blakean visionary traveler who passes through the center of a globe to find it has become a vortex. Like that traveler, too, she has entered into full relationship with the object of her perception. Thus the "Orb within orb" Asia sees in Panthea's eyes is not only the anticipation but the birth of that "multitudinous Orb" (4.253) later described by Panthea, whose "Ten thousand orbs involving and involved / . . . / Sphere within sphere" (4.241, 243) is a symbol of a universe completely interrelated.

Now able to see deeply into her sister's mind, Asia perceives the image of Prometheus there, which upon fading draws her even farther inward. Huge reserves of psychic energy are released by Asia's momentary reunion with Prometheus through the mediating power of Panthea. Indeed, Asia's mental voyaging makes the internal external, freeing from Panthea's mind a forgotten dream that urges "Follow, follow!" (2.1.131) as it retreats back into the depths of her subconscious. Associational logic now governs exchanges far beyond mere rational discourse as first Panthea and then Asia remember forgotten dreams in which the landscape becomes script—flowers, tree, and mountains all offer the same written message: "Follow!"

Clearly, through their remembered dreams the two are already beginning to "follow." And a portion of Asia's dream reveals the source of this command:

> A wind arose among the pines—it shook
> The clinging music from the boughs, and then
> Low, sweet, faint sounds, like the farewell of ghosts,
> Were heard—*O follow, follow, follow me.*
> (2.1.156–59)

In the "Ode to the West Wind," "the leaves dead / Are driven, like ghosts from an enchanter fleeing" (ll. 2–3). These same leaves are later described as the poet's own thoughts: "Drive my dead thoughts over the universe / Like withered leaves to quicken a new birth!" (ll. 63–64). The similarity between the images here is revealing: it is the apocalyptic voice of the creative imagination, loosed by Asia's brief vision of the apotheosized Prometheus, which beckons her on to Demogorgon's realm to "quicken a new birth." Once loosed, this voice is echoed everywhere throughout a terrain that has become equivalent to a mental landscape, has in fact become a mental landscape, through which Asia and Panthea travel to the volcanic regions of power. Though not yet utterly transformed, Asia has been changed by her encounter with Panthea's dream. Indicative of her revitalized capacity for relationship, she asks Panthea to join hands with her as they begin their journey: "Come, sweet Panthea, link thy hand in mine, / And follow, ere the voices fade away" (2.1.207–8).

Transformation is the theme underlying both Act 2 and Act

3 of “Prometheus Unbound.” Panthea’s dream of Prometheus is crucial to the change at the heart of the drama. It not only acts as a catalyst for all that is to lead Asia and Panthea to Demogorgon but also as the key to that climactic confrontation. In this dream Prometheus first appears as the “morning sun,” an image that Asia retains as metonymical for a liberated and transformed universe. Later she uses it to structure the question that is the immediate cause of that transformation: “Prometheus shall arise / Henceforth the Sun of this rejoicing world: / When shall the destined hour arrive?” (2.4.126–28). To convert a wasteland into paradise, Asia, like a grail questor, must ask the right question. Indeed, in “Prometheus Unbound” a question properly structured contains the power to compel an appropriate response: “Ask and they must reply,” the Earth tells Prometheus (1.215). Asia, then, must and does ask the question to which the only response is “Behold!” (2.4.128). The potency of her question depends upon its structuring trope, received from Panthea’s dream.

Asia’s metaphoric equation of the unbound Prometheus with the sun shows her intuitive understanding of Promethean potentiality: it conflates Prometheus with both Apollo and the primary symbol of liberty in the volume. Like Apollo, Prometheus is to become the god of the human imagination, the hypostasis of all creative thought. Thus, he is later to depict his relationship with man in terms of love given and received through the mediating forms of art (3.3.49–62). In such art and the visionary imaginations that create it are the sources of all liberty. Hence, Prometheus is also like the rising morning sun, a symbol of liberty Shelley uses elsewhere in the volume: in the “Ode to Liberty,” for instance, liberty “like heaven’s sun girt by the exhalation / Of its own glorious light, . . . didst arise” (ll. 159–60).[22] Able to see so clearly the transformation of the universe in Prometheus’s unbinding and subsequent arising as the sun, Asia serves notice in her question to Demogorgon that the mind is prepared for this unbinding. In “Prometheus Unbound” the readiness is all: the ability to envision and will such a transformation becomes its immediate cause. The destined hour arrives.

The apocalypse Asia precipitates also requires her participation. William Hildebrand has commented upon the "equivocal nature of the destined Hour, one aspect of which is the destruction of Jupiter and one the transformation of Asia. Both natures signify phases of the potential activity of Demogorgon, who, like the West Wind, destroys in order to preserve."[23] Destruction and creation are the rhythms of apocalypse; attendant upon Demogorgon's dark chariot is Asia's ivory one. The Asia who by ascending in her "ivory shell inlaid with crimson fire" (2.4.157) repeats her moment of birth "[w]ithin a veined shell" (2.5.23), is love being reborn into the world as an active power.

"Some good change / Is working in the elements" (2.5.18–19), Panthea tells Asia, after having already remarked, "How thou art changed!" (2.5.16). A world is being reformed by the now radiant Asia, whose own lyric of transformation ends Act 2. In this song, which describes love assuming its place at the center of being, Asia transforms Prometheus's tragic refrain—"pain ever, forever!" (1.30)—into a description of her "enchanted" soul floating "ever—forever" (2.5.78) on the waves of song that transport her. And Asia's triumph is Jupiter's undoing. As Jove is converted by Demogorgon from kinetic back to potential energy, it is he, not Prometheus, who must lament: "I sink . . . / Dizzily down—ever, forever, down" (3.1.80–81).[24] Reflected in the transformation of this refrain, then, is the transformation of a cosmos.

Appropriately, the sun, which has been in the act of dawning throughout the drama, begins to rise at Jupiter's overthrow. Panthea's prefigurative dream of the liberated Prometheus as the "morning sun" is thus realized. Here metaphoric logic postpones the scene of Prometheus's unbinding for a scene in which three symbols—Apollo, Ocean, and Atlantis—converge to represent the change in which that unbinding is implicit.

Shelley's Ocean meets Apollo at "The Mouth of a great River." By placing Ocean in conjunction with a river, Shelley is at his syncretic best. For as he knew by reading the notes to Thomas Taylor's translation of Pausanias's *Description of*

Greece: "[W]hen Homer calls Ocean a *river*, he alludes to the deity of this name . . . who is a fontal deity *πηγαιος Θεος*, and is therefore very properly denominated a *river*, . . . being . . . the source of the sea and the all-various streams that flow upon the earth."[25] Shelley's Ocean is also a fontal deity; he writes in the "Ode to Liberty": "One ocean feeds the clouds, and streams, and dew" (l. 87). The perpetual transformation of Ocean's waters through the hydrogen cycle is a perfect symbol for mental flux. Taylor notes that Ocean "belongs to that order of gods which is called intellectual"[26] and goes on to quote Proclus's *Commentaries on the Timaeus* "that *Ocean* in fine is the cause of all motion, intellectual, . . . and natural."[27]

At its most fundamental level of meaning, "Prometheus Unbound" insists that mind, like Proclus's Ocean, is the cause of all intellectual and natural motion. In particular, Asia—in her role as "daughter of Ocean" or love, the most potent offspring of the human mind—is the cause of that motion which transforms the mind and all that it beholds. Asia's own lyric of transformation, as she passes below the structures of the mind, fittingly describes those structures in terms of oceanic imagery:

> We have past Age's icy caves,
> And Manhood's dark and tossing waves
> And Youth's smooth ocean, smiling to betray;
> Beyond the glassy gulphs we flee
> Of shadow-peopled Infancy,
> Through Death and Birth to a diviner day . . .
> (2.5.98–103)

With an offspring like Asia, the mind Shelley portrays can be self-transforming, finally at home in a world of its own creation.

As symbolic of the relative organization of the human mind, the ocean can be either a disorganized chaos or an integrated and harmonious body, a fractured surface distorting all it reflects or a true mirror of heaven. The Promethean revolution, therefore, leaves

> Man, who was a many-sided mirror
> Which could distort to many a shape of error
> This true fair world of things—a Sea reflecting Love;
> Which over all his kind, as the Sun's Heaven
> Gliding o'er Ocean, smooth, serene, and even,
> Darting from starry depths radiance and light, doth move . . .
> (4.382–87)

Once "so dusk and obscene and blind," the human mind is now "an Ocean / Of clear emotion, / A Heaven of serene and mighty motion" (4.95, 96–98). "Henceforth," Ocean tells Apollo, "the fields of Heaven-reflecting sea / Which are my realm, will heave, unstain'd with blood" (3.2.18–19). Indeed, the ocean has been transformed into a medium for true commerce from a site of tyranny, where Proteus and his nymphs tracked ships "by blood and groans; / And desolation, and the mingled voice / Of slavery and command" (3.2.29–31). No longer a barrier hiding heaven from the nymphs in its depths, the ocean now not only reflects heaven but becomes analogous to it.[28]

Succeeding this change in ocean is the resurfacing of Atlantis. As Asia explains to Demogorgon, the city is one of the gifts Prometheus gave to humanity. A place of infinite human possibility, the city can be either the artistic and architectural expression of the fulfillment and perfection of a human community, or the ruin expressive of the fallen form of human consciousness in which community is no longer possible. Atlantis, an archetype of human community, reemerges into the world, repeating the pattern of Asia's rebirth from the depths of a no longer chaotic ocean, a buoyant product of the Promethean mind's reintegration. The reunion of Apollo and Ocean at Atlantis, then, is a perfect symbol of this reintegration.[29] By symbolically bringing together here sun and ocean, Shelley also depicts the reunion of imagination and love, Prometheus and Asia.

Representative, too, of this reunion is the cave to which the now unbound Prometheus and the three Oceanides are led by the Spirit of the Earth. Formerly hostile and mysterious, the natural world gives up its opacities for transparencies. The Spirit of the Earth reports:

> There was a change . . . the impalpable thin air
> And the all-circling sunlight were transformed
> As if the sense of love dissolved in them
> Had folded itself round the sphered world.
> My vision then grew clear, and I could see
> Into the mysteries of the Universe.
> (3.4.100–105)

A symbol of the natural world opening up to the mind, the rock upon which Prometheus was suspended turned inside out, the cave is also symbolic of much more.

For the cave is to be the womb of the Promethean universe, a center to which "come, sped on the charmed winds / Which meet from all the points of Heaven . . . / The echoes of the human world" (3.3.40–41, 44). "In exchanging mountain for cave, an external and unresponsive nature for a world of intellectual symbols," comments Stuart Curran, "Prometheus commits himself to the destiny of man, to a human fellowship and the love that renders it possible."[30] Indeed, as Prometheus and the Oceanides begin their occupancy of the cave, they establish the returned form of the creative imagination. "Painting, Sculpture, and rapt Poesy / And arts, though unimagined, yet to be" become "the mediators / Of that best worship, love" (3.3.55–56, 58–59) given and returned between the cave's inhabitants and humanity. The Earth explains that during Prometheus's enslavement to Jupiter, the cave was a site

> where my spirit
> Was panted forth in anguish whilst thy pain
> Made my heart mad, and those who did inhale it
> Became mad too, and built a Temple there
> And spoke and were oracular, and lured
> The erring nations round to mutual war
> And faithless faith, such as Jove kept with thee . . .
> (3.3.124–30)

Tempering pure inspiration with love, the Promethean imagination is able to inspire, instead of madness, "calm and happy thoughts" in a mind that like the "unpastured sea" hungers "for calm" (3.3.146; 3.2.49). So potent are the transformative powers of the newly inhabited cave that Demogorgon in his final speech refers to the earth as the "calm empire of a happy Soul" (4.519).

The Earth provides yet another context for understanding the significance of the Promethean cave when she instructs the Spirit of the Earth to lead the Promethean entourage near a temple in Greece that "once . . . bore / Thy name, Prometheus; there the emulous youths / Bore to thine honour through the divine gloom / The lamp, which was thine emblem" (3.3.167–70). Here the Earth refers to the temple established for Prometheus in the Academy, the grove just outside of Athens where Plato instructed his students. From this temple was run the Lamadephoria, the race that as Shelley knew from Pausanias was an important part of the Attic Promethean rites:

> In the Academy is an altar to Prometheus, and it is from it they run to the city carrying burning torches. The contest is while running to keep the torch alight; if the torch of the first runner goes out, he no longer has any claim to victory but the second runner has. If his torch also goes out, then the third man is the victor. If all torches go out, no one is left to be winner.[31]

Analogous to this contest, says the Earth, is Prometheus's bearing of "the untransmitted torch of hope . . . / To this far goal of Time" (3.3.171, 174).

But the temple in the Academy is not Prometheus's final destination. Edward Hungerford notes: "There were two places in ancient times connected with the Attic cult of Prometheus: one was his sanctuary in the Academy; the other was the sacred grove at Colonus, a deme outside the walls of Athens, about a mile and a quarter to the northwest, and contiguous with the grove of the Academy."[32] "Beside that Temple is the destined cave," says the Earth (3.3.175), indicating that Prometheus's journey will bring him finally to Colonus, the site, Hungerford reports, of "a chasm or fissure reputed to lead down to the lower world."[33]

Shelley makes symbolic use of the Athenian worship of Prometheus. By locating the Promethean cave next to Athens he is able to associate it with a society he thought "the most memorable in the history of the world" (*Prose*, 7:223). Indeed, from the Athens extant between the years 490 and 322 B.C., Shelley shaped a symbol in both his poetry and prose of the highest possible human development. In Athens he saw a unified and harmonious community, both nurtured by and nurturing art:[34] "[N]ever at any other period has so much energy, beauty, and virtue been developed; never was blind strength and stubborn form so disciplined and rendered subject to the will of man, or that will less repugnant to the dictates of the beautiful and true" (*Prose*, 7:119). And Athenian art is dependent upon Athenian liberty, as Shelley makes clear in the "Ode to Liberty." In *Hellas* he writes: "Let there be light! said Liberty, / And like sunrise from the sea, / Athens arose!" (ll. 682–84). As the embodiment of the first creative words spoken by Liberty, the original site of the liberated human imagination, Athens is appropriately connected to the reemergent form of that imagination.

Those arts that Prometheus lists as mediators between humanity and himself all flourish in Athens. Yet "it is Poetry alone, in form, in action, or in language, which has rendered this epoch memorable above all others, and the storehouse of examples to everlasting time" (*Prose*, 7:119). That the greatest classical depiction of the human transformed to the divine—*Oedipus at Colonus*—was among the treasures of this storehouse allowed Shelley to create in the very location of the cave in Colonus, rather than in Athens proper, a symbol of transformation, of the divine potentiality of the human imagination. Moreover, Colonus itself, the mythological home of the Furies, is converted in "Prometheus Unbound," where vengeance and hatred are conquered by pity and love, into the regenerative center of a regenerated world, the hub of a changing universe.

The word "change" is the keynote of the reports given by

the Spirit of the Earth and the Spirit of the Hour, ending Act 3. Both of their speeches have roots in the biblical notions of apocalypse found in Revelation, and particularly 1 Corinthians, where Paul writes:

> Behold, I shew you a mystery; We shall not all sleep, but we shall all be changed,
> In a moment, in the twinkling of an eye, at the last trump: for the trumpet shall sound, and the dead shall be raised incorruptible, and we shall all be changed.
> For this corruptible must put on incorruption, and this mortal *must* put on immortality.
> So when this corruptible shall have put on immortality, then shall be brought to pass the saying that is written, Death is swallowed up in victory. (15:51–54)

"[A]nd all / Were somewhat changed," says the Spirit of the Earth, "All things had put their evil nature off" (3.4.70–71, 77). The Shelleyan version of the "corruptible" putting on "incorruption," this change finds its immediate cause in Shelley's revision of the last trump, the seashell that Proteus, after "breathing within it / A voice to be accomplished" (3.3.66–67), gives to Asia as a wedding gift.

Like the "voice unspoken" of Demogorgon, the transforming voice within the shell awaits Asia's own reawakening. Thus, the "hollow rock" (3.3.68) under which the shell is hidden by Ione until it can be used is an anticipation of the Promethean cave, a prophetic symbol of the transformation to come. Connected also with the shell in which Asia first arises from the ocean and the shell-chariot in which she is reborn, this "mystic shell" (3.3.70) contains a "mighty music" (3.3.81)—the ocean's epithalamium for Prometheus and Asia, the mind's celebration of its own reborn creative powers. Such music is itself all-creative. Heard as "thunder mingled with clear echoes" (3.3.82), the voice of the shell shakes "The towers amid the moonlight" (3.4.55), transforming all in its path.

The effects of a "sceptred curse" that produced "looks of firm defiance, and calm hate, / And such despair as mocks itself with smiles, / Written as on a scroll" (1.259–61) are thus erased: "hate, disdain or fear, / Self-love or self-contempt on human brows" are "No more inscribed" (3.4.133–34, 135). Prometheus's refusal to utter that "fatal word" has led at last to a new basis for language: "None talked that common, false, cold, hollow talk / Which makes the heart deny the *yes* it breathes" (3.4.149–50). Finally, humanity achieves its greatest victory over death. For death, as the Earth explains to Asia, is "the veil which those who live call life" (3.3.113). But now the mental death that once was called life has been replaced by true life: "The painted veil, by those who were, called life, / Which mimicked, as with colours idly spread, / All men believed and hoped, is torn aside" (3.4.190–92). Revealed to man are his own Promethean possibilities. Though not exempt from "chance, and death, and mutability" (3.4.201), man can now rule them like slaves, for he is at last, "the King / Over himself": "Sceptreless, free, uncircumscribed" (3.4.196–97, 194). The overthrow of the "sceptred curse" is the happiest of all the "happy changes" reported in Act 3 (3.4.84).

Implied in Act 3 of "Prometheus Unbound," as Shelley himself discovered, is Act 4.[35] A yet happier change awaited description: attending human transformation is universal relationship. The "multitudinous Orb" (4.253) of the earth described by Panthea in Act 4 is the drama's primary symbol of this relationship, identifying microcosm with macrocosm, the atom with the cosmos, the mind with all.[36] The orb appears to Panthea with "loud and whirlwind harmony," and its description, though lengthy, is important:

> A sphere, which is as many thousand spheres,
> Solid as chrystal, yet through all its mass
> Flow, as through empty space, music and light;
> Ten thousand orbs involving and involved,
> Purple and azure, white and green and golden,
> Sphere within sphere, and every space between
> Peopled with unimaginable shapes, . . .
> Yet each intertranspicuous, and they whirl

Over each other with a thousand motions
Upon a thousand sightless axles spinning
And with the force of self-destroying swiftness,
Intensely, slowly solemnly roll on . . .
(4.238–44, 246–50)

Here, as Richard Holmes has written, is a "prevision of electron shells in the atomic structure of matter."[37] Indeed, Carl Grabo first located as a source for Shelley's orb a discussion by Sir Humphrey Davy which concludes that atomic motion "must be a vibratory or undulatory motion, or a motion of the particles round their axes, or a motion of particles around each other."[38] That the orb is so clearly modeled after atomic structure should not prevent one from seeing that it is also modeled after Renaissance conceptions of the cosmos.

The most important Renaissance cosmological model was Ptolemaic, based "upon a belief that the sphere is the standard form in the universal structure—in Aristotle's phrase, the primary shape in nature."[39] Robert Recorde in his *Castle of Knowledge*, written in 1556, explicates this system: "The whole world is round exactlye as anye ball or globe, and so are all the principall partes of it, every sphere severallye and joyntlye, as well of the Planetes, as of the Fixed starres. . . . And they are aptely placed together, not as a number of round balles in a nette but every sphere includeth others."[40] The Ptolemaic system and many of its Renaissance variations have interesting analogies to Shelley's orb. Not only do they depict the sphere as the basic unit of all structures, but they also show the heavens to be structured around the divine number ten: seven planetary spheres, a "cristalline" sphere, a sphere of fixed stars, and the "primum mobile." Shelley's "ten thousand orbs involving and involved" is a more complex reworking of this common pattern. Mythographers like Natalis Comes drew diagrams of the universe in which the spaces between the cosmic spheres were filled by mythological creatures, like the "unimaginable shapes" peopling the spaces between Shelley's spheres. And the music flowing between the turning spheres of Shelley's "multitudinous Orb" is, of course, similar to Pythagorean-Platonic concepts of the music proceeding from the turning of Ptolemy's spheres.

Though we now picture the Ptolemaic universe as a static series of concentric circles, Shelley would have had a different perspective. He was probably familiar with the armillary sphere, a common Renaissance teaching tool, which was a three-dimensional model of the Ptolemaic universe, "the celestial globe in all its detail, the macrocosm made momentarily static."[41] In the interinvolved spheres of this celestial globe, Shelley would have found a close visual analog to his own orb. At the center of the armillary sphere, the focal point of the turning heavens, lay, very much like Shelley's Spirit of the Earth, the earth.

This infant human form, lying within an orb that is at once atom and cosmos, is a symbol of rebirth, or a universe restructured and rehumanized—that is, reseen—from the level of the atom up.[42] For the orb, both as described by Panthea and as compared to her eyes (2.1.117), is also a symbol of her altered eye in which Asia first perceives the apotheosized Prometheus. In "Prometheus Unbound," as in Blake, the eye altering alters all. A symbol of universal process and harmony, the orb is also a symbol of the mind responsible for producing this harmony by being, at last, able to perceive it.

"Let us recollect our sensations as children," writes Shelley. "We less habitually distinguished all that we saw and felt, from ourselves. They seemed as it were to constitute one mass" (*Prose*, 6:195). Shelley could thus provide no better symbol of a universe reborn into complete relationship, a microcosm that is a macrocosm, than the child in the earth and that "winged Infant" (4.219) in the lunar orb described by Ione. Moreover, it is a comparison of man to a leprous child who has been miraculously restored to health that ushers in the most triumphant assertion of relationship in the drama:

> Man, oh, not men! a chain of linked thought,
> Of love and might to be divided not, . . .
> . . . .

> Man, one harmonious Soul of many a soul
> Whose nature is its own divine controul,
> Where all things flow to all, as rivers to the sea . . .
> (4.394–95, 400–402)

Humanity, and hence the cosmos, becomes organized into a titanic oceanic network in which "all things flow to all"—and the ocean is Asia's element. A revitalized moon makes clear the source of the universal transformation underway: " 'Tis Love, all Love!" (4.369). Thus, the cosmic masque of love to which Panthea and Ione are audience through most of Act 4 seems to each of them to be a "stream of sound" (4.506). From this "stream" the Oceanides emerge to hear instead a "universal sound like words" (4.518), the voice of Demogorgon, the harmony from which all harmonies ultimately derive.

The blank verse of Panthea and Ione gives way to the rhymed pentameter of Demogorgon's seven summonses to the powers of the universe, within whose structure Shelley fashions a final symbol of universal relationship. Each summons consists of a quatrain rhyming ABAB, answered by a one-line response that ends also with the B rhyme, forming a concluding couplet between summons and response—a harmony. The only variation of this pattern is in the fourth and numerically central summons to the "happy dead" (4.534), where Demogorgon is interrupted by "A Voice: from beneath" before he can complete his quatrain. Instead of producing a rhyme word for "portray," his shortened line ends on the dissonant word "suffered" (4.537). This break emphasizes a line that refers back to the pre-apocalyptic universe: "which once ye saw and suffered— . . ." (4.537), a reference Demogorgon enlarges into the entire content of his final summons to man, who was "once a despot and a slave,— / A dupe and a deceiver,—a Decay, / A Traveller from the cradle to the grave / Through the dim night of this immortal Day" (4.549–52).

Demogorgon's summonses thus prefigure his final speech, where he is to emphasize the tenuousness of the Promethean revolution. For even in the midst of being all that he might become, man must never forget that he is in a constant state of becoming and may revert to all that he once was. Structurally, Shelley has reinforced this point by interrupting an otherwise perfectly symmetrical pattern of summons and response.

The process of transformation in "Prometheus Unbound" points in two directions simultaneously. On man's will alone rests the condition of his universe; on his imaginative ability to love, all things depend. Hence Demogorgon's summons to man dwells most on the unhappy past. So, too, unlike the other responses, where only those summoned replied, "All" answer Demogorgon's call to man. The universe is at last firmly united under the name of man. And the one voice with which all things speak is the last voice but one to speak in the poem. In response to its request for his "strong words" (4.553), Demogorgon addresses a universal congregation for which he is a bonding agent both productive of and produced by its unity.

Defining themselves against Prometheus's curse, which the Earth once preserved as a "treasured spell" (1.184), Demogorgon's words provide "the spells" by which man, if need be, can once more liberate himself from the ruinous power of his own words. Especially interesting here is Shelley's use of stanzaic patterning to achieve formal and thematic closure for his drama. Of the three stanzas composing Demogorgon's final speech the first two consist of eight lines: surrounding a quatrain rhyming BCCB are an opening and closing couplet. The nine-line third stanza resembles the other two in everything but its extra line. This, the last line of the drama, is the only alexandrine in a succession of pentameter lines, a final reminder of the imaginative expansion of the Promethean universe. Moreover, it creates, from the couplet in the eight-line stanza, a triplet whose rhyming words—"be," "free," and "Victory"—reiterate the theme of the entire poem. The ontological condition of the liberated mind is the greatest victory humanity can gain. And it is with this "Victory" that both Demogorgon and Shelley wish to end. The volume, however, continues.

[III]

Though few Romanticists would now support Douglas Bush's accusation that Shelley is guilty of "sentimental optimism" in "Prometheus Unbound," most would grant that it is an apparently optimistic play—even considering Demogorgon's final warning.[43] But this is largely to ignore how the other poems in the volume purposefully condition the drama's optimism. Read together, the 1820 poems present a complex mapping of human potentiality that is in no way finally optimistic. Reiman and Powers conjecture that "The Sensitive-Plant" was the first of the "other poems" included in the *Prometheus Unbound* volume, "perhaps because it is both the longest of these poems and a mythopoeic fable that harmonizes with *Prometheus* itself."[44] In particular, however, the thematic grounds of this harmony might have led Shelley to link the poems together: over the course of "Prometheus Unbound" paradise is regained only to be unmade in "The Sensitive-Plant," the first poem to follow; once lost, this paradise will not reappear in the volume.

Asia's first appearance in "Prometheus Unbound" occurs simultaneously with the appearance of spring. Similarly, the spring that begins "The Sensitive-Plant" arises like "The Spirit of love felt everywhere" (1.6). Creative of an "undefiled Paradise" (1.58), this spirit of love is personified in an Asia-like "Lady," who, to the flowers of the garden, "was as God is to the starry scheme" (2.4). Like Asia's "step" ("Prometheus Unbound," 2.1.192), which alone can break the sleep of Demogorgon, there is a special potency in the "step" of this Lady, which not only seems "to pity the grass it prest" (2.21), but also spreads joy throughout a garden in which the awakened power of Demogorgon is everywhere evident. Complete relationship exists between the flowers of the garden:

> For each one was interpenetrated
> With the light and the odour its neighbour shed

> Like young lovers whom youth and love makes dear
> Wrapt and filled by their mutual atmosphere.
> (1.66–69)

Like the young lovers within the orbs of the moon and earth, the major symbols of relationship in "Prometheus Unbound," the flowers are "Wrapt and filled by their mutual atmosphere." And, as we have seen, Shelley identifies the ability to achieve this kind of relationship with the child. Thus the flowers are not only described as "young lovers," but are compared to "an infant's awakening eyes" (1.59), and the sensitive plant, the flower most desirous of relationship, is "A sweet child . . . / The feeblest and yet the favourite" (1.112–13).

The prototype for this interinvolved "garden fair" (1.5) may well be the forest surrounding the Promethean cave, where one finds

> . . . the dark linked ivy tangling wild
> And budding, blown, or odour-faded blooms
> Which star the winds with points of coloured light
> As they rain through them, and bright, golden globes
> Of fruit, suspended in their own green heaven;
> And, through their veined leaves and amber stems,
> The flowers whose purple and translucid bowls
> Stand ever mantling with aereal dew . . .
> (3.3.136–43)

Here is the first connection between flowers and stars in the volume, the image pattern Wasserman locates as central to the meaning of "The Sensitive-Plant."[45] Moreover, within this same description, the breath of the earth is said to rise throughout the forest as "A violet's exhalation" ("Prometheus Unbound," 3.3.132), just as the "fresh odour, sent / From the turf" (1.15–16) mixes with the "breath" of the snowdrop and violet in the garden.

These metaphoric similarities align the "garden fair" with the sacred grove at Colonus, the site of the Promethean cave and the transformational center of the world. Yet, as Demogorgon reminds us, transformation is a two-way process; producing a hell made heaven in "Prometheus Unbound," it can also make the "sublunar Heaven" (2.10), that is the garden in "The Sensitive-Plant," into a hell:

> The garden once fair, became cold and foul
> Like the corpse of her who had been its soul
> Which at first was lovely as if in sleep,
> Then slowly changed, till it grew a heap
> To make men tremble who never weep.
> (3.17–21)

The change the garden undergoes is thus likened to the decomposition of a corpse. More specifically, it is like the death and decay of the spirit of love.

The life and death of the Lady are described specifically in seasonal imagery: she appears in spring, tends the garden throughout the summer, and dies "ere the first leaf looked brown" (2.60). However, she is not a nature goddess who dies with the dying year and returns in the spring. Rather, Shelley deliberately sets up tension between nature's cyclical progression and the human mind's metaphoric, noncyclical seasons: the harmonious mind still perceives nature's winter as humanity's spring. The death in "The Sensitive-Plant" is not that of the Lady but of the mind's ability to perceive the Lady—to experience the kind of love that makes a garden of this world: "That garden sweet, that lady fair / . . . In truth have never past away— / 'Tis we, 'tis ours, are changed—not they" (Conclusion, 17, 19–20). As metaphorical conception, then, the Lady's death represents the mind's failure of vision and signals the inevitable approach of autumn and winter.

In a similar way, Prometheus's curse not only forces the exile of Asia, a counterpart to the Lady, but initiates winter. As the Earth explains: "black blight [fell] on herb and tree, / And in the corn and vines and meadowgrass / Teemed ineradicable poisonous weeds / Draining their growth, for my wan breast was dry / With grief" (1.173–77). So, in "The Sensitive-Plant," "All loathliest weeds began to grow" upon the death of the Lady (3.51). Once again, the earth is cursed into winter; Promethean potentiality becomes bound: "Winter came— . . . / His breath was a chain which without a sound / The earth and the air and the water bound" (3.90, 94–95).

A northern whirlwind wanders appropriately about the ruined garden, "Like a wolf that had smelt a dead child out" (3.111). That dead child is a world now devoid of relationship. For such a world no renewal comes with the returning spring. And no renewal is possible until humanity recognizes that the garden is a form imposed upon the world by a mind harmonized through love. To "Fate, Time, Occasion, Chance, and Change . . . / All things are subject but eternal Love" (2.4.119–20), says Demogorgon. "For love, and beauty, and delight / There is no death nor change" (Conclusion, 21–22), likewise concludes the narrator of "The Sensitive-Plant." Attendant upon a changing human mind, however, is the changing of all things. Though love and the garden remain eternally available to the mind, it nonetheless allows itself to contract the perspective of its vision and, like Prometheus, become bound to a wintry world of death.

"A Vision of the Sea," the third poem in the collection, is a Shelleyan exercise in the sublime, difficult to interpret because its exposition (virtually all description) breaks off before reaching any thematic statement or denouement.[46] Yet if, on the one hand, we are tempted to dismiss the poem as an anomaly, its placement in the volume invites us to discover continuities with the other poems and highlights thereby its metaphoric substructure. The "terror of the tempest" (l. 1) with which "A Vision of the Sea" begins thus recalls the disorganization of the ocean caused by Prometheus's curse: "the sea / Was lifted by strange tempest" (1.165–66).[47] However, in "Prometheus Unbound" man's will is eventually triumphant, becoming "as a tempest-winged ship, whose helm / Love rules, through waves which dare not overwhelm" (4.409–10), while that same will appears shipwrecked in "A Vision of the Sea": "The heavy dead hulk / On the living sea rolls an inanimate bulk, / Like a corpse on the clay which is hungering to fold / Its corruption around it" (ll. 31–34).

Read in the symbolic context of the volume, then, "A Vision of the Sea" seems a fit companion to the preceding "Sensitive-

Plant"; here the ocean, as that poem's earth, might be seen as representing the hostile, unhumanized natural world that results from the mind's own disintegration. Both poems, in fact, abound with images of ruin and corruption. Perhaps the death and decay characterizing the death of love in "The Sensitive-Plant" is most strongly depicted in a passage appearing in the 1820 volume and deleted from most subsequent editions of the poem, in which the moss rotting off the stalks of fungi is compared to a body rotting on a gibbet: "Where rags of loose flesh yet tremble on high, / Infecting the winds."[48] The second line of "A Vision of the Sea" echoes this image, transposing it in terms of the ruined ship, where "The rags of the sail / Are flickering in ribbons within the fierce gale." Later in "A Vision of the Sea," the image cluster culminates when an oak splinter from the deck of the ship pierces through the breast and back of the last living sailor, "And hung out to the tempest, a wreck on the wreck" (l. 65). The moss and the sail are not only equated with human flesh, but are, in a sense, human flesh. They are symbols of the corruption and decay of a once healthy and united body that universally responded to the name of man at the end of "Prometheus Unbound." And the gibbet, upon which criminals were hanged and then left to rot, is a fit symbol of human miscreative will, a will once more enslaved to the tyrant Jove.

In contrast to Ocean's claim that "Henceforth the fields of Heaven-reflecting sea / Which are my realm, will heave, unstain'd with blood" (3.2.18–19) is the bloody shipwreck of "A Vision of the Sea," during which, as the sailors dying "One after one" (l. 58) are thrown into the ocean, "the sharks and the dogfish their grave-clothes unbound, / And were glutted like Jews with their manna rained down / From God on their wilderness" (ll. 56–58). Unbound in this poem is not Prometheus nor the human race, but the "grave-clothes" of the dead seamen by the sharks and dogfish to whom they are thrown. Corpses blasted by the tempest and "smitten" by thunder (l. 61) are the only kind of manna the thunderer is capable of providing his true worshipers.

There is, however, a force in the poem opposed to Jove's

destructive reign. In "Prometheus Unbound" it is "Love" which guides the helm of the ship that is man's will. Likewise, in "A Vision of the Sea," "At the helm sits a woman more fair / Than Heaven" (ll. 66–67). This nameless woman is the third of three successively more naturalistic and powerless avatars of love in the volume. Like Asia and the also nameless "Lady" of "The Sensitive-Plant," she, too, is coupled with an infant: "She clasps a bright child on her upgathered knee" (l. 69). And just as the young Spirit of the Earth is said by Ione to mock the sublime harmony of the orb within which he lies, this infant "laughs at the lightning" and "mocks the mixed thunder / Of the air and the sea" (ll. 70–71). In Shelley's 1820 volume it is only the adult mind that perceives the natural world as threatening; the child sees all as an extension of itself, viewing the sublime as a source of heightened joy rather than fear. The young Earth is thus able to speak metaphorically of the "tyger Joy" (4.501), and the infant in "A Vision" actually beckons to the tigers lying on the deck of the ruined ship "to rise and come near, / It would play with those eyes where the radiance of fear / Is outshining the meteors" (ll. 72–74).

Mother and child, love and relationship, alone survive the wreck of the ship—but only tenuously. Holding on to the last piece of the ship with her left hand, the mother struggles to sustain her infant with her right, while they both await rescue. At this point the poem ends abruptly, balancing hope for the survival of the mother and child against knowledge of the sudden and treacherous shifts of which the "false deep" (l. 167) is capable: though now appearing tranquil and "smiling," the sea appeared to smile similarly just before the onset of the tempest. Jove, as the poem ends, still seems to control the ocean.

Its abrupt ending reminds the reader that "A Vision of the Sea," like any vision, is subject to fragmentation. It should also be remembered that the poem is entitled "A Vision of the Sea," not "The Vision of the Sea." The ocean, after all, can be perceived quite differently. Like the ruined garden at the end of "The Sensitive-Plant" and the tempest-tossed ocean of "Prometheus Unbound," the chaotic ocean of "A Vision of the Sea" might be read as symbolic of humanity's contracted and chaotic perspective. In the *Prometheus Unbound* volume, as demonstrated graphically in the "Ode to Heaven," perspective is everything.

The "Ode to Heaven" is a cosmic exercise in perspective revealing that the mind inhabits only the universe of its perception. The three descriptions of heaven juxtaposed in this poem range from a constricted Newtonian view to an imaginative vision of the visible universe as a mere fraction of the infinite cosmos, a "globe of dew" in whose "frail and fading sphere" "Constellated suns unshaken, / Orbits measureless, are furled" (ll. 46, 52, 50–51). This "globe of dew" not only suggests Panthea's eyes in which Asia sees "the deep blue, boundless heaven / Contracted to two circles" and the "multitudinous Orb" in whose spheres microcosm and macrocosm are likewise identified, but also the "clear dew" through which the eye of the lily gazes "on the tender sky" in "The Sensitive-Plant" (1.35–36). However, rather than in its third vision alone, the meaning of the "Ode to Heaven" is to be found in the competing positions of its three speakers, in the conflicting statements of voices increasingly "remote."[49] For these are three specifically poetic visions: their words are not only markers of a perspective, but, in effect, makers as well. Each of the three universes described is just as real as its speaker believes it to be and vies with the others for predominance. In the *Prometheus Unbound* volume, to articulate is to shape—and to transform.

With so much dependent on the transformative powers of words, there can be nothing static in the 1820 volume about Shelley's symbols or the world they represent. The sun whether rising or setting, the ocean calm or in storm, the west wind preserving or destroying, Prometheus himself unbound or enchained: all of these function as constants with variable values. Each fluctuates between and is defined by its capacity for good or ill; each is capable of ceaseless change. Hence, "The Cloud," placed eighth, is a lesson in the symbolic calculus governing the entire volume; delighting most in its ability to change continually without losing its essential identity, Shelley's cloud finds self-definition in perpetual transformation: "I change, but I cannot die" (l. 76).

Like the various characters in "Prometheus Unbound," the cloud speaks from its own dramatic point of view. Primarily, the cloud understands itself in terms of agency. As a storm cloud, it is an agent of destruction: "I wield the flail of the lashing hail" (l. 9). But, like Asia, the cloud is also a daughter of Ocean, a form of love capable of annihilating itself to replenish and renew the earth. Both destroyer and creator, the cloud enacts the rhythms of the apocalyptic imagination, providing in the description of its own destruction an image of rebirth (ll. 81–84). More than one critic has therefore agreed with Donald Pearce's conclusion that "in the image of the cloud . . . we have a most precise symbolization of the mind's creative power, as Shelley conceived it."[50] Yet as the volume as a whole demonstrates, Shelley was a good deal more cautionary about the "mind's creative power" than such an identification allows. Indeed, the cloud is portrayed as a child, with attendant limitations. Shape-shifter though it may be, the cloud exhibits an unself-conscious reflexiveness that prevents it from seeing its effects on the world as much more than a gauge of its own powers. Moreover, the underside of the cloud's playful exuberance and self-assurance is its complete ignorance of the forces controlling its transformations. In other words, the strength of the cloud is also a form of blindness baneful to the mature poetic mind.

For the poet in the 1820 collection, as for the cloud, "being" is a matter of "becoming." The primary imaginative agent in the world, the poet is thus also the main catalyst of change. He is at once perpetually transformed by his world and perpetually trying to transform it. Change is his element. As Shelley explained to the Gisbornes, "Poets, the best of them—are a very camaeleonic race" (*LS*, 2:301). In Act 3 of "Prometheus Unbound" we are told that Proteus had breathed "A voice to be accomplished" within the shell blown by the Spirit of the Earth. Proteus can therefore be understood as an avatar of the poetic imagination; his voice, the agent of apocalypse. As Shelley would have known, Renaissance Neoplatonists had remarked with interest the correspondences between Proteus and the chameleon. According to tradition, Proteus dwelled within an underwater cave. This helps to explain why, in "An Exhortation," "Poets are on this cold earth, / As chameleons might be, / Hidden from their early birth / In a cave beneath the sea" (ll. 10–13).[51] Nurtured from their birth by Proteus, both the chameleon and the poet understand fully the importance of change. The poet alone, however, recognizes its hazards.

Poetic chameleons, after all, can be subject to debilitating changes. "An Exhortation," a poem that Shelley claimed "is itself a kind of excuse for Wordsworth" (*LS*, 2:195), concerns the difficulty the poet-prophet faces in remaining true to his own vision when that vision is ignored by the public: "Where light is, chameleons change: / Where love is not, poets do: / Fame is love disguised: if few / Find either, never think it strange / That poets range" (ll. 14–18). Ignored by their contemporaries, poets must fight to prevent their chameleonic imagination from binding its liberated energies into acceptably popular forms and ideas:

> Yet dare not stain with wealth or power
>   A poet's free and heavenly mind:
> If bright chameleons should devour
>   Any food but beams and wind,
> They would grow as earthly soon
>   As their brother lizards are.
>   Children of a summer star,
> Spirits from beyond the moon,
>   Oh, refuse the boon! (ll. 19–27)

By most standards a minor poem, "An Exhortation" becomes important in the *Prometheus Unbound* volume, where it serves as a fit preface to the thematically central "Ode to the West Wind" by asking that poets suffer the ignominy of the prophet to retain the clarity of their vision, the freedom of their imagination. For, as Shelley's greater exhortation to the west wind reveals, much depends on the unfettered mind of the poet.

While informing his prophet Ezekiel that he will be scorned by the Hebrews, the Lord also admonishes him to "be not afraid of their words, though briers and thorns *be* with thee" (2:6). The Shelley who falls upon the "thorns of life" (l. 54) and bleeds in the "Ode to the West Wind" is similarly engaged in a prophetic mission. If most people see from a single perspective, poets possess double vision. Like his cloud, Shelley knows that death and rebirth, destruction and creation, are the necessary rhythms of transformation; each of the contraries implies the other. Like the prophets and the Christ recalled in the poem's imagery, he also knows that his attempt to transform humanity demands his martyrdom. "Shelley's poem," writes James Rieger, "concerns the *vates* who immolates himself for the regeneration of his fellows."[52]

During the composition of the "Ode to the West Wind," Shelley first wrote a passage in his notebook he later refined and used in the "Ode to Liberty":

> Within the surface of the fleeting river
> The wrinkled image of the   lay
> Immoveably, unquiet; it
> and forever
> It trembles but it cannot pass away[53]

This passage is based upon lines from Wordsworth's "Elegiac Stanzas: Suggested by a Picture of Peele Castle, in a Storm, Painted by Sir George Beaumont": "Thy Form [i.e., Peele Castle] was sleeping on a glassy sea. / . . . / Whene'er I looked, thy Image was still there; / It trembled, but it never passed away" (ll. 4, 7–8).[54] While composing a poem demanding that the imagination revitalize its world, Shelley has in mind a poem in which Wordsworth's imagination begins to falter: "I have submitted to a new control: / A power is gone, which nothing can restore" ("Peele Castle," ll. 34–35).

Replacing imagination for Wordsworth is endurance: "But welcome fortitude and patient cheer, / And frequent sights of what is to be borne!" ("Peele Castle," ll. 57–58). For Shelley, there was little fundamental difference between the passive endurance of the Wordsworth in "Peele Castle" and the defiant endurance of Byron in "Prometheus." Both positions result in the mind's resigning itself to a world beyond its control; both lack the will for change. Wordsworth's man finds his prototype in Beaumont's painting of Peele Castle standing steadfast against the constant assault of "The lightning, the fierce wind, and trampling waves" (l. 52). The storm-buffeted landscape that Wordsworth approvingly terms "well chosen," depicts a "sea in anger" in which a ship "labours in the deadly swell" against a "rueful sky"—all together forming a "pageantry of fear" (ll. 46, 44, 45, 48). Reacting in this poem against his former conception of nature's benevolence, Wordsworth embraces instead a vision of natural malevolence. He, in effect, seems to accept as ultimate reality the universe of "A Vision of the Sea"—and by doing so, becomes one of Jupiter's subjects.

Unlike Wordsworth in "Elegiac Stanzas," Shelley in the "Ode to the West Wind" sees in the power of an upcoming storm a means to dethrone Jupiter. It is, after all, a storm that undoes Jupiter in "Prometheus Unbound," where he is described as

> An eagle so caught in some bursting cloud
> On Caucasus, his thunder-baffled wings
> Entangled in the whirlwind, and his eyes
> Which gazed on the undazzling sun, now blinded
> By the white lightning, while the ponderous hail
> Beats on his struggling form which sinks at length
> Prone, and the aerial ice clings over it. (3.2.11–17)

Appropriately, Jove's most awful weapon is made the instrument of his defeat. Shelley's attempt to unite with the west wind, then, is an effort once again to wrest control of the storm from Jove and unleash its powers against him, to fashion from a rapidly approaching winter the prophecy of spring. As in "Elegiac Stanzas," natural imagery provides a model of the mind in "West Wind." However, in place of Wordsworth's battered mind and battering sea is Shelley's self-annihilating mind and a sea in which the waves "Cleave themselves" (l. 38) before the voice of the wind. The west wind that the poet would have carry his words is thus an agent of transformation, the externalized power of the poet's transformative imagination. As such, the "trumpet" (l. 69) through which it is to spread his apocalyptic prophecy is like the Protean seashell through which the Spirit of the Hour blows the trumpet of human apocalypse.

Yet the wind carries a prophecy of uncertain potency. Contrasting ironically with the triumphant question by which Asia precipitates the apocalypse in "Prometheus Unbound" is Shelley's unanswered question ending the "Ode to the West Wind": "If Winter comes, can Spring be far behind?" (l. 70). Balanced precariously in this single line are the enormous dialectical tensions of the entire volume. If, in the "Ashes and sparks" (l. 67) that are his words, the Promethean poet attempts to restore the gift of fire to humankind, his efforts are subject to the same initial fate as those of his prototype. Promethean flames are all too easily extinguished by an obstinate humanity or the poet's own despair. Ice, after all, not fire, dominates the wintry world in which "Prometheus Unbound" begins.

Within the Indian Caucasus, the birthplace of humanity, Shelley conceives the symbolic polarities of human potentiality: the icy ravine upon which Prometheus endures winter and the lovely vale in which Asia welcomes the coming of a long-awaited spring. Though Shelley himself may well have to endure Promethean-like suffering, there are no guarantees that he will similarly succeed in gaining Prometheus's victory. True spring, as "The Sensitive-Plant" demonstrates, need not follow winter. For the buds of spring to blossom from the seeds of winter, the voice of the poet-prophet must not only be heard but followed. Perhaps, then, the most courageous aspect of Shelley's address to the west wind is that it ends in a question. Unsure of the ultimate power of his words, certain only that they must be spoken, Shelley, at the end of the poem, is trapped between the urgency of his vision and a recalcitrant humanity.

The "Ode to the West Wind" is in many ways about "the human voice, which sets stones dancing and echoes the spheres,"[55] whose utterance might compel reality into new and renewed forms. Shelley's faith in the power of the human voice led him to inquire of Leigh Hunt if he knew "of any bookseller who would like to publish a little volume of *popular songs* wholly political, & destined to awaken & direct the imagination of the reformers" (*LS*, 2:191). Though this "little volume" was never assembled, a poem that might have been included appeared instead in the *Prometheus Unbound* collection. Immediately following Shelley's request that the west wind bring his words to an "unawakened Earth" (l. 68) is "An Ode, written October 1819, before the Spaniards Had Recovered Their Liberty," which opens with the repeated imperatives, "Arise," "Awaken" (ll. 1, 8). Despite its elaborate and somewhat misleading title,[56] this poem is a direct appeal to the potential reformer in every person to begin the difficult task of personal and political liberation.

The overtly political significance of "An Ode" both highlights the political implications of "Ode to the West Wind" and conditions the violent immediacy of its imagery. Shelley correctly saw that, late in 1819, the Reform movement in England was foundering for want of leadership and vision. Directionless, the movement threatened to become merely futile or, even worse, senselessly violent. Shelley was convinced that any attempt at violent revolution risked succumbing, as did the French Revolution, to its own violence. He depicts the dangers of returning hate for hate in "Prometheus Unbound." This theme is refashioned into an explicit political warning in "An Ode": "Conquerors have conquered their foes alone, / Whose revenge, pride, and power they have overthrown: / Ride ye, more victorious, over your own" (ll. 26–28). The kind of revolution Shelley demanded begins with a willed change of mind and heart, with humanity realizing its potentiality for being truly humane. And if this were ever actually possible, it would never be easy.

Indeed, "To a Sky-Lark" concerns the gap that has developed between the human voice and song, between humanity and its own potentiality for harmony. Only the poet can bridge this gap. Although "To a Sky-Lark" is frequently read as an aesthete's poem, its context within the volume gives it political implications as well: Shelley goes to school to the skylark because its "music sweet as love" (l. 45) proceeds from a voice that is the last vestige of the Promethean paradise left in a hellish world. As such, the joy that it expresses has the power to compel the attention of its listeners "Till the world is wrought / To sympathy with hopes and fears it heeded not" (ll. 39–40). The ability to cause this transformative response is a skill that to a poet is "Better than all measures / Of delightful sound— / Better than all treasures / That in books are found" (ll. 96–99). Consequently, from the middle ground upon which he stands, Shelley tries to locate this "Scorner of the ground" (l. 99) in order to learn the secret of its song.

But the distance between the ontological states of the skylark and of humanity creates a problem in epistemology: how is the poet to know this "Sprite or Bird" (l. 61)? Failing, first visually and then through a series of similes, to define the skylark adequately, Shelley learns only of his inability to know: "What thou art we know not . . . / I know not how thy joy we ever should come near" (ll. 31, 95). Yet when his attempt at definition fails, the poet is still in command of the rhetorical resources of poetry, which, as evidenced by the "Ode to the West Wind," include supplication. If Shelley cannot teach himself the secret of the skylark's song, then perhaps the skylark itself will consent to become his teacher. He asks, therefore, not only that the skylark give humanity in general a lesson in joy—"Teach us . . . / What sweet thoughts are thine" (ll. 61–62)—but, more specifically, that it teach him the power to transfix and hence transform his audience: "The world should listen then—as I am listening now" (l. 105). "To a Sky-Lark," then, is an invocation to a muse, a request for the inspiration necessary to remake the human voice into song. The penultimate poem of the collection, it is succeeded by the "Ode to Liberty," a poem designed by Shelley to climax the volume, with an even more ambitious supplication and an even more disturbing failure of voice.

One of the greatest agonies Prometheus must endure is the failure of the French Revolution. The "present is spread / Like a pillow of thorns for thy slumberless head," taunt the Furies (1.562–63). Taken from Byron's response in *Childe Harold IV* to the failure of the French Revolution, the epigraph to the "Ode to Liberty"—"Yet, Freedom, yet, thy banner, torn but flying, / Streams like a thunder-storm against the wind" makes clear that Shelley is here accepting that same "pillow of thorns," confronting the possibility that the present world, despite his own exhortations and the seemingly successful revolution in Spain, will fail to liberate itself from the reign of Jupiter. The degree of pain the poet must endure, then, is finally and convincingly presented in the "Ode to Liberty," a summary of human history that is clearly intended to balance "Prometheus Unbound" both thematically and imagistically, providing a fit ending for the volume.[57]

As the "Ode to Liberty" begins, the inspiration Shelley called for in "To a Sky-Lark" seizes him. The control over the storm, for which he had asked in the "Ode to the West Wind" and which man had gained in "Prometheus Unbound," where the "Lightning is his slave" (4.418), becomes manifested again in the Spanish people, whose revolution has "vibrated again / The lightning of the nations" (ll. 1–2). Buoyed by the hope this revolution engenders, Shelley's soul "spurns the chains of its dismay" to "Clothe itself, sublime and strong" in the "rapid plumes of song" (ll. 5–7). But this image of Promethean unbinding is misleading. For Shelley's song of liberty and the "voice out of the deep" (l. 15) that sustains it soon falter, their appeal for liberty unheeded.

In the version of history given by the "Ode to Liberty," liberty and the imaginative vision necessary to foster it exist originally as unrealized potentiality, "like unfolded flowers beneath the sea" (l. 54), hidden below consciousness within the depths of the mind.[58] Unsurprisingly, however, from the "enchanted caves" of Greece come "Prophetic echoes" (ll. 49, 50) of its emergence. For, as we have seen, Greece is the location of the Promethean cave and the setting for the celebration of liberty that forms the entire Act 4 of "Prometheus Unbound."

In the "Ode to Liberty" it is the Prometheus-worshiping

Athenians who, through their determined will and art, first plumb the depths of the human mind, releasing liberty into the world. Within a historical moment the Promethean paradise becomes briefly incarnated in the form of Athens. And although Athenian liberty is lost through time, Shelley insists that what has once been achieved can be accomplished again. Here the oceanic imagery he had created and rejected for the "Ode to the West Wind" provided Shelley with a model of the mind:

> Within the surface of Time's fleeting river
> Its [Athens's] wrinkled image lies, as then it lay
> Immovably unquiet, and for ever
> It trembles, but it cannot pass away. (ll. 76–79)

Like the Atlantis of "Prometheus Unbound," Athens is submerged within the mind, as well as distanced from us in time, existing as an archetype—though in a "wrinkled image" as if seen through great depths of water—ready to be reimposed upon the world once the human mind is again liberated.

The oceanic imagery of the volume culminates in the final stanzas of the "Ode to Liberty," in an echoing of the imagery of "Prometheus Unbound." Indeed, much of the imagery of these final stanzas echoes the opening poem of the collection. The eighteenth stanza of the "Ode to Liberty" is particularly allusive. It begins with a plea to liberty: "Come Thou, but lead out of the inmost cave / Of man's deep spirit, as the morning-star / Beckons the Sun from the Eoan wave, / Wisdom" (ll. 256–59). The image of the Promethean cave is thereby reinvoked: no longer the center of a transformed universe, the cave is hidden deep within the mind. Moreover, by once again juxtaposing the sun and the ocean, these lines recall Apollo's reunion with Ocean.

In the harmonious world of Act 3 of "Prometheus Unbound," the "small, clear, silver lute of the young spirit / That sits i' the Morning star" (3.2.38–39) beckons Apollo to rise from his congress with Ocean. Attempting to reconstruct such a world, Shelley asks liberty to lead wisdom into a new sunrise, "as the morning-star / Beckons the Sun from the Eoan wave." However, though "the wise and free" have "Wept tears, and blood like tears" (ll. 269, 270), such a sunrise has not yet dawned. "[L]et that thorn-wounded brow / Stream not with blood—it mingles with thy tears!" (1.598–99), a tormented Prometheus cries to the image of a crucified Christ presented him by the Furies. The poet in the "Ode to Liberty" is similarly tormented. To him the tears wept by the "wise and free" seem to confirm the Furies' statement that "those who do endure / Deep wrongs for man, and scorn and chains, but heap / Thousand-fold torment on themselves and him" (1.594–96). For, though in "Prometheus Unbound" the collapse of Jove allows new dialogue between Ocean and Apollo, a dissonance still remains between the sun and the ocean in the world pictured at the end of the "Ode to Liberty." The mediatory song that might reconcile the two ceases like a "wild swan . . . / When the bolt has pierced its brain" (ll. 273–77), stifled by the thunderer who yet remains in power.

Shelley's song of liberty, a victim of the tyranny that still dominates the human mind, becomes submerged beneath the fading echoes of the voice that once sustained it, "As waves which lately paved his watery way / Hiss round a drowner's head in their tempestuous play" (ll. 284–85). The oceanic imagery of the volume thus culminates in a drowning. Here is a reversal of the "all-prophetic song" issued by the "harmonious mind" in "Prometheus Unbound," whose apotheosizing power "lifted up the listening spirit / Until it walked . . . / God-like o'er the clear billows of sweet sound" (2.4.76, 74, 77–79). That this drowning ends the volume gives it added importance. Although the "Ode to Liberty" begins in hope, it ends in frustration, its song failed, its final supplication to liberty left unanswered. Despite the poet's desperate exhortations, all Promethean possibilities for humanity seem remote. Nowhere in the volume do the poet's efforts seem more futile.

Like the amphisbaenic serpent described in Act 3 of "Prometheus Unbound," "Prometheus Unbound" and the "Ode to Liberty" seem to give the 1820 collection a body with two heads facing in opposite directions. But perhaps the form of the volume more closely resembles an ouroburos, the serpent residing beneath Demogorgon's throne, which bites its own tail. For the "Ode to Liberty" ends by depicting the kind of world with which "Prometheus Unbound" begins. Harold Bloom has called "Prometheus Unbound" a "giant ode to the spring."[59] This is in many ways a just analogy. Shelley's vision, however, demanded that he balance the spring and full bloom of summer represented in "Prometheus Unbound" with the autumnal tones of the "West Wind" and the wintry bleakness at the end of "The Sensitive-Plant" and the "Ode to Liberty." Beginning with a vision of spring and ending with a vision of winter, Shelley's 1820 volume covers the gamut of human potentiality. Throughout, whether the individual poems are predominantly optimistic, pessimistic, or poised between the two positions, there remains the openness of a mind that refuses to deny any possibility.

Thus, it would be wrong to imply that the shape of the book is merely circular. In fact, the earth orb of "Prometheus Unbound" provides the best metaphor for the volume. Like that "multitudinous Orb," structured by "Sphere within sphere" (l. 243), the poems in the *Prometheus Unbound* collection not only support but interpenetrate one another thematically and imagistically. As an interrelated unit, they make a plea for relationship: their theme is the need for liberating those imaginative powers that enable the mind to circumvent selfhood and relate to its world with love. Like the earth orb, too—which continuously transforms the ground it passes over—the 1820 poems provide an education in the dynamics of transformation, showing that through our words and thoughts we call up worlds that constantly need recalling, reimagining. As Demogorgon warns, the Promethean paradise must be perpetually remade, or again it will be lost. Only by imaginatively re-creating itself and its world through love can the mind, with Shelley's cloud, "arise like a ghost from the tomb" (l. 83). The vitality, the very freedom of our minds and societies depend upon such knowledge—and the chameleonic poets who teach it. Perhaps, then, there is yet more meaning to the epigraph prefacing the collection. For it is an address directed to an underground spirit to awaken and take notice:

"Do you hear this, Amphiarus, hidden away under the earth?" In *Prometheus Unbound, with Other Poems*, Shelley urges British liberty, lying deep within its tomb, once again to arise.

The culmination of Shelley's poetic achievement, the *Prometheus Unbound* volume ranks with *Lyrical Ballads* and Keats's *Lamia* volume as one of the greatest poetic collections of the age. It was through their volumes that the major Romantics presented themselves to contemporary readers, focusing thematic concerns and fashioning public personas. Through their volumes, too, the Romantics influenced not only one another but subsequent poets as well.[60] In short, their books often are revealing structures that provide us with valuable contexts for understanding both the poets and their canons. Nor will these contexts be recovered until—as editors, critics, and readers of the Romantics—we attend more closely to the interplay between the poem and the book.

Notes

CHAPTER 1

1. One interesting example of this interaction can be found in the second edition of *Tottel's Miscellany*, where several poems have been moved from their original positions and placed after others they appear to "answer" thematically. Such "paired poems" are not uncommon in sixteenth-century volumes. See Rollins, *Tottel's Miscellany*, 2:10, 77n. Similar pairings of poems occur in Romantic volumes. In *Clifton Grove, a Sketch in Verse, with Other Poems* (1803), for instance, Henry Kirk White prints a poem addressed to him by Coppell Loft in the midst of a series of numbered sonnets and goes on to "answer" it in the following sonnet, "Recantatory, in Reply to the Foregoing Elegant Admonition." However, as we shall see, it is more common to find paired poems written by the same poet in a Romantic book.

2. Common in seventeenth-century usage but now rare, "contexture" denotes an "interwoven structure," according to the OED, which also lists a specifically literary application: "the construction or composition of a writing as consisting of connected and coherent members." Perhaps no word adequately conveys the special qualities of the poetic collection as an aggregate: that is, the "contextuality" provided for each poem by the larger frame within which it is placed; the "intertextuality" between poems so placed; and the resultant "texture" of resonance and meanings. I have appropriated "contexture" for its usefulness in suggesting all three of these qualities without being restricted to any one.

3. Erdman, *Poetry and Prose of William Blake*, pp. 713–14. Erdman also notes that though Blake assembled seven volumes of *Songs of Innocence and of Experience* in the same order, "this 'final' order may represent only a final weariness. For when he took pains to write out instructions as to 'The Order in which the Songs . . . ought to be paged & placed'—an order followed in one copy, on 1818 paper, though the

list is checked over twice as if for two bindings—Blake contrived yet one more unique arrangement" (p. 714).

4. Even Blake never reordered the poems in *Poetical Sketches*, the only one of his books published by traditional methods. Nor, for that matter, did he reissue the volume in any form.

5. Rollins, *Letters of John Keats* (hereafter cited in the text as *LK*), 2:26. Here Keats is reacting to the failure of *Endymion*. His desire to produce a "volume of some worth" was realized in the *Lamia* collection; see chapter 4 below. Jack Stillinger in *Texts of Keats's Poems* entertains "the notion that each of Keats's volumes constitutes a separate literary work in which the arrangement of the pieces within the volume in a sense represents one more stage of composition, and consequently that we ought to read the poems ... in the order in which Keats put them." He concludes that "the individual poems of *1817* and *1820* do take on additional meanings by their relationships with the poems that precede and follow them in the original volumes, and Keats, like other poets, must have been aware of the fact" (p. 284).

6. Griggs, *Collected Letters of Samuel Taylor Coleridge* (hereafter cited in the text as *LC*), 1:545.

7. Jones, *Letters of Percy Bysshe Shelley* (hereafter cited in the text as *LS*), 2:196. "Julian and Maddalo" was reserved for a volume that Shelley never lived to publish but which would have contained, he explains to Ollier, "all my saddest verse raked up into one heap" (*LS*, 2:246).

8. This statement, of course, appears in the preface to *The Excursion* (1814). See Owen and Smyser, *Prose Works of William Wordsworth*, 3:5–6. One might usefully recall here Coleridge's remarks in a lecture on the Gothic Mind (27 January 1818): "Gothic architecture impresses the beholder with a sense of self-annihilation; he becomes, as it were, a part of the work contemplated. An endless complexity and variety are united into one whole, the plan of which is not distinct from the execution." See Hill, *Imagination in Coleridge*, p. 101.

9. The Alexandrians were certainly not the first Western poets to arrange groups of their own poems, however. Although our evidence is sketchy, Sappho, Mimnermos, and Theognis—among others—may all have done so before the rise of the poetry book in Alexandria. See, for example, Rose, *Handbook of Greek Literature*, pp. 83, 85–88, 97, and passim.

10. Van Sickle, "The Book-Roll," p. 6. I have found Van Sickle's entire discussion of the book-roll enlightening, pp. 5–42.

11. See Santirocco, "Horace's *Odes*," pp. 46–47.

12. In "Horace's *Odes*," Santirocco notes about *Iambs* that "on metrical grounds two groups of stichic poems (1–4, 8–13) surround a group of epodes (5–7). On thematic grounds, 7–11 are placed together since

all offer aetiologies, whereas 11 and 12 are set side by side to juxtapose their forms, an epitaph and genethliacon" (p. 46). In addition, see the discussions of *Iambs* in Dawson, "The Iambi of Callimachus"; and Clayman, "Callimachus' Thirteenth Iamb," pp. 29–35.

13. Indeed, the idea of a garland is in itself suggestive of artful arrangement and, of course, appears frequently in volumes in the Renaissance and after. Although it is tempting to add Theocritus (the first seven *Idylls*) and Herodas (*Mimiaboi*) to the list of Hellenistic poets who organized their books, it is uncertain just how responsible either poet is for the arrangement of his poems. See, for example, Giangrande, review of Lawall, *Theocritus' Coan Pastorals*," pp. 170–73.

14. Van Sickle, "The Book-Roll," p. 16.

15. The connections between Horace's *Odes* and the formally and thematically heterogeneous poems in Alexandrian books are elaborated in Cody, *Horace and Callimachean Aesthetics*. For the general influence of Callimachus on the Augustans, see Clausen, "Callimachus and Latin Poetry," pp. 181–96. Van Sickle in "Book-Roll" considers the influence of the Alexandrian poets on Virgil's *Eclogues*, pp. 16–29. In *Petrarch's Lyric Poems*, Durling notes that Horace's *Odes* and Virgil's *Eclogues*, as well as the elegies of Propertius and Ovid, are classical models for Petrarch's *Canzoniere* (p. 10).

16. The Catullan corpus begins with a sequence of poems (2–11) designed to trace the progression and final dissolution of a love affair. See Santirocco, "Horace's *Odes*," p. 49. We cannot be sure, however, that Catullus arranged his corpus as we now know it.

17. Needless to say, *La vita nuova* is not the first work to combine prose and poetry. This practice, for instance, was not uncommon in Latin didactic texts. Although the *vidas* and *razos* often found in manuscript collections of Provençal poets have been cited as vernacular precedents for the prose explanations in *La vita nuova*, Sarah Sturm-Maddox distinguishes between these earlier examples and Dante's innovation by noting that the former were not provided by the poet himself. See her "Transformations of Courtly Love Poetry," p. 129. In one of the earliest English sequences, *The Hekatompathia; or Passionate Centurie of Love* (1582), Thomas Watson may well be following Dante by including his own commentary in the headnote to each poem. S. K. Heninger, Jr., suggests, moreover, that Watson is probably influenced by the Continental vogue of annotating sonnets, two prominent examples of which are Bembo's commentary on Petrarch and that of Muret and Belleau on Ronsard's *Amours*. See Heninger's edition of Watson's book, p. ix. The impact on English collections of this Continental vogue and of Dante's own critical prose in *La vita nuova* has not, to my knowledge, been sufficiently explored.

George Gascoigne, for example, seems to draw from both traditions in *The Adventures of Master F. J.*, where he uses a fictitious editor "G. T." to provide the critical and "biographical" commentary linking a sequence of love poems written by the equally fictitious "F. J." It is interesting to note as well Michael McCanles's recent assertion that E. K.'s commentary in *The Shepheardes Calendar* ought to be regarded as part of the larger fiction of the book. See "*The Shepheardes Calendar* as Document and Monument," pp. 5–19.

18. Rosalie Colie has commented aptly upon the "aspirations" of the sonnet, the way "this little form had always aspired to be what it was not, to keep up with the Joneses of more spacious forms." See *Resources of Kind*, p. 103.

19. E. H. Wilkins writes that the "tradition that *canzoni* and sonnets should be kept separate remained so strong that it prevailed, even against the authority of Petrarch, among some of the copyists of his poems." See *Making of the "Canzoniere,"* p. 266.

20. In *Petrarch's Lyric Poems*, Durling observes that Petrarch derived from *La vita nuova* "the idea of placing canzoni as structural nodes or pillars at varying intervals among the shorter poems" (p. 11).

21. For instance, in what may be the first complete love sequence in English, Turbervile's *Epitaphs, Epigrams, Songs, and Sonets* (1567), a variety of kinds and subjects is subsumed by the larger pattern of love poems addressed to "Pyndara" by the speaker "Tymetes." Carol Thomas Neely speculates that the Renaissance sonnet sequence became the "chief repository for particular pastoral forms like the ode and elegy . . . and for the eclogue structure—a group of arranged and interconnected lyrics on selected themes." See "The Structure of English Renaissance Sonnet Sequences," p. 389n.

22. Thomas Roche argues strongly that in addition to reading such poems as Spenser's *Epithalamion* as the proper conclusion to the *Amoretti*, and Daniel's *Complaint of Rosamond* as the culmination of the *Delia* sequence, we ought to view *A Lover's Complaint* as the appropriate ending to Shakespeare's sonnets. See "Shakespeare and the Sonnet Sequence," p. 107.

23. See, for instance, Sturm-Maddox, "Transformations of Courtly Love Poetry," pp. 128–32.

24. For the evolving and open form of the *Canzoniere*, see Wilkins, *Making of the "Canzoniere,"* pp. 145–89.

25. These volumes provide excellent examples of contextural forms determined by time (*The Shepheardes Calendar*) as well as those determined by spatial trope (*The Forest*, *Underwoods*, *The Temple*). Spatial tropes might be further divided between architectural metaphors—that is, those that define form (e.g., *The Temple*)—and topographical metaphors, which give no clearly circumscribed form of

space (e.g., *The Forest*, *Underwoods*, *Hesperides*, and the related forms of silvae, meadows, and gardens).

26. See Miner, "Dryden's Admired Acquaintance," pp. 21–22.

27. Harrison, *Complete Works of Edgar Allan Poe*, 14:195–96.

28. See Cohen, *Art of Discrimination*, p. 85. Cohen notes that the "shift in the kind of unity developed in *The Seasons* was indicated by the increased looseness of connection between parts in contrast to the need for a dominant plot unity in a drama or epic" (p. 96).

29. See Rosenthal and Gall, *The Modern Sequence*, p. 9. The scope of this recent study demonstrates the remarkable extent to which (and virtuosity with which) modern poets practice sophisticated contextural strategies.

30. Nor, to be fair, is this their intention. In fact, Rosenthal and Gall see modern poets as replacing the traditional long poem with a form that seems at once integrated aggregate and long poem, whose unity depends not on plot or theme but on "lyrical structure" (i.e., a dynamic "progression of tonalities and affects"). For an extended definition and discussion of lyrical structure, see *The Modern Sequence*, pp. 11–18.

31. By "part" I mean a portion of the whole with its own distinct beginning and end. For a valuable discussion of poetic parts and wholes, see Miner, "Integrated Collections."

32. See Allport, *Theories of Perception*, p. 561.

33. Smith, *Poetic Closure*, p. 119.

34. Ibid., p. 13.

35. Fish, *Is There a Text in This Class?*, p. 105.

36. Iser, "The Reading Process," p. 64.

37. Santirocco, "Horace's *Odes*," p. 43. Segal, "Ancient Texts and Modern Literary Criticism," p. 13.

38. Colie, *Resources of Kind*, p. 52.

39. Gleckner, *Poetical Sketches*, p. 153.

40. Culler, *Structuralist Poetics*, p. 170.

41. Heninger, "Sidney and Milton," p. 94.

42. Sonnet sequences especially depend upon the persona as a unifying and organizing agent. Not only do the poems of a sequence manifest the speaker's mind and voice, but they are also generally arranged to simulate the chronology of his experience. Michael Drayton gives particular attention to the persona of his *Idea* sequence (1594): his revisions for the second edition (1599) in effect alter the persona from a conventional Petrarchan lover to a playful rationalist. See St. Clair, "Drayton's First Revision of His Sonnets," pp. 49–50. With a strategy not unlike that of sonneteers, Thomas Whythorne in *Autobiography* (ca. 1576) weaves together approximately two hundred poems into the fabric of a fictive autobiography.

43. Quoted from Furst, *European Romanticism*, p. 147.

44. J. W. Saunders states that for professional poets of the Tudor period, poetic volumes were essentially acts of "self-advertisement. As careerists their concern was to ensure that as many people as possible should realize how different they were from other members of the middle class." See "The Stigma of Print," p. 164. Though the courtly poets of the Tudor and Elizabethan periods shunned print, poets such as Jonson became increasingly involved with the printing process. According to Phoebe Sheavyn, "When a manuscript had been openly agreed for, the author usually superintended its passage through the press. In fact, unless absent from London, or unless a personage of too great importance, he was expected personally to supervise during the actual printing." See *The Literary Profession in the Elizabethan Age*, p. 82. Of course, the greater a poet's control of the press, the more we can be sure that his poems are printed in the order he preferred. For Pope's fashioning of a public image through his collections, see Vincent Carretta, "Images Reflect from Art to Art." See chapter 2 below for Byron's efforts in this vein. Perhaps Yeats, of all poets, best shows how one can not only fashion and project an identity through his individual books, but actually remodel and sophisticate this persona by revising the shape of his canon. For the shaping of Yeats's canon, see, for example, Kenner, "The Sacred Book of the Arts."

45. Parker, *Milton*, 1:631.

46. Although this pattern is more clearly defined in the second section than in the first, the English poems do seem to be arranged in distinct groupings internally ordered by chronology—even if these groups are sometimes thematic rather than generic. For an elaboration of these groupings, see, for instance, Parker, "Some Problems in the Chronology of Milton's Early Poems," pp. 279–83.

47. Martz, "The Rising Poet," p. 12. Martz provides in this fine essay a fuller reading of *Poems* than can be given here, pp. 3–33. See also Waddington, "Milton among the Carolines," pp. 340–45; Nitchie, "Milton and His Muses," pp. 75–84; and Wittreich's brief but suggestive discussion in *Visionary Poetics*, pp. 127–28. Wittreich sees the organization of *Poems* as making explicit a progression implicit in the *Justa Edovardo King Naufrago* volume: both collections reveal Milton as "a poet who, though indebted to his English predecessors, is ready to move beyond them" (p. 127).

48. These lines are spoken by Thyrsis in his singing contest with Corydon. They read in context, as translated by E. V. Rieu: "Bring ivy-leaves to decorate your rising poet, shepherds of Arcady, and so make Codrus burst his sides with envy. Or, if he tries to harm me with excessive praise, twine foxglove round my brows, to stop his evil tongue from hurting your predestined bard." See Martz, "Rising Poet,"

p. 8. Wittreich's observation that Milton is competitively engaging tradition in *Poems* could thus find support in the epigraph itself, which sets up the entire volume as Milton's own entry in a singing contest. It is interesting to note as well that Pope, who owned a copy of *Poems*, similarly constructs his 1717 *Works* to represent his own Virgilian ascent from pastoral poet to prophet.

49. Milton's poetic birth is heralded by Humphrey Moseley's prefatory address to the reader, which immediately precedes the "Ode on Christ's Nativity." Moseley claims that as publisher of *Poems* he is "bringing into the Light as true a Birth, as the Muses have brought forth since our famous Spencer wrote."

50. Martz, "Rising Poet," p. 10. The "Epitaphium Damonis," of course, contains the famous passage in which Milton dedicates himself to writing a British epic rather than Latin pastoral verse. Martz notes the progression throughout the Latin and Greek poems from light elegy to a mature Virgilian mode, p. 9. The entire second section of the volume is itself framed by its opening poem, the lighthearted "Elegia Prima," which is addressed to Charles Diodati, and the concluding "Epitaphium Damonis," which mourns Diodati's death.

51. Wittreich, *Visionary Poetics*, p. 128. Whereas each section of the volume has its own integrity, there are enough continuities among the poems for the whole to be seen as a unified structure. Indeed, Milton begins "Ad Joannem Rousium" by referring to *Poems* as a "Twin-membered book rejoicing in a single cover, yet with a double leaf." See Hughes, *John Milton: Complete Poems and Major Prose*, p. 146 (hereafter all quotations and translations from Milton cited in the text will be taken from this edition).

52. Because "Ad Joannem Rousium"—dated 23 January 1646—already looks back at *Poems* from a mature perspective, it renders more vivid the growth implied by the organization of that volume.

53. Without actually considering their context within the same volume, S. K. Heninger traces a progression in which the Nativity Ode and "The Passion" as companions are a "dry (and incomplete) run" for "L'Allegro" and "Il Penseroso," while the latter pair are themselves "an *étude* for *Lycidas*." See "Sidney and Milton," pp. 80–86.

54. Wittreich observes that, as a sign of its importance, "Milton has *Lycidas* call attention to itself by the boldness of the typeface given this poem in 'The Table of the Poems' included in *Poems upon Several Occasions*." See *Visionary Poetics*, p. 127. Moreover, Nitchie points out that "if we take the maske [i.e., "Comus"], with its title page, as giving the poem a separate significance," "Lycidas" becomes the final poem of the first section. See "Milton and His Muses," p. 84n. In "Milton among the Carolines," Waddington also claims that the separate title page gives "Comus" status as "an independent unit between English and Latin sections" (p. 360). He speculates that the poem is placed out

of chronological sequence because of its length and because of its genre. That is, after Milton rejected the poet-patron relationship implied by the masque as a form, "Comus" "may have seemed to represent a dead end or a miscalculation in his development" (p. 360).

55. Hartman, "Blake and the 'Progress of Poesy,'" p. 61.

56. See chapter 2 below, especially sections III and VI, for several important Romantic collections, similarly miscellaneous, that resemble Milton's in their form of thematic coherence, their probings about the appropriate role for poetry and the poet, and their self-portrayal of the poet as prophet. Whereas these resemblances might well be explained by Milton's general influence on the major Romantics, it is also quite possible that Milton's volumes directly influenced Romantic contextural practices. Although no documentary evidence exists to confirm this point, both *Poems* and *Poems upon Several Occasions* would have been available to any of the major poets and Wordsworth, for one, owned a copy of each volume. See Shaver and Shaver, *Wordsworth's Library*, p. 300.

57. Durling, *Petrarch's Lyric Poems*, p. 26.

58. Gleckner, *Poetical Sketches*, p. 150.

CHAPTER 2

1. See the preface to *Imitations and Translations from the Ancient and Modern Classics, Together with Original Poems Never before Published* (1809), p. iv. Throughout the eighteenth century, the growing number of poetic volumes published each year was boosted by the profitable and increasingly widespread practice of publication by subscription. In fact, as early as 1790, Alexander Wilson bemoaned in the preface to his *Poems* "those numerous and formidable [poetic] volumes that now march through the land" (p. iv). I have looked at some three hundred poetic volumes published between 1789 and 1830 for the survey in this chapter.

2. Contemporary poets in general were almost excruciatingly aware of reviewers. Attempting to protect themselves, the minor poets in particular resorted to clumsily apologetic prefaces and other forms of self-disparagement. The Reverend Charles Edward Stewart, for instance, preempts critics of *A Collection of Trifles in Verse* (1797) by providing in the table of contents a pithy list of "Friendly Criticisms" next to the title of each poem, which includes such judgments as "Long and dull" for one poem and "Stuff" for another. This, in a volume that has for its epigraph the self-damning (but accurate) couplet: "My verse so miserably flows, / 'Tis less like Poetry than Prose." The Reverend John Black publishes as the opening poem to *Poetical Pieces, Chiefly Sacred to Friendship and Virtue* (1799) a piece

entitled "The Author's Apology for Presuming to Call These Trifles, Poems," which contains the following prediction: "The Criticks will me sorely maul, / And dip their pens in bitter gall" (p. 6). No one, however, outdoes J. J. Vassar, who ends *Poems on Several Occasions* (1799) with a note in which he writes three separate reviews of his own volume (in the styles of the *Monthly* and *Analytic* reviews, as well as *The European Magazine*).

3. Jack, "Poems of John Clare's Sanity," p. 213. Although such matters were generally left to the discretion of the poet, a few publishers of the day actively encouraged poets to organize coherent collections. "Talking . . . with Hessey," writes John Taylor to Clare, "it occurred to me that a good Title for another Work would be—'The Shepherd's Calendar'—a Name which Spenser took for a poem or rather Collection of Poems of his.—It might be like his divided into Months, & under each might be given a descriptive Poem & a Narrative Poem." This largely unpublished letter is quoted in Jack, p. 209. Taylor was, of course, instrumental in shaping Clare's collections. Jack notes about *The Shepherd's Calendar* volume: "Taylor probably wanted Clare to take his time and produce a volume that would not be a mere collection of unconnected pieces" (p. 208).

4. In "On Poesy or Art" Coleridge writes: "In order to derive pleasure from the occupation of the mind, the principle of unity must always be present, so that in the midst of the multeity the centripetal force be never suspended, nor the sense be fatigued by the predominance of the centrifugal force. This unity in multeity I have elsewhere stated as the principle of beauty. It is equally the source of pleasure in variety, and in fact a higher term including both." See Shawcross, *Biographia Literaria*, 2:262 (hereafter cited in the text as *BL*). Cf. Coleridge's comments about the poet's state of mind while composing: "This is the state which permits the production of a highly pleasurable whole, of which each part shall also communicate for itself a distinct and conscious pleasure." See Raysor, *Coleridge's Shakespeare Criticism*, 1:164.

5. See Rollins, *Letters of John Keats*, 2:26.

6. Tibble and Tibble, *Letters of John Clare*, p. 57.

7. Thomas Moore organizes *Fables for the Holy Alliance* (1823) entirely as a response to the pervasive fear of contemporary reviewers. Writing under the pseudonym "Thomas Brown, the Younger, Secretary of the Poco-Curante Society," Moore concludes the preface: "It may be as well also to state for the information of those critics, who attack with the hope of being answered, and of being, thereby, brought into notice, that it is the rule of this Society to return no other answer to such assailants, than is contained in the three words 'Non curat Hippoclides' (meaning, in English, 'Hippoclides does not care a fig') which were spoken two thousand years ago by the first founder of

Poco-curantism, and have ever since been adopted as the leading *dictum* of the set" (pp. viii–ix). Within the larger fiction of the book, "Thomas Brown" avers that "except in the 'painful preeminence' of being employed to transcribe their [the members of the Society] lucubrations," he has no more claim as author than "any other gentleman, who has contributed his share to the contents of the volume" (p. vii). As the final poem, Moore prints "Genius and Criticism," which urges that poets free themselves from the false canons of taste upheld by reviewers.

8. These distinctions are developed by Vincent Carretta in his forthcoming essay, " 'Images Reflect from Art to Art.' "

9. The characteristic contents of such books are suggested in the title of George Huddesford's *Salmagundi: A Miscellaneous Combination of Original Poetry, Consisting of Illusions of Fancy: Amatory, Elegiac, Lyrical, Epigrammatical and Other Palatable Ingredients.*

10. Felicia Hemans defends her decision to include "Elysium" in *Scenes and Hymns of Life* even though the poem had already been published elsewhere because "the train of thought it suggests ... [appears] not unsuitable to the present work" (p. 247). Mrs. Hemans, who dedicates her book to Wordsworth, explains her theologic purpose in the preface: "It has been my wish to portray the religious spirit, not alone in its meditative joys and solitary aspirations ... but likewise in those active influences upon human life, so often called into victorious energy by trial and conflict, though too often also, like the upward-striving flame of a mountain watch-fire, borne down by tempest showers, or swayed by the unrest of opposing winds" (p. vii).

11. One might mention in this connection the later fad for collections of national songs touched off, in particular, by Byron's *Hebrew Melodies.*

12. More than a few poets, on the other hand, appear to have intentionally kept their volumes free from political controversy. George Dyer reserves his political poems for a future collection which will be "consecrated to liberty," explaining to the reader of *Poems* (1800): "I proceed systematically; confining the present volume to subjects at least inoffensive, which will, I hope, afford some amusement, and which ought to give no one offence. But let no man misunderstand my meaning. In the second volume I shall attempt, at least, a bolder strain. The principles of freedom are too sacred, to be surrendered for trifles; too noble, to be exchanged for a song" (pp. xlii, xxxvii).

13. Jones, *Letters of Percy Bysshe Shelley*, 2:191. Poems that seem to have been written for this uncompleted project include "To Sidmouth and Castlereagh," "Lines written during the Castlereagh Administration," "England in 1819," "Song to the Men of England," and "A New National Anthem."

14. Typical of the book intended for a private audience is William Hayley's *Poems on Serious and Sacred Subjects, Printed Only as Private Tokens of Regard, for the Particular Friends of the Author* (1817). One might add that even Byron's first collection went through two privately printed editions before it was published as *Hours of Idleness*. Byron writes to Dr. T. Falkner in a note accompanying a copy of the second edition, *Poems on Various Subjects* (1807): "Such '*Juvenilia*,' as they can claim no great degree of approbation. . . . They were written on many, & various Occasions, and are now published merely for the perusal of a friendly Circle." See Marchand, *Byron's Letters and Journals*, 1:103. The tendency of some minor poets to court their subscribers and supporters is satirized in an anonymous volume falsely attributed to Byron, *Poems Written by Somebody; Most Respectfully Dedicated (by Permission) to Nobody; and Intended for Everybody Who Can Read!!!* (1816). "Spring," the most noteworthy poem in the book, travesties the byplay between poet and audience when, with a Shandyesque twist, it halts abruptly with a note inviting the reader to supply the ending in a manner agreeable to his own imagination and taste.

15. See Abrams, *Mirror and the Lamp*, pp. 226–41, esp., pp. 226–27.

16. *Poems of Thomas Little*, 6th ed. (1806), sig. A3^{v}. McGann and others have noted the influence of Moore's collection on Byron in *Hours of Idleness*, especially in terms of the poet's self-dramatization. See, for example, McGann, *Fiery Dust*, p. 14. That Moore resorts in a poetic volume to a device that had been primarily exploited by novelists is underscored when he goes so far as to claim that among Little's papers he has found a "novel, in rather an imperfect state, which, as soon as I have arranged and collected it, shall be submitted to the public eye" (sig. A3^{v}). Shelley resorted to a similar device in the *Posthumous Fragments of Margaret Nicholson* (1810), in which he appears as "John Fitzvictor," the "editor" of the ravings of his aunt, a mad washerwoman who, presumably during a rare moment of sanity, attempted to assassinate George III. See chapter 3 of this volume for Wordsworth and Coleridge's creation of a fictive author for *Lyrical Ballads* (1798).

17. McGann, *Fiery Dust*, p. 21. Critics have, of course, long argued over Byron's relative sincerity as a poet. Upon this subject I agree with McGann, who asks that we set aside our concern for Byron's sincerity and accept his poetry as a "self-dramatizing vehicle." See *Fiery Dust*, p. 25. McGann is also quite right to note in particular the "self-propagandizing" quality of *Hours of Idleness* (p. 23). I have found his entire discussion of the volume enlightening, pp. 3–28.

18. See Marchand, *Byron*, 1:152.

19. As was previously noted, the first two editions were privately

printed and distributed. The changing titles of the collection are themselves indicative of the poet's changing poses, from the somewhat reluctant young author of "Fugitive Poems" to the well-educated aristocrat of "Poems Original and Translated." "Hours of Idleness," the most affected title of the group, was chosen not by Byron but his publisher John Ridge. However, as Gleckner observes, it accurately reflects the substance and tone of the preface in suggesting that the poems are products of the left hand from a young lord with more important uses for his time. See Gleckner, *Ruins of Paradise*, p. 1. In a letter written to Ridge on 11 November 1807, Byron asks that the title "Hours of Idleness" be changed "simply to 'poems' by Ld. Byron &c. &c." He thus rids the book of its affectations in title and preface in the final version. See Marchand, *Byron's Letters and Journals*, 1:137.

20. Gleckner, *Ruins of Paradise*, p. 15. For Gleckner's fine reading of the thematic groupings in *Hours of Idleness*, see pp. 3–26.

21. To be sure, the Byronic hero so depicted is in his formative stages. As McGann argues in *Fiery Dust*, Byron at this point is still conventional in much of his posturing (pp. 21–22). With greater notoriety and more experience at manipulating the public, Byron in 1816 agreed to the publication of *Poems*, a volume containing ten short pieces: six concerning his own personal woes and exile from England and four about Napoleon's defeat and exile. Even if the reader were slow at first to make the desired conflation of the two titans, he could hardly overlook the fact that the book ends with "Napoleon's Farewell" in a direct echo of the sixth and last poem explicitly about Byron, "Fare Thee Well."

22. McGann, *Fiery Dust*, pp. 7–8. He is quoting here from Burns's preface.

23. See Stillinger, *Hoodwinking of Madeline*, p. 5.

24. Stillinger, *Poems of John Keats*, p. 72. In chapter 4 I provide a lengthy reading of the self-discovery dramatized in Keats's 1820 volume.

25. Although the "Voice of the Ancient Bard" appears as a *Song of Innocence* in other arrangements, I take this apparently final ordering as Blake's preferred form. I would argue, moreover, that as a *Song of Innocence* the piece asks to be read differently and thus serves as an excellent example of how context within a book can condition the meaning of a poem.

26. See Averill, "Shape of *Lyrical Ballads*," p. 389. Averill notes that the opening poem of the 1796 volume, "Monody to Chatterton," "places Coleridge as the heir . . . to Chatterton's genius" (p. 389). For a reading of the changing shape of the 1796 collection in the second edition, see Averill, pp. 389–90. Coleridge's well-known comment from *Table Talk* is quoted in Whalley, "Coleridge's Poetical Canon," p. 19. As Whalley reminds us, despite what Coleridge says

here, he never attempted a chronological arrangement of his own collected poems.

27. See Grosart, *Prose Works of William Wordsworth*, 3:474. Graves comments upon "the feeling akin to indignation" that Wordsworth manifested at the suggestion that his poems be printed in the order of their composition (3:474).

28. See Curtis, *Poems, in Two Volumes*, p. 27. Wordsworth was clearly jarred by critical complaints about the triviality of several personal pieces in the 1807 volumes. See, for example, the letter he writes to Lady Beaumont on 21 May 1807, De Selincourt, Moorman, and Hill, *Letters of William and Dorothy Wordsworth: The Middle Years*, 1:147 (hereafter cited in the text as *MY*).

29. Wordsworth was certainly aware of this difficulty while grouping poems for the 1807 collection, which apparently he first planned as a single volume. In his edition of *Poems, in Two Volumes*, Curtis notes that "To overcome the problem of presenting sixty to seventy poems in a single run, as he had done in *Lyrical Ballads*, Wordsworth developed the method of presenting 'a few at once' so as to guide the reader's response by the surrounding context" (p. 36). For a valuable discussion of Wordsworth's early manuscript groupings as well as a consideration of the design of the printed volumes, see Curtis, pp. 3–39, esp., 35–39, and pp. 703–8.

30. In *Imagination and Fancy*, Scoggins writes: "The history of Wordsworth's reputation has not, but should have been, the history of critical attitude toward the system of organization that he devised so carefully for editions of his poems" (p. 15). But, as Scoggins notes, few critics have taken the organization of *Poems* (1815) as seriously as did Wordsworth himself. See Scoggins for a summary of critical response, pp. 15–24; for an extended discussion of the shape of *Poems* see pp. 53–138. Four brief but provocative essays have more recently joined the debate over the significance of the 1815 arrangement: see Ruoff, "Critical Implications of Wordsworth's 1815 Categorization"; Herman, "The Poet as Editor"; Heffernan, "Mutilated Autobiography"; and Ross, "Poems 'Bound Each to Each.' "

31. Waller even uses separate half-title pages for each generic division: "Epistles," "Imitations," "Sonnets," "Epigrams," "Descriptive Poems," "Sacred Poems," and a final section of "Miscellaneous Poetry." Although Waller did not choose to do so, Romantic poets frequently presented generic groupings—especially sonnets and odes—in numbered sequences.

32. Marrs, *Letters of Charles and Mary Anne Lamb*, 2:111. Suffering from ill health and grave personal problems, Coleridge left the selection and arrangement of the poems in this third edition to his publisher Longman, who in turn delegated these matters to Lamb—a natural choice, since Lamb's own poems had been mixed with Cole-

ridge's in the two preceding editions (acknowledged only by the initials "C. L." in 1796). Nevertheless, Lamb did not wish to make such decisions without learning Coleridge's own wishes.

33. Cowper's *The Task* would appear to have prompted many volumes similar in organization to Gisborne's *Walks*. Of all the Romantic collections I have seen, Richard Polwhele's *Poetic Trifles* (1798) most closely conforms in a superficial way to the Petrarchan paradigm. After a section of "Lyric and Elegiac Pieces," Polwhele prints "Canzones and Sonnets, Occasioned by the Amours of Montauban," which he follows with a long poem on a related subject: "The Flight of Montauban; A Mock Heroic Poem in Three Cantoes."

34. The widespread penchant for using spatially contiguous, discrete poems as parts of a larger whole is reflected in the work of Henry Boyd who, in *Poems, Chiefly Dramatic and Lyric* (1793), groups together four separate but continuously plotted odes to create "The Wanderer, a Lyric Poem, in Four Irregular Odes." Utilizing a narrative framework and the figure of an extemporaneous narrator, Thomas Beddoes binds together three contiguous poems in *The Improvisatore, in Three Fyttes, with Other Poems* (1821).

35. James Averill remarks that in volumes by Wordsworth and by Coleridge "the first poem tends to be about poetry and the poet. Both men have a passion for introduction, one not entirely satisfied by the prefaces they chronically attach to their works." See "Shape of *Lyrical Ballads*," p. 391. Some contemporaries even composed pieces explicitly to open or close miscellaneous collections. For example, "Perdita" Robinson prints "Ode: To the Muse" at the start of *Poems* (1796), and both Thomas Park in *Sonnets, and Other Smaller Poems* (1797) and John Clare in *The Rural Muse* (1835) open with poems addressed "To the Rural Muse." Likewise, Bernard Barton closes *Poems, by an Amateur* with "The Author's Parting Address to the Muse." "A Parting Song" provides closure for Mrs. Hemans's *Records of Woman, with Other Poems* (1828); and William Parson's *Fidelity, Or Love at First Sight, with Other Poems* (1798) ends theatrically with a verse Epilogue, succeeded by a prose passage in which the poet bids the "GENTLE READER, farewell for the present" (p. 92).

36. McGann, *Lord Byron: Complete Poetical Works*, 3:453.

37. Newstead Abbey is pictured on the frontispiece of these books. One cannot help but notice that from the introductory poem of his first volume onward, Byron's poetry is consciously self-referential.

38. Shilstone, "The Lyric Collection as Genre," p. 50. With cause, Shilstone views the *Hebrew Melodies* as "an attempt to create a new genre from the piecemeal framework of the collection of national songs" (p. 49). It would be appropriate to state here that a "contexture" as I have defined it is no more a genre in itself than is a "text": it is simply a form in which poetic texts are presented to the public. A

contexture may be a cabinet of genres—as is so often the case in Romantic books—or the vehicle for a single genre, as in *Hebrew Melodies*. One of the more enduring uses of the book as vehicle for a single kind of poem is the funeral collection. This tradition—perhaps best known to modern readers through the *Justa Edovardo King Naufrago* volume, to which Milton contributed "Lycidas"—appears in such contemporary books as *Verses on the Death of Percy Bysshe Shelley* (1822), in which Bernard Barton mourns Shelley's passing, but is scarcely able to forgive the poet's apparent lack of religion. Charles Lloyd makes public a more private grief by assembling a collection of poems he had written to eulogize his late grandmother—for which Coleridge and Lamb each provided one piece—*Poems on the Death of Priscilla Farmer* (1796).

39. Smith, *Poetic Closure*, p. 172.

40. A number of volumes end with a flourish of patriotism, in particular those written during the height of hostilities with France near the turn of the century, like Thomas Maurice's *Poems, Epistolary, Lyric, and Elegiacal* (1800): "Britons, the Crisis of her fate draws near, / *Advance* your standards, launch th'avenging spear; / In radiant arms and indissolubly join'd, / Your firmness hath subdued the world combin'd" (p. 284). Cf. the less militant patriotism ending James Montgomery's *Greenland, and Other Poems* (1819), published, of course, after hostilities with France had ceased: "So may thy [i.e., Britain's] wealth and power increase: / So may thy people dwell in peace; / On thee the Almighty glory rest / And all the world in thee be blest" (p. 207).

41. Even less sophisticated arrangements by minor poets sometimes returned in the final poem to a significant theme or formal element that began the book. For instance, "Prayer to the Parcae," the closing poem of Hannah Brand's 1798 *Plays, and Poems*, concerns the sister to whom the volume was dedicated. Charles Edward Stewart, whose *A Collection of Trifles in Verse* began with "Epistle to Mr. Burke," printed as his last poem "Lines to Mr. Burke on the Loss of His Son." Works based on stories from Boccaccio, moreover, both opened and closed John Hamilton Reynolds's *The Garden of Florence, and Other Poems* (1821). Reynolds and Keats had at one time planned to publish a joint volume of poems based on Boccaccio—for which Keats wrote "Isabella"—but as Reynolds acknowledged with poignance in the Advertisement: "[I]llness on his part, and distracting engagements on mine, prevented us from accomplishing our plan at the time; and Death, now, to my deep sorrow, has frustrated it forever" (p. xii).

42. In *The Idea of Coleridge's Criticism*, R. H. Fogle explains: "In a totality pure homogeneity is impossible, as a negation of the basic ideas of order and structure. A uniform intensity would be not harmony but monotony" (p. 57).

43. Thus besides examining what the major Romantics included in their collections, we can sometimes ascertain their principles for selection by noting what works they would have had on hand but chose to omit (e.g., Coleridge's exclusion of "Lewti" from the second issue of *Lyrical Ballads* and Shelley's of "Julian and Maddalo" from the *Prometheus Unbound* volume).

44. Coleridge to Southey, 10 November 1799, Griggs, *Collected Letters of Samuel Coleridge*, 1:545.

45. Because of complaints about the extravagance of "Ancient Mariner," Wordsworth almost dropped the poem from *Lyrical Ballads* in 1800. Instead, however, he moved it to the back of the first volume (still in a significant position, as I argue in chapter 3), and chose as the new opening "Expostulation and Reply" and "The Tables Turned." A letter Wordsworth writes on 24 June 1799 to his publisher Joseph Cottle sums up his predicament: "From what I can gather it seems that The Ancyent Marinere has upon the whole been an injury to the volume, I mean that the old words and the strangeness of it have deterred readers from going on. If the volume should come to a second edition I would put in its place some little things which would be more likely to suit the common taste." See De Selincourt and Shaver, *Letters of William and Dorothy Wordsworth: The Early Years* (hereafter cited in the text as *EY*), 1:264. Wordsworth's notion here of using the opening poem as a sop to public taste is echoed in Coleridge's letter to Southey and is in line with much contemporary practice.

46. For evidence that Wordsworth and Coleridge were both well acquainted with Southey's 1797 volume, see Jacobus, *Tradition and Experiment*, p. 33n. Considering, however, Coleridge's close friendship with Southey and the fact that he had even contributed a stanza to "The Soldier's Wife," such evidence is hardly necessary.

47. McFarland, *Romanticism and the Forms of Ruin*, p. 49.

48. Shawcross, *Biographia Literaria*, 2:262.

CHAPTER 3

1. Until quite recently, most scholars agreed with Emile Legouis's opinion that *Lyrical Ballads* (1798) is a "somewhat random and incongruous assemblage." See "Some Remarks on the Composition of the *Lyrical Ballads* of 1798," p. 3. Even Ruth Cohen, who has read the 1800 edition as a coherent structure, calls the 1798 edition a "scattered and random selection . . . which, we must remember, had been published quickly under the pressure of financial need." See "The 1800 Ordering of *Lyrical Ballads*," p. 33. Opposing such views are R. L. Brett and Alun R. Jones, who insist "that it is as a *body* of poetry that

Lyrical Ballads first influenced the course of English poetry and that it is as a body of poetry that it should be studied." See "*Lyrical Ballads*," p. x. Stephen Prickett, in his short but suggestive "*The Lyrical Ballads*," argues that the 1798 volume possesses an organic unity in which each poem "changes the nature of the whole, and therefore of all the other parts" (p. 28). Yet to the detriment of his thesis, Prickett concerns himself primarily with five poems scattered throughout. James Averill, who has published the best discussion of the book's coherence to date, finds that although *Lyrical Ballads* "is not a seamless work, it is stitched together in workmanlike fashion." See "Shape of *Lyrical Ballads*," p. 402. Although Averill's consideration of *Lyrical Ballads* as an "odal volume" highlights spatial contiguity among the poems and my own focus is on the thematic and verbal resonances running throughout the whole, I believe our points of view are generally compatible.

2. See Jacobus, *Tradition and Experiment*, p. 4.

3. For the seminal statement of this viewpoint, see Reed's carefully argued "'Plan' of *The Lyrical Ballads*."

4. Jordan, *Why "The Lyrical Ballads"?*, p. 38.

5. For Wordsworth's comment, see De Selincourt, *Poetical Works of William Wordsworth*, 1:x. For Coleridge, see Schulz, *The Poetic Voices of Coleridge*, p. 23.

6. Averill convincingly demonstrates that both poets cared from the start about the details and arrangement of their volumes. See "Shape of *Lyrical Ballads*," pp. 388–90. He concludes, "There is no reason to think that a book put together by two such poets would be more random or structurally unconsidered than those each put together on his own" (p. 390). Wordsworth and Coleridge's concern for the format of *Lyrical Ballads* is apparent in Coleridge's letter to Cottle on 4 June 1798; see Griggs, *Collected Letters of Samuel Taylor Coleridge*, 1:412.

7. In a similar way, Wordsworth wrote "Michael" specifically to conclude the 1800 edition. He informs Cottle on 23 December 1800: "By the same post I send you two other sheets containing a poem entitled, *Michael*. This poem contains 493 or 4 lines. If it be sufficient to fill the volume to 205 pages or upwards, printing it at 18 lines, or never more than 19 in a page as was done in the first Edition of Lyrical Ballads you will print this poem immediately after the *Poems on the Naming of Places* and consider it as, (with the two or three Notes adjoined) finishing the work. If it does not fill up so much space as to make the volume 205 pages you must not print immediately the Poem of Michael, as I wish it to conclude the volume. If what I have sent does not make the vol: amount to 205 pages let me know immediately *how many* pages it amounts to, and I will send you something to insert between Michael and the Poems on the *Naming of Places*." See De Selincourt and Shaver, *Letters of William and Dorothy Words-*

worth: The Early Years, p. 307. Wordsworth apparently felt that "Tintern Abbey" was in its proper place, for it remains the closing poem in the first volume of the 1800 edition, though he shifted the order of several others. For the reordering of this edition, see Cohen, "The 1800 Ordering of *Lyrical Ballads*," and Scoggins, *Imagination and Fancy*, pp. 27–38. Jared Curtis, in his recent edition of Wordsworth's *Poems, in Two Volumes* (1807), remarks that the Intimations Ode was deliberately chosen to close the 1807 collection "just as 'Tintern Abbey' was placed to conclude *Lyrical Ballads* in 1798" (p. 22).

8. See Owen, *Wordsworth and Coleridge: "Lyrical Ballads" 1798*, p. 136 (hereafter all quotations from the poems of and notes to the 1798 edition will be cited in the text as Owen).

9. Shawcross, *Biographia Literaria*, 2:5.

10. Jordan, *Why "The Lyrical Ballads"?*, p. 12.

11. Jordan in *Why "The Lyrical Ballads"?* argues persuasively that this desire is responsible for the omission from the volume of "Lewti," a poem incongruous with the others in style and concerns (p. 43). For a more detailed discussion of the publication of *Lyrical Ballads* (1798), see Jordan, pp. 33–52. For bibliographical details of the issue containing "Lewti," see Foxon, "The Printing of *Lyrical Ballads*, 1798."

12. This letter, quoted more fully in the epigraph to chapter 3, was written to Cottle on 28 May 1798. Coleridge has introduced some confusion by referring here to "the volumes" of *1798*. See Owen, *"Lyrical Ballads" 1798*, p. xiii, for a possible explanation of his reference. Parrish, in *Art of "The Lyrical Ballads,"* believes that Coleridge claimed the collection was like an ode in order to placate Cottle's fears "that the contents of the volume would not be homogeneous" (p. 40). Even if this were so, however, it would not necessarily negate the truth of Coleridge's statement or indicate that he was being insincere. Indeed, such an observation is characteristic of Coleridge. Some thirty-five years later, for instance, Coleridge remarks that Shakespeare's "extraordinary sonnets form, in fact a poem of so many stanzas of fourteen lines each." See H. N. Coleridge, *Table Talk* (entry for 14 May 1833), 1:93.

13. I would agree with Averill, who in "Shape of *Lyrical Ballads*" understands Coleridge as implying that the volume "read correctly becomes a single poem" (pp. 390–91). Whereas Averill is more interested in the overall structure than in the theme of such a "poem," theories about the "theme" of *Lyrical Ballads* abound and are produced even by those who do not fully believe in the unity of the volume. For instance, Danby in *The Simple Wordsworth* argues that *Lyrical Ballads* is devoted mainly to pointing out "the dislocation between man and nature" (p. 130). Gérard, in *English Romantic Poetry*, writes that the major concern in *Lyrical Ballads* is "the evil present in the human condition" (p. 185). In *Why "The Lyrical Bal-*

lads"?, Jordan suggests that perhaps "the turns on gratitude (and ingratitude)—familiar, neighborly, tribal, social—are close to the 'theme' of the 1798 *Lyrical Ballads*" (p. 185). My own sense of the volume comes closest to that of Sheats, who finds in "The *Lyrical Ballads*" that the whole is fundamentally concerned with the "liberation of the reader from his own 'pre-established codes of decision'" (p. 133).

14. Jordan comments, "Probably Wordsworth and Coleridge were chiefly interested in keeping their names off the title page, particularly *two* names." See *Why "The Lyrical Ballads"?*, p. 43.

15. McFarland, *Romanticism and the Forms of Ruin*, p. 57. McFarland's entire first chapter closely examines the symbiosis between Wordsworth and Coleridge, pp. 56–103. See also Parrish, *Art of "The Lyrical Ballads,"* pp. 34–79.

16. Parrish, of course, discusses the dramatic nature of *Lyrical Ballads* throughout *Art of "The Lyrical Ballads."* For Heath, see *Wordsworth and Coleridge*, p. 36.

17. See Sheats, "The *Lyrical Ballads,*" p. 140.

18. Unless otherwise designated, all quotations from Wordsworth's poetry other than the *Lyrical Ballads* are taken from De Selincourt and Darbishire, *Poetical Works of William Wordsworth* (hereafter cited in the text as *PW*). All quotations from Coleridge's poems, other than those in *Lyrical Ballads*, are from E. H. Coleridge, *Complete Poetical Works of Samuel Taylor Coleridge.*

19. In his fine edition *"The Ruined Cottage" and "The Pedlar,"* James Butler traces the development of the Pedlar as a character, linking this process to Wordsworth's "growing fascination with his own past experience and the way in which it affected his apprehension of reality" (p. 17). Indeed, Butler calls the Pedlar sequence Wordsworth's "first autobiographical work" (p. 17), and notes that feelings initially attributed to the Pedlar were later transferred to *The Prelude* (pp. 17–18).

20. In "Wordsworth's Contrarieties," Swingle has argued convincingly that Wordsworth's poems are designed as dramatic constructions through which he can exert pressures upon the reader's mind. If this is true of Wordsworth's canon in general, it is certainly true of his contributions to *Lyrical Ballads*, where in poems like "Simon Lee" and "The Idiot Boy" the reader is even addressed directly. In fact, *Lyrical Ballads* is one of the earliest works of the high Romantics to function—in W. J. T. Mitchell's well-chosen words about Blake's *Milton*—as "an exploration of the limits of poetry as a force for inciting people to imaginative action, and a prophecy of the breaking-down of those limits." See "Blake's Radical Comedy," p. 282.

21. See Jones, "The Compassionate World," p. 8.

22. Little, *Barron Field's Memoirs*, p. 120n.

23. Wolfson, who arrives independently at the importance of questioning in *Lyrical Ballads*, argues that each speaker of these paired poems "fails to understand what is important about the answers he dismisses." See "The Speaker as Questioner," p. 552.

24. Prickett similarly observes: " 'Tintern Abbey' . . . shows us the version of Nature that lies behind 'Expostulation and Reply'; it provides an answer and a reassurance to the metaphysical terror of 'The Ancient Marinere.' " See "*The Lyrical Ballads*," p. 50. Averill, who also recognizes the importance of these framing poems, claims: "*Lyrical Ballads* is not a volume where the different placement of any single poem (except 'The Ancyent Marinere' or 'Tintern Abbey') would radically change one's perception of the whole work." See "Shape of *Lyrical Ballads*," p. 402. I think, however, that Averill is wrong to ignore the significance of "The Thorn" as a centerpiece.

25. Marrs, *Letters of Charles and Mary Anne Lamb*, 1:80, 82.

26. Jonathan Wordsworth, *Music of Humanity*, p. 195. For an account of the changing roles of the mariner and the Female Vagrant in the various manuscripts of the Salisbury Plain poems, see Gill, *Salisbury Plain Poems*, pp. 3–16. If the wandering mariner of *Adventures on Salisbury Plain* is indeed a naturalistic prototype for the more mythically treated Ancient Mariner, important differences also exist between the two characters. Whereas Wordsworth's mariner finally accepts hanging as a relief to his tortured conscience, the Ancient Mariner suffers without cease: he "hath penance done / And penance more will do" (ll. 413–14).

27. See Jonathan Wordsworth, *Music of Humanity*, p. 98. See also Butler, *"The Ruined Cottage" and "The Pedlar,"* p. 18.

28. My discussion of the "Ancient Mariner" is, of course, based on the 1798 text. For an excellent consideration of the subsequent forms of the text, see McGann, "Meaning of 'The Ancient Mariner.' " McGann provides an overview of critical responses to the poem, pp. 48–55.

29. My discussion of causality in the "Ancient Mariner" has been influenced by James D. Boulger's excellent introduction to "*The Rime of the Ancient Mariner*," pp. 1–20.

30. John Jordan in *Why "The Lyrical Ballads"?* notes the tendency of both Coleridge and Wordsworth to write in a "descriptive mode [that] is existential: it describes a state of being." As examples of his point in *Lyrical Ballads*, he offers Coleridge's "It is an ancyent Marinere" and Wordsworth's "There is a thorn" as well as "it is the first mild day of March" (p. 170).

31. In "The Old Cumberland Beggar," a poem written in 1798 and published in *Lyrical Ballads* (1800), the Old Beggar, described as being "in the eye of Nature" (l. 196), similarly sits on a stone. All

quotations cited in the text from the 1800 edition are from Brett and Jones.

32. The key passage here is Acts 28:25–28.

33. Rollins, *Letters of John Keats*, 1:193.

34. Coleridge seems to have conceived of "The Ancient Mariner" and "The Foster-Mother's Tale" as companion poems. Although Wordsworth separates the two in 1800, Coleridge re-pairs them as the first and second poems, respectively, in *Sibylline Leaves*. In "Shape of *Lyrical Ballads*," Averill notes that the first sixteen lines of "The Foster-Mother's Tale" seem to refer the reader back to the "Ancient Mariner" and that these lines were dropped in 1800 when the two poems were no longer juxtaposed (p. 398). One might add that they were restored in *Sibylline Leaves*.

35. These two poems are, in fact, grouped together in 1800 as the fifth and fourth poems, respectively, of the first volume.

36. This point is made by Hartman in his convincing discussion of "The Last of the Flock" in *Wordsworth's Poetry*, p. 144.

37. However similar in effect, their alienation differs significantly in cause. That is, the Female Vagrant, unlike the Mariner, is a victim of unjust political and social conditions. Indeed, as originally conceived in 1793, the Female Vagrant's story was an overt attack on contemporary oppression of the poor, with which Wordsworth linked other injustices, such as England's entry into war against France. See Gill, *Salisbury Plain Poems*, p. 5. As presented in 1798, "The Female Vagrant" retains much of its force as a protest against social oppression and war. Its attack on wealthy landowners and enclosure, in particular, make it one of the most overtly political poems of *Lyrical Ballads*, though one might argue that, even so, it is more a psychological or ontological study than a political one. Beginning with *Lyrical Ballads* (1802), and throughout subsequent revisions, Wordsworth muted the political elements of the poem. For the changing states of the manuscript, see Gill's edition.

38. I am grateful to Joseph Wittreich for bringing the stanzaic patterning of "The Thorn" to my attention.

39. See Sheats's brief but excellent consideration of "The Thorn" in "The *Lyrical Ballads*," pp. 141–45. See also Wolfson's discussion, which parallels my own at some points, in "The Speaker as Questioner," pp. 553–57.

40. Sheats, "The *Lyrical Ballads*," p. 143.

41. Gérard establishes this point in *English Romantic Poetry*, p. 83.

42. Ashton first discovered the echo in " 'The Thorn,' " p. 186.

43. Murray, *Wordsworth's Style*, p. 142.

44. De Selincourt and Hill, *Letters of William and Dorothy Wordsworth: The Later Years*, 1:245.

45. This passage is located in De Selincourt and Darbishire, *The Prelude*, p. 525.

46. Ibid.

47. Ibid.

48. Indeed, its context in the volume provides for "The Idiot Boy" much of what unhappy readers have found lacking in it. However, for an excellent discussion of the poem on its own merit, see Storch, "Wordsworth's Experimental Ballads," pp. 621–39.

49. Clearly, Wordsworth recognized the essential congruity of the two poems. Although many critics note that Wordsworth seriously considered dropping "Ancient Mariner" from *Lyrical Ballads* (1800), and in fact removed it from its position as the opening poem of the collection, few mention that—significantly—he placed it immediately before "Tintern Abbey" as the penultimate poem of the first volume.

50. In *Wordsworth: A Philosophical Approach*, Rader comments: "In contrast to the passive, material content of the world, the '*natura naturata*,' or God as product, stands the '*natura naturans*,' or God as action, motion, and life. As Helen Darbishire remarks: 'Wordsworth seems to find in motion the very essence of life. God Himself, the divine principle in things, *is* motion' " (p. 65).

51. Maniquis's "Comparison, Intensity, and Time," pp. 373–79, contains an excellent discussion of time and memory in the poem.

52. This is a resolution prefigured in many ways by the Mad Mother, whose love for her child allows her to accept a world of flux and constant loss. In *Lyrical Ballads* (1800), "The Mad Mother" fittingly precedes "Ancient Mariner" and "Tintern Abbey."

53. These thematic tensions might be reformulated in terms of genre, as suggested by Wordsworth's subsequent reorganizations of *Lyrical Ballads*, highlighted by the title change in 1802 to *Lyrical Ballads, with Pastorals and Other Poems*. That is, the volume might be read as moving thematically from antipastoral to a freshly conceived idea of pastoral that accounts for human suffering, one that has at its center the thorn. In fact, rather than diminishing the significance of the 1798 edition, the changing shapes of *Lyrical Ballads* in 1800 and 1802 develop the possibilities opened by the original ordering, as I hope to show at length in a future study. Later arrangements of a collection, then, may reveal (or even conceal) what the poet has already made.

CHAPTER 4

1. Rollins, *Letters of John Keats*, 2:174.

2. Stillinger, *Hoodwinking of Madeline*, p. 5. For a more detailed

reading of the 1817 volume than can be given here, see Stillinger's first chapter, "The Order of Poems in Keats's First Volume," pp. 1–13.

3. All quotations from Keats's poetry are taken from Stillinger, *Poems of John Keats* (hereafter cited in the text as *Poems*).

4. According to Stillinger in *Poems*, it is likely that "Hyperion" is the only poem in the *Lamia* volume for which Keats "did not prepare, or directly supervise the preparation of, printer's copy" (p. 10).

5. See, for instance, ibid., pp. 11–13.

6. Ibid., p. 11. Stillinger excepts Keats's titillating revision of the "Eve of St. Agnes," which Taylor refused to print. However, in his review of Stillinger's *Poems of John Keats*, John Barnard argues that even the decision to omit this revision should be seen as fulfilling Keats's intention (pp. 544–46). For Taylor's interest in the organization of poetic volumes, see chapter 2. Apparently, Keats at first planned to include "Song of Four Fairies" (*Poems*, p. 12), but probably both he and Taylor later agreed that the poem was inappropriate for the collection. Similarly, Keats at one time wished to begin the volume with the "Eve of St. Agnes" rather than "Lamia." Although it is difficult to say whether he later changed his mind or was overruled by Taylor, I lean toward the former view for reasons just supplied in the text. For Charles Brown's letter notifying Taylor that Keats wished the "Eve of St. Agnes" to open the volume, see Rollins, *The Keats Circle*, 1:105.

7. Stillinger, *Poems*, p. 737. The Advertisement concludes by stating that "Hyperion" "was intended to have been of equal length with ENDYMION, but the reception given to that work discouraged the author from proceeding." Across from this sentence in the Burridge copy, Keats wrote, "This is a lie" (*Poems*, pp. 736–37).

8. Rollins, *Keats Circle*, 1:116. Early in 1820, Keats may have briefly considered publishing "Hyperion" jointly with a poem or poems by Hunt. Perhaps this helps explain his initial reluctance to include "Hyperion" in the *Lamia* volume. See *Keats Circle*, 2:234.

9. See Stillinger, *Poems*, p. 737. Stillinger conjectures that the layout excluding "Hyperion" preceded the other.

10. As a caveat to critics who read the six great odes as a limited canon, Robert Gleckner observes that the "two most interesting aspects of the [1820] volume are Keats's exclusion of the 'Ode to Indolence' and the fact that the other odes are not grouped together." See "Keats's Odes," p. 584. If, as it seems, Keats did control, or at least approve, the organization of the volume, then the *Lamia* collection valuably illuminates his own sense of the shape of his canon.

11. Fish, *Is There a Text in This Class?*, p. 51.

12. Sperry, *Keats the Poet*, p. 246.

13. See Wittreich, *The Romantics on Milton*, p. 553.

14. Bruce Haley is a notable exception to this general neglect. In his

study of the influence of *Troilus* on the "Ode to a Nightingale," Haley writes: "Without question Keats knew Shakespeare's *Troilus and Cressida* thoroughly. His letters are sprinkled with allusions to and quotations from the work, and if the amount of underscoring and annotation is an indication, he gave more attention to *Troilus* than to any of the other plays in the folio reprint he acquired in 1817." See "The Infinite Will," p. 19. Miriam Allott notes that the opening stanzas of "Isabella" were written in this folio: see "'Isabella,' 'The Eve of St. Agnes,' and 'Lamia,'" p. 44.

15. Spurgeon, *Keats's Shakespeare*, p. 45.

16. All quotations from Shakespeare are taken from Harbage, *William Shakespeare: The Complete Works* (hereafter cited in the text by act, scene, and line).

17. The relevant passage here is from Act 3, where Troilus recognizes the danger of his rapture:

> I am giddy; expectation whirls me round.
> Th' imaginary relish is so sweet
> That it enchants my sense. What will it be
> When that the wat'ry palates taste indeed
> Love's thrice-repurèd nectar? Death, I fear me,
> Sounding destruction, or some joy too fine,
> Too subtle, potent, tuned too sharp in sweetness
> For the capacity of my ruder powers.
> I fear it much. (3.2.16–24)

18. Throughout *Troilus and Cressida*, honey and sweetness stand as symbols of erotic pleasure. For example, Cressida coyly pleads with Diomed: "Sweet honey Greek, tempt me no more to folly" (5.2.17). In response to Helen labeling him "My . . . honey-sweet lord" (3.1.62), Pandarus, punning, taunts back, "Sweet Queen, sweet queen; that's a sweet queen i' faith" (3.1.67–68). And Priam thus scolds Paris: "Like one besotted on your sweet delights / You have the honey still, but these [the Trojans] the gall" (2.2.143–44).

19. Bloom, *The Ringers in the Tower*, p. 23.

20. So Crete is described by Donald Reiman in "Keats and the Humanistic Paradox," p. 23.

21. Matthews, "A Volcano's Voice in Shelley," p. 112.

22. Stewart, "*Lamia* and the Language of Metamorphosis," p. 21.

23. Indeed, the debate over the meaning of "Lamia" has raged since Victorian readers began to view it as an allegorical attack on science. See Bate, *John Keats*, pp. 547–48, for a history of the poem's interpretation. Earl Wasserman's fascinating chapter on "Lamia" in *The Finer Tone* is the best place to begin reading contemporary arguments about the poem.

24. Sperry, *Keats the Poet*, p. 292.

25. Emphasizing the unfruitfulness of their love, Bernard Blackstone, in *The Consecrated Urn*, says: "From first to last Isabella is presented as the potential mother. . . . Her tragedy is the tragedy of frustrated motherhood" (p. 269).

26. Stillinger, *Hoodwinking of Madeline*, p. 43.

27. Herbert G. Wright has noted the poem's resemblance to "The Thorn" in *Boccaccio in England*, p. 407.

28. De Selincourt and Darbishire, *Poetical Works of William Wordsworth*, 5:36.

29. In "Lamia" Apollo's song is described as a "long, long melodious moan" (1:75); in "Hyperion" it is described as containing a "living death" in "each gush of sounds" (2:281).

30. See Ragusis's fine article on the poem, "Narrative Structure and the Problem of the Divided Reader."

31. Writing on the three romances in *John Keats: A Reassessment*, Miriam Allott locates a common pattern: a lover falls into a swoon from which he " 'awakens' into enchantment. . . . At last, suddenly and without warning, the trance is over and the lover awakens to a world not only deprived of beauty but transformed into something repellent and hostile" (pp. 48–49). Roger Sharrock discusses a similar pattern underlying the romances in "Keats and the Young Lovers," p. 80.

32. Dickstein, *Keats and His Poetry*, p. 217.

33. This has been suggested also by Allott, " 'Isabella,' 'The Eve of St. Agnes,' and 'Lamia,' " p. 48.

34. Indeed, in "Fancy" we are told that fancy "has vassals to attend her" (l. 28).

35. Hughes, *John Milton*, pp. 258–59.

36. Sperry, *Keats the Poet*, p. 269.

37. This wariness is perhaps responsible for W. J. Bate's opinion, shared by other critics, that the "Ode on a Grecian Urn" "is in every way a more considered poem than the 'Nightingale' " (*John Keats*, p. 510).

38. For example, see Sperry, *Keats the Poet*, p. 269.

39. K. Allott, "The 'Ode to Psyche,' " p. 86.

40. Bloom, *The Visionary Company*, p. 403. Bate makes a similar observation in *John Keats*, p. 494.

41. Cf. Freud's later observation: "When any situation that is desired by the pleasure principle is prolonged, it only produces a feeling of mild contentment." *Civilization and Its Discontents*, p. 23.

42. Ende, *Keats and the Sublime*, p. 8.

43. In an earlier letter to his brother and sister-in-law, Keats had made a comparison of his own between Smollett and Scott, stating that "Scott endeavours to th[r]ow so interesting and ramantic [*sic*] a colouring into common and low Characters as to give them a touch of the sublime" (*LK*, 1:200).

44. "On Visiting The Tomb of Burns," l. 10.

45. Jack Stillinger recognizes this relationship, claiming in *Hoodwinking of Madeline* that the two poems "are intimately related in theme and imagery" (p. 2). David Perkins also discusses the two poems together, though in the reverse order from their positions in the volume; see *Quest for Permanence*, pp. 282–94. Both critics emphasize the acceptance of concrete reality in the poems. Neither of them sees the odes as raising as many questions as they would answer. A very different reading of the volume would result, however, if "To Autumn" were its final poem or even if it followed instead of preceded the "Ode on Melancholy," a reading more amenable to both Stillinger and Perkins.

46. Sperry, *Keats the Poet*, p. 284.

47. Critics have tended to see Oceanus's speech as the thematic center of the entire poem, identifying his point of view with that of Keats himself. However, as Brian Wilkie in *Romantic Poets and Epic Tradition* reminds us: "Oceanus's advice, in its quietism and apparent reasonableness, is almost certainly based on Belial's speech in the Miltonic council. . . . Keats may well have intended this scene to be, like Milton's, objectively dramatic" (p. 176). Sperry, in *Keats the Poet*, agrees: "to accept his [Oceanus's] speech as the point of the poem is to ignore the dramatic context in which it is delivered" (p. 185). I view Oceanus's speech as a product of his own limitations; yet insofar as he presents a dynamic rather than a static ideal of beauty he advances the understanding of the other Titans—and approaches Keats's own perspective.

48. Hartman, *Fate of Reading*, p. 326n.

49. Whatever Keats's original reasons for leaving "Hyperion" a fragment, its ending is dramatically appropriate to the volume. The rows of asterisks ending the poem in 1820 do not appear in any of the manuscripts. However, as Stillinger notes in *Poems of John Keats*, we must assume that any new readings appearing in the *Lamia* volume represent Keats's preferences (p. 15).

50. Sperry, *Keats the Poet*, pp. 182, 187.

51. Kroeber, *Romantic Narrative Art*, p. 87.

52. For example, Jack Stillinger carries his sense of Keats's maturation into his reading of the *Lamia* collection itself. Stillinger, who writes on the shape of the volume, sees the poems progressing to an unquestioning acceptance of the natural world: "the tone of these last poems makes clear that nature suffices" (*Hoodwinking of Madeline*, p. 117).

CHAPTER 5

1. Jones, *Letters of Percy Bysshe Shelley*, 2:196. For the bibliographical background of the *Prometheus Unbound* collection, see the introduction to my forthcoming critical edition of the volume.

2. For a discussion of the sophisticated organization of Shelley's *Alastor* collection, see Fraistat, "Poetic Quests and Questioning."

3. Michael Scrivener provides a very recent exception to this general neglect in *Radical Shelley*, where he briefly discusses the other poems in the collection along with Act 4 of "Prometheus Unbound," pp. 233–46. Scrivener, of course, is interested primarily in the political implications of the book.

4. White, *Shelley*, 2:192.

5. Wasserman, *Critical Reading*, pp. 282–83. For the original context of the epigraph, see J. E. King's translation of Cicero's *Tusculan Disputations*, p. 215. Wasserman further discusses "Prometheus Unbound" as Shelley's response to Aeschylus, pp. 284–91. There have, in fact, been many fine studies comparing Shelley's poem with Aeschylus's *Prometheus Bound* and what is known of his lost *Prometheus Unbound*. The most useful articles among these are Weaver, "*Prometheus Bound* and *Prometheus Unbound*," and Hurt, "*Prometheus Unbound* and Aeschylean Dramaturgy." For other helpful comparisons between the dramas, see Zillman, *Variorum*, pp. 63–66, and Butter, *Shelley's Idol*, pp. 165–69.

6. Curran, *Shelley's Annus Mirabilis*, p. 32.

7. Reiman and Powers, *Shelley's Poetry and Prose*, p. 133. Unless otherwise noted, all quotations from Shelley in the text will be from this edition.

8. Following Susan Hawk Brisman's splendid article, "'Unsaying His High Language,'" to which I am indebted throughout my discussion of "Prometheus Unbound," a number of interesting studies have illuminated Shelley's equation between language and ontology. See, especially, Hall, *Transforming Image*, and Burwick, "Language of Causality." Hall's concern with the transforming power of song most closely approaches my own, although she concentrates primarily on the function of lyric in "Prometheus Unbound" (pp. 68–101). Scant attention has as yet been given to the affective properties of Shelley's language on the reader. Shelley, after all, seems to be straining for a poetic language that bridges the gap between mere words and "spells" or "incantations," special orderings and choices of words that compel transformations regardless of the will of those upon whom they act.

9. For Shelley's first developed arguments identifying selfhood with solipsism, see the lengthy disquisitions on self running throughout his 1811–12 letters to Hogg and Elizabeth Hitchener.

10. Shelley first elaborates an analogous metaphoric schema in "On the Death of Princess Charlotte," his eloquent appeal for English liberty, written shortly before he left that country forever: "But *man* has murdered Liberty, and whilst the life was ebbing from its wound, there descended on the heads and on the hearts of every human thing, the sympathy of an universal blast and curse. Fetters heavier than iron weigh upon us, because they bind our souls. . . . Let us follow the corpse of British Liberty slowly and reverentially to its tomb: and if some glorious Phantom should appear, and make its throne of broken swords and sceptres and royal crowns trampled in the dust, let us say that the Spirit of Liberty has arisen from its grave and left all that was gross and mortal there, and kneel down and worship it as our Queen." See Ingpen and Peck, *Complete Works of Percy Bysshe Shelley* (hereafter cited in the text as *Prose*), 6:82.

11. Bloom, *Mythmaking*, p. 48. Here, one might also recall Shelley's claims to independence from the Lake poets in the preface to "Prometheus Unbound."

12. Robinson, *Shelley and Byron*, p. 126. For an extensive discussion of the relationship between Byron's poetry and "Prometheus Unbound," see pp. 113–27.

13. E. H. Coleridge, *Works of Lord Byron*, 4:195 (hereafter all quotations in the text from Byron's poetry will be taken from this edition).

14. Perhaps it should be emphasized that in the preceding discussion I have been trying to articulate Shelley's sense of Byron rather than my own. (Byron, it seems to me, moves beyond "contempt & desperation" in *Childe Harold IV*.) Yet it would be misleading to imply that Shelley saw self-defeating Promethean defiance, or even hopelessness, as Byron's most characteristic positions. More accurately, he viewed them as dangerous tendencies of an otherwise admirable mind—and tried to check them whenever he could. Cf., for instance, his deep admiration of *Don Juan* and *Cain*.

15. In *Radical Shelley*, Scrivener argues that the volume is organized around three themes: "ontology, the libertarian poet, and liberty." He sees "Prometheus Unbound" as dealing with all these themes, but breaks the other nine poems into groups of three: one concerning ontology—"The Sensitive-Plant," "A Vision of the Sea," and "Ode to Heaven"; one the libertarian poet—"An Exhortation," "Ode to the West Wind," and "To a Sky-Lark"; and one liberty—"An Ode," "The Cloud," and "Ode to Liberty." Thus, the order of the poems corresponds with their thematic grouping, "with the exception of 'To a Sky-Lark,' which, like 'Ode to Liberty,' was added to the volume shortly before it was published." See p. 234. This is a plausible thesis, not altogether incompatible with my own, especially in terms of the primary themes of the volume. As should be clear by now, however, I

believe that there are far more points of contact between the poems than Scrivener's groupings would suggest.

16. The longstanding debate over the definition of Demogorgon is too well known to need lengthy rehearsing here. My own definition can be glossed best by reference to two of Shelley's finest readers. First, Wasserman's contention in *Critical Reading* that Demogorgon is "infinite potentiality, needing only to be roused in order to release his force into existence as a chain of events" (p. 319). Second, and even more important, Curran's demonstration in *Shelley's Annus Mirabilis* that Demogorgon represents a hypostatic "principle of attraction" (p. 110) that is manifested in the natural world through such forces as electricity, magnetism, and gravitation, and operant psychologically through the power of love. Curran, moreover, has shown persuasively that it is reductive to view Demogorgon simply as Necessity (i.e., when understood as a principle of cause and effect), although neither his position nor mine would exclude such a reading. However, neither of us would assent to this identification if Necessity were defined as a deterministic principle utterly indifferent and external to mind. As Curran observes, "Demogorgon is a power always present: he alters the universe only if the mind alters" (*Shelley's Annus Mirabilis*, p. 110). For a brief history of critical perspectives on Demogorgon, including Mary Shelley's remark that he is "the Primal Power of the world," as well as subsequent claims that he is Eternity, Destiny, and Necessity, see Zillman, *Variorum*, pp. 317–19. For an excellent summary of sources and analogs for Shelley's use of the name "Demogorgon," see Cameron, *Golden Years*, pp. 512–13. Cameron, of course, has long advocated viewing Demogorgon as the deterministic force of Necessity. See, for example, ibid., pp. 514–15. For other succinct discussions of Demogorgon as Necessity or a power akin to Necessity, see Kuhn, "Shelley's Demogorgon," and Sperry, "Role of the Hero" (esp. p. 248).

17. Because the following discussion of "Prometheus Unbound" is intended primarily to highlight the elements most important to the volume as a whole, it could not be organized as a scene-by-scene explication. For a good elaboration of the poem's intricately symmetrical structure, though, see Reiman, *Percy Bysshe Shelley*, pp. 75–87.

18. This similarity is underscored by one of his early lines: "No change, no pause, no hope!—Yet I endure" (1:24). Aeschylus's Prometheus is, of course, the prototype for both the Byronic Prometheus and the Titan who first appears in Shelley's drama.

19. Baker, *Shelley's Major Poetry*, p. 103. In a note on this page, Baker provides a good, but by now somewhat dated, critical history of the three sisters.

20. In "'Unsaying His High Language,'" Brisman draws attention to

Panthea's key role as mediator; see esp. pp. 78–79.

21. See Wasserman, *Critical Reading*, p. 289.

22. In "Lines written among the Euganean Hills," a poem composed at the same time as Act 1 of "Prometheus Unbound," Shelley similarly equates the rising sun with liberty: "the sun floats up the sky / Like thought-winged Liberty" (ll. 206–7).

23. Hildebrand, *Polar Paradise*, p. 113.

24. For an understanding of this interchange between potential and kinetic energy I am indebted to Daniel J. Hughes, "Potentiality in *Prometheus Unbound*."

25. See Taylor, *Description of Greece* (1794), 3:262. Shelley ordered Taylor's Pausanias from Ollier on 24 July and, again, 3 August 1817. And though there is no extant record of Shelley's receiving or reading it, his use of the temple of Prometheus at the end of Act 3 almost certainly derives from Pausanias. For Shelley's knowledge of Taylor's work, see Notopulos, "Shelley and Thomas Taylor."

26. Ibid.

27. Ibid., p. 263.

28. In *Study of English Romanticism*, Frye comments: "The struggle between Prometheus and Jupiter is thus in part a struggle for the control of the ocean, represented on the one side by Prometheus' love for Asia, a daughter of the Oceanides, and on the other by Jupiter's marriage to Thetis the Nereid" (p. 111).

29. Compare this with Blake's similar use of Atlantis in *America*, 10:5–10.

30. Curran, *Shelley's Annus Mirabilis*, p. 77.

31. See Pausanias, *Description of Greece*, 1:167.

32. Hungerford, *Shores of Darkness*, p. 197.

33. Ibid., p. 198.

34. For excellent discussions of Shelley's view of Athens, and Greece in general, see Webb, *Voice Not Understood*, pp. 191–228, and Bornstein, *Yeats and Shelley*, pp. 175–98.

35. Though months passed before Shelley added Act 4 to what had seemed to be a completed effort, one should also keep in mind Stuart Curran's caution in *Shelley's Annus Mirabilis* that evidence from Shelley's notebook indicates that "Act 4 of *Prometheus Unbound* was no mere afterthought" (p. 209).

36. Shelley critics have located a plethora of sources and analogs for the earth orb, ranging from Ezekiel, Bacon, and Milton to contemporary scientific theorists. Perhaps the most complex and syncretic of all symbols in "Prometheus Unbound," the orb seems to substantiate most of these critical hypotheses. Thomas Reisner, in "Some Scientific Models," notes: "The symbol of the multitudinous orb has all the intellectual genesis, yet none of the actual attributes of a hybrid. It demonstrates Shelley's power to bring radically heterogeneous con-

cepts into fertile imaginative conjunction, a power which (as *A Defense of Poetry* has it) 'subdues to union under its light yoke all irreconcilable things'" (p. 59). See the first few pages of Reisner's article for a critical history of the orb. See also Oras, "The Multitudinous Orb," and Zillman, *Variorum*, pp. 585–93.

37. Holmes, *Shelley*, p. 506.

38. For this and Davy's entire discussion, see Grabo, *Newton among Poets*, p. 142.

39. See Heninger, *Cosmographical Glass*, p. 34.

40. Ibid.

41. Ibid., p. 41.

42. The orb thus might be understood as Shelley's vital response to the mechanistic visions of Newton and Paley.

43. See Bush, *Mythology*, p. 155. More than a few critics have perceived this optimism as a failure of vision. For example, although Tilottama Rajan, who has recently discussed the darker implications of passages in the earlier acts of "Prometheus Unbound," cites as extreme Bostetter's charge that Act 4 represents a "'switching off' of the critical intelligence," she nonetheless sees Shelley straining here "to press beyond the ambiguities of skepticism to the finality of a holistic vision of the universe." See *Dark Interpreter*, pp. 88–89.

44. Reiman and Powers, *Shelley's Poetry and Prose*, p. 210.

45. See Wasserman's brilliant chapter on "The Sensitive-Plant," in *Critical Reading*, pp. 154–79. The context of the poem within the *Prometheus Unbound* volume leads me to a different reading than that of Wasserman and previous critics, however. For other commentaries, see St. George, "Good and Evil in 'The Sensitive Plant,'" and Caldwell, "The Sensitive Plant as Original Fantasy." Caldwell notes parallels between "Prometheus Unbound" and "The Sensitive-Plant" on pp. 248 and 252.

46. For one of the few detailed readings of the poem, see Ketcham, "Shelley's 'A Vision of the Sea.'" Ketcham sees the poem as demonstrating "that Nature at her worst is no final barrier to establishing the realm of hope and love which is the theme of *Prometheus Unbound*" (p. 59).

47. All quotations of "A Vision of the Sea" are taken from Hutchinson and Matthews, *Shelley: Poetical Works*. I will also be quoting "An Exhortation" and "An Ode" from this edition.

48. By omitting this stanza from their texts, these editors (including Hutchinson) follow the lead of Mary Shelley, who cancelled it in her transcript of the poem and deleted it from her collected editions of Shelley's poetry. In the 1820 volume and in the Reiman and Powers edition, these lines appear as 3.65–66.

49. The Reiman and Powers text of "Ode to Heaven" accepts manuscript authority for the second voice to be labeled as "A Remoter

Voice" and the third "A Louder and Still Remoter Voice." See p. 220 of this edition.

50. Pearce, "Riddle of Shelley's Cloud," p. 217. Reiman first identified the cloud as "an analogue of the human mind" in *Percy Bysshe Shelley*, p. 116.

51. I am grateful to Theresa M. Kelley for pointing out to me the Neoplatonist connections between Proteus and the chameleon. See her "Proteus and Romantic Allegory."

52. Rieger, *Mutiny Within*, p. 182.

53. This passage from Shelley's notebook can be found in Rogers, *Shelley at Work*, p. 221.

54. De Selincourt and Darbishire, *Poetical Works of William Wordsworth*, 4:258.

55. Rieger, *Mutiny Within*, pp. 181–82.

56. The primary targets for Shelley's appeal were, of course, the English, not the Spanish people.

57. Judith Chernaik has argued that the "'Ode to Liberty' can be read as a 'Prometheus Unbound' in miniature, with a specifically political focus." See *Lyrics of Shelley*, p. 100. It seems to me, however, that the "Ode to Liberty," with its historical focus and bleak ending, is designed to be antithetical to the mythic comedy of "Prometheus Unbound."

58. Similarly, the Lady of "The Sensitive-Plant," the unused potentiality for love, has a mind described as being "Like a sea-flower unfolded beneath the Ocean" (2.8). These are the plants that despoil themselves in the third stanza of the "Ode to the West Wind."

59. Bloom, *Mythmaking*, p. 93.

60. Bornstein vividly elaborates this point in "Victorians and Volumes," pp. 5–7.

Bibliography

Abrams, M. H. *The Mirror and the Lamp: Romantic Theory and the Critical Tradition.* London: Oxford University Press, 1953.

Allott, Kenneth. "The 'Ode to Psyche.'" In *John Keats: A Reassessment,* edited by Kenneth Muir, pp. 75–102. 2d ed. Liverpool: Liverpool University Press, 1969.

Allott, Miriam. "'Isabella,' 'The Eve of St. Agnes,' and 'Lamia.'" In *John Keats: A Reassessment,* edited by Kenneth Muir, pp. 40–63. 2d ed. Liverpool: Liverpool University Press, 1969.

Allport, Floyd H. *Theories of Perception and the Concept of Structure.* New York: John Wiley, 1955.

Ashton, Thomas L. "'The Thorn': Wordsworth's Insensitive Plant." *Huntington Library Quarterly* 35 (1971–72): 171–87.

Averill, James. "The Shape of *Lyrical Ballads* (1798)." *Philological Quarterly* 60 (1981): 387–407.

Baker, Carlos. *Shelley's Major Poetry: The Fabric of a Vision.* Princeton, N.J.: Princeton University Press, 1948.

Barnard, John. Review of Jack Stillinger, *The Poems of John Keats. Studies in Romanticism* 21 (1982): 541–46.

Bate, Walter Jackson. *John Keats.* Cambridge, Mass.: Harvard University Press, Belknap Press, 1963.

Blackstone, Bernard. *The Consecrated Urn: An Interpretation of Keats in Terms of Growth and Form.* New York: Longmans, Green, and Co., 1959.

Bloom, Harold. *The Ringers in the Tower: Studies in Romantic Tradition.* Chicago: University of Chicago Press, 1971.

______. *Shelley's Mythmaking.* Ithaca, N.Y.: Cornell University Press, 1959.

______. *The Visionary Company: A Reading of English Romantic Poetry.* 1961. Reprint. Ithaca, N.Y.: Cornell University Press, 1971.

Bornstein, George. "Victorians and Volumes, Foreigners and First Drafts: Four Gaps in Postromantic Influence Study." *Romanticism Past and Present* 6 (1982): 1–9.

———. *Yeats and Shelley*. Chicago: University of Chicago Press, 1970.

Boulger, James D. "'The Rime of the Ancient Mariner'—Introduction." In *"The Rime of the Ancient Mariner": A Collection of Critical Essays*, edited by James D. Boulger, pp. 1–20. Englewood Cliffs, N.J.: Prentice-Hall, 1969.

Brett, R. L., and Jones, Alun R., eds. *Wordsworth and Coleridge, "The Lyrical Ballads": The Text of the 1798 Edition with the Additional 1800 Poems and the Prefaces*. Rev. ed. London: Methuen, 1965.

Brisman, Susan Hawk. "'Unsaying His High Language': The Problem of Voice in *Prometheus Unbound*." *Studies in Romanticism* 16 (1977): 51–86.

Burwick, Frederick. "The Language of Causality in *Prometheus Unbound*." *Keats-Shelley Journal* 31 (1982): 136–58.

Bush, Douglas. *Mythology and the Romantic Tradition*. Cambridge, Mass.: Harvard University Press, 1937.

Butler, James, ed. *"The Ruined Cottage" and "The Pedlar" by William Wordsworth*. The Cornell Wordsworth. Ithaca, N.Y.: Cornell University Press, 1979.

Butter, Peter H. *Shelley's Idols of the Cave*. Edinburgh: Edinburgh University Press, 1954.

Caldwell, Richard S. "'The Sensitive Plant' as Original Fantasy." *Studies in Romanticism* 15 (1976): 221–52.

Cameron, Kenneth Neill. *Shelley: The Golden Years*. Cambridge, Mass.: Harvard University Press, 1974.

Carretta, Vincent. "'Images Reflect from Art to Art': Alexander Pope's Collected Works of 1717." In *Poems in Their Place*, edited by Neil Fraistat. Chapel Hill: University of North Carolina Press, forthcoming.

Chernaik, Judith. *The Lyrics of Shelley*. Cleveland: Case Western Reserve University Press, 1972.

Cicero. *Tusculan Disputations*. Translated by J. E. King. Loeb Classics Editions. 1927. Reprint. Cambridge, Mass.: Harvard University Press, 1975.

Clausen, W. V. "Callimachus and Latin Poetry." *Greek, Roman, and Byzantine Studies* 5 (1964): 181–96.

Clayman, D. L. "Callimachus' Thirteenth Iamb: The Last Word." *Hermes* 104 (1976): 29–35.

Cody, J. V. *Horace and Callimachean Aesthetics*. Collection Latomus 147. Brussels: Latomus, 1976.

Cohen, Ralph. *The Art of Discrimination: Thomson's "The Seasons" and the Language of Criticism*. Berkeley: University of California Press, 1964.

Cohen, Ruth. "The 1800 Ordering of *Lyrical Ballads*: Its Moral Purpose." *Caliban* 13 (1977): 31–44.

Coleridge, Ernest Hartley, ed. *The Complete Poetical Works of Samuel Taylor Coleridge*. 2 vols. Oxford: Clarendon Press, 1912.

______. *The Works of Lord Byron: Poetry*. 7 vols. London: John Murray, 1900–1904.

Coleridge, Henry Nelson, ed. *Specimens of the Table Talk of the Late Samuel Taylor Coleridge*. 2 vols. New York: Harper and Brothers, 1835.

Colie, Rosalie. *The Resources of Kind: Genre-Theory in the Renaissance*. Berkeley: University of California Press, 1973.

Culler, Jonathan. *Structuralist Poetics*. Ithaca, N.Y.: Cornell University Press, 1975.

Curran, Stuart. *Shelley's Annus Mirabilis: The Maturing of an Epic Vision*. San Marino, Calif.: Huntington Library Press, 1975.

Curtis, Jared, ed. *Poems in Two Volumes, and Other Poems, 1800–1807, by William Wordsworth*. The Cornell Wordsworth. Ithaca, N.Y.: Cornell University Press, 1983.

Danby, John F. *The Simple Wordsworth*. London: Routledge and Kegan Paul, 1960.

Dawson, C. M. "The Iambi of Callimachus." *Yale Classical Studies* 11 (1950): 1–168.

De Selincourt, Ernest, ed. *The Poetical Works of William Wordsworth*. Vol. 1. Oxford: Clarendon Press, 1940.

______, and Darbishire, Helen, eds. *The Poetical Works of William Wordsworth*. 5 vols. Oxford: Clarendon Press, 1940–52.

______. *The Prelude, or The Growth of a Poet's Mind*. 2d ed. Oxford: Clarendon Press, 1959.

______, and Hill, Alan G., eds. *The Letters of William and Dorothy Wordsworth: The Later Years, Part 1, 1821–1828*. 2d ed. Oxford: Clarendon Press, 1978.

______; Moorman, Mary; and Hill, Alan G., eds. *The Letters of William and Dorothy Wordsworth: The Middle Years, 1806–1820*. 2 vols. 2d ed. rev. Oxford: Clarendon Press, 1969–70.

______, and Shaver, Chester L., eds. *The Letters of William and Dorothy Wordsworth: The Early Years, 1787–1805*. 2d ed. rev. Oxford: Clarendon Press, 1967.

Dickstein, Morris. *Keats and His Poetry: A Study in Development*. Chicago: University of Chicago Press, 1971.

Durling, Robert. *Petrarch's Lyric Poems: The "Rime Sparse" and Other Lyrics*. Cambridge, Mass.: Harvard University Press, 1976.

Ende, Stuart. *Keats and the Sublime*. New Haven: Yale University Press, 1976.

Erdman, David V., ed. *The Poetry and Prose of William Blake*. Garden

City, N.Y.: Doubleday, 1965.

Fish, Stanley. *Is There a Text in This Class?: The Authority of Interpretive Communities*. Cambridge, Mass.: Harvard University Press, 1980.

Fogle, Richard Harter. *The Idea of Coleridge's Criticism*. Berkeley: University of California Press, 1962.

Foxon, David Fairweather. "The Printing of *Lyrical Ballads*, 1798." *The Library*, 5th ser. 9 (1954–55): 221–41.

Fraistat, Neil. "Poetic Quests and Questioning in Shelley's *Alastor* Collection." *Keats-Shelley Journal* 33 (1984): 161–81.

———, ed. *Poems in Their Place*. Chapel Hill: University of North Carolina Press, forthcoming.

———. *Shelley's "Prometheus Unbound, with Other Poems": A Critical Edition*. English Text Series. New York: Garland Publishing, forthcoming.

Freud, Sigmund. *Civilization and Its Discontents*. Translated by James Strachey. New York: W. W. Norton, 1961.

Frye, Northrop. *A Study of English Romanticism*. New York: Random House, 1968.

Furst, Lillian R., ed. *European Romanticism, Self-Definition: An Anthology*. London: Methuen, 1980.

Gérard, Albert. *English Romantic Poetry: Ethos, Structure, and Symbol in Coleridge, Wordsworth, Shelley, and Keats*. Berkeley: University of California Press, 1968.

Giangrande, G. Review of G. Lawall, *Theocritus' Coan Pastorals*. *Journal of Historical Studies* 88 (1968): 170–73.

Gill, Stephen, ed. *The Salisbury Plain Poems of William Wordsworth*. The Cornell Wordsworth. Ithaca, N.Y.: Cornell University Press, 1975.

Gleckner, Robert. *Blake's Prelude: Poetical Sketches*. Baltimore: Johns Hopkins University Press, 1982.

———. *Byron and the Ruins of Paradise*. Baltimore: Johns Hopkins University Press, 1967.

———. "Keats's Odes: The Problem of the Limited Canon." *Studies in English Literature, 1500–1900* 5 (1965): 577–85.

Grabo, Carl. *A Newton among Poets: Shelley's Use of Science in "Prometheus Unbound."* Chapel Hill: University of North Carolina Press, 1930.

Griggs, Earl Leslie, ed. *The Collected Letters of Samuel Taylor Coleridge*. 6 vols. Oxford: Clarendon Press, 1956–71.

Grosart, Alexander, ed. *The Prose Works of William Wordsworth*. 3 vols. 1876. Reprint. New York: AMS Press, 1967.

Haley, Bruce. "The Infinite Will: Shakespeare's *Troilus* and the 'Ode to a Nightingale.'" *Keats-Shelley Journal* 21 (1972): 18–23.

Hall, Jean. *The Transforming Image: A Study of Shelley's Major Poetry*. Urbana, Ill.: University of Illinois Press, 1980.

Harbage, Alfred, ed. *Shakespeare: The Complete Works*. Baltimore: Penguin Books, 1969.

Harrison, James A., ed. *The Complete Works of Edgar Allan Poe*. 17 vols. 1902. Reprint. New York: AMS Press, 1965.

Hartman, Geoffrey. "Blake and the 'Progress of Poesy.'" In *William Blake: Essays for S. Foster Damon*, edited by Alvin Rosenfeld, pp. 57–68. Providence: Brown University Press, 1969.

———. *The Fate of Reading, and Other Essays*. Chicago: University of Chicago Press, 1975.

———. *Wordsworth's Poetry, 1787–1814*. 1964. Reprint. New Haven: Yale University Press, 1971.

Heath, William. *Wordsworth and Coleridge: A Study of Their Literary Relations in 1801–1802*. Oxford: Clarendon Press, 1970.

Heffernan, James A. W. "Mutilated Autobiography: Wordsworth's *Poems* of 1815." *Wordsworth Circle* 10 (1979): 107–12.

Heninger, S. K., Jr. *The Cosmographical Glass: Renaissance Diagrams of the Universe*. San Marino, Calif.: Huntington Library Press, 1977.

———. "Sidney and Milton: The Poet as Maker." In *Milton and the Line of Vision*, edited by Joseph Anthony Wittreich, Jr., pp. 57–95. Madison: University of Wisconsin Press, 1975.

———, ed. *The Hekatompathia: or Passionate Centurie of Love*. Gainesville, Fla.: Scholar's Facsimile and Reprints, 1964.

Herman, Judith B. "The Poet as Editor: Wordsworth's Edition of 1815." *Wordsworth Circle* 9 (1978): 82–87.

Hildebrand, William H. *Shelley's Polar Paradise: A Reading of "Prometheus Unbound."* Salzburg Studies in English Literature. Salzburg: Institut für Englische Sprache und Literature, 1974.

Hill, John Spencer, ed. *Imagination in Coleridge*. Totowa, N.J.: Rowman and Littlefield, 1978.

Holmes, Richard. *Shelley: The Pursuit*. London: Weidenfeld and Nicolson, 1974.

Hughes, Daniel J. "Potentiality in *Prometheus Unbound*." *Studies in Romanticism* 2 (1963): 107–26.

Hughes, Merritt Y., ed. *John Milton: Complete Poems and Major Prose*. Indianapolis: Bobbs-Merrill Co., Odyssey Press, 1957.

Hungerford, Edward B. *Shores of Darkness*. New York: Columbia University Press, 1941.

Hurt, James R. "*Prometheus Unbound* and Aeschylean Dramaturgy." *Keats-Shelley Journal* 15 (1966): 43–48.

Hutchinson, Thomas, and Matthews, G. M., eds. *Shelley: Poetical Works*. 2d ed. London: Oxford University Press, 1970.

Ingpen, Roger, and Peck, Walter E., eds. *The Complete Works of Percy*

Bysshe Shelley. 10 vols. The Julian Edition. London: Ernest Benn, 1926–30.

Iser, Wolfgang. "The Reading Process: A Phenomenological Approach." In *Reader Response Criticism from Formalism to Post-Structuralism*, edited by Jane Tompkins, pp. 50–69. Baltimore: Johns Hopkins University Press, 1980.

Jack, Ian. "Poems of John Clare's Sanity." In *Some British Romantics: A Collection of Essays*, edited by James V. Logan, John E. Jordan, and Northrop Frye, pp. 191–232. Columbus: Ohio State University Press, 1966.

Jacobus, Mary. *Tradition and Experiment in Wordsworth's "Lyrical Ballads" 1798*. Oxford: Clarendon Press, 1976.

Jones, Alun R. "The Compassionate World: Some Observations on Wordsworth's *Lyrical Ballads* of 1798." *English* 19 (1970): 7–12.

Jones, Frederick L. *The Letters of Percy Bysshe Shelley*. 2 vols. Oxford: Clarendon Press, 1964.

Jordan, John E. *Why "The Lyrical Ballads"?* Berkeley: University of California Press, 1976.

Kelley, Theresa M. "Proteus and Romantic Allegory." *Journal of English Literary History* 49 (1982): 623–52.

Kenner, Hugh. "The Sacred Book of the Arts." In *Gnomon: Essays on Contemporary Literature*, pp. 9–29. New York: McDowell, Obolensky, 1951.

Ketcham, Carl H. "Shelley's 'A Vision of the Sea.' " *Studies in Romanticism* 17 (1978): 51–59.

Kroeber, Karl. *Romantic Narrative Art*. Madison: University of Wisconsin Press, 1966.

Kuhn, Albert J. "Shelley's Demogorgon and Eternal Necessity." *Philological Quarterly* 13 (1934): 309–11.

Legouis, Emile. "Some Remarks on the Composition of the *Lyrical Ballads*, 1798." In *Wordsworth and Coleridge: Studies in Honor of George McLean Harper*, edited by Earl L. Griggs, pp. 3–11. Princeton, N.J.: Princeton University Press, 1939.

Little, Geoffrey, ed. *Barron Field's Memoirs of Wordsworth*. Australian Academy of the Humanities, Monograph 3. Sydney: Sydney University Press, 1975.

McCanles, Michael. "*The Shepheardes Calendar* as Document and Monument." *Studies in English Literature, 1500–1900* 22 (1982): 5–19.

McFarland, Thomas. *Romanticism and the Forms of Ruin: Wordsworth, Coleridge, and Modalities of Fragmentation*. Princeton, N.J.: Princeton University Press, 1981.

McGann, Jerome J. *Fiery Dust: Byron's Poetic Development*. Chicago: University of Chicago Press, 1968.

———. "The Meaning of 'The Ancient Mariner.'" *Critical Inquiry* 8 (1981): 35–67.

———, ed. *Lord Byron: The Complete Poetical Works*. 7 vols. Oxford: Clarendon Press, 1980–.

Maniquis, Robert M. "Comparison, Intensity, and Time in 'Tintern Abbey.'" *Criticism* 11 (1969): 358–82.

Marchand, Leslie A. *Byron: A Biography*. 3 vols. New York: Alfred A. Knopf, 1957.

———, ed. *Byron's Letters and Journals*. 12 vols. Cambridge, Mass.: Harvard University Press, Belknap Press, 1973–82.

Marrs, Edwin W., Jr. *The Letters of Charles and Mary Anne Lamb*. 6 vols. Ithaca, N.Y.: Cornell University Press, 1975–.

Martz, Louis. "The Rising Poet, 1645." In *The Lyric and Dramatic Milton*, edited by Joseph H. Summers, pp. 3–33. New York: Columbia University Press, 1965.

Matthews, G. M. "A Volcano's Voice in Shelley." In *Twentieth-Century Interpretations of Shelley: A Collection of Critical Essays*, edited by George Ridenour, pp. 111–31. Englewood Cliffs, N.J.: Prentice-Hall, 1965.

Miner, Earl. "Dryden's Admired Acquaintance, Mr. Milton." *Milton Studies* 11 (1978): 3–27.

———. "Some Issues for Study of Integrated Collections." In *Poems in Their Place*, edited by Neil Fraistat. Chapel Hill: University of North Carolina Press, forthcoming.

Mitchell, W. J. T. "Blake's Radical Comedy: Dramatic Structure as Meaning in *Milton*." In *Blake's Sublime Allegory: Essays on "The Four Zoas," "Milton," and "Jerusalem,"* edited by Stuart Curran and Joseph Anthony Wittreich, Jr., pp. 281–307. Madison: University of Wisconsin Press, 1973.

Murray, Roger N. *Wordsworth's Style: Figures and Themes in the "Lyrical Ballads" of 1800*. Lincoln: University of Nebraska Press, 1967.

Neely, Carol Thomas. "The Structure of English Renaissance Sonnet Sequences." *Journal of English Literary History* 45 (1978): 359–89.

Nitchie, George W. "Milton and His Muses." *Journal of English Literary History* 44 (1977): 75–84.

Notopulos, James A. "Shelley and Thomas Taylor." *Publications of the Modern Language Association* 51 (1936): 502–17.

Oras, Ants. "The Multitudinous Orb: Some Miltonic Elements in Shelley." *Modern Language Quarterly* 16 (1955): 247–57.

Owen, W. J. B., ed. *Wordsworth and Coleridge: "Lyrical Ballads" 1798*. 2d ed. Oxford: Clarendon Press, 1967.

———, and Smyser, Jane Worthington, eds. *The Prose Works of William Wordsworth*. 3 vols. Oxford: Clarendon Press, 1974.

Parker, William Riley. *Milton: A Biography*. 2 vols. Oxford: Clarendon Press, 1968.

———. "Some Problems in the Chronology of Milton's Early Poems." *Review of English Studies* 11 (1935): 276–83.

Parrish, Stephen Maxfield. *The Art of "The Lyrical Ballads."* Cambridge, Mass.: Harvard University Press, 1973.

Pausanias. *Description of Greece*. Translated by William Henry Samuel Jones. Loeb Classics Editions. 5 vols. Cambridge, Mass.: Harvard University Press, 1918.

Pearce, Donald. "The Riddle of Shelley's Cloud." *Yale Review* 62 (1972): 202–20.

Perkins, David. *The Quest for Permanence: The Symbolism of Wordsworth, Shelley, and Keats*. Cambridge, Mass.: Harvard University Press, 1959.

Prickett, Stephen. *Wordsworth and Coleridge: "The Lyrical Ballads."* London: Edward Arnold, 1975.

Rader, Melvin. *Wordsworth: A Philosophical Approach*. Oxford: Clarendon Press, 1967.

Ragusis, Michael. "Narrative Structure and the Problem of the Divided Reader in 'The Eve of St. Agnes.'" *Journal of English Literary History* 42 (1975): 379–94.

Rajan, Tilottama. *Dark Interpreter: The Discourse of Romanticism*. Ithaca, N.Y.: Cornell University Press, 1980.

Raysor, Thomas M., ed. *Coleridge's Shakespeare Criticism*. 2 vols. London: Dent, 1960.

Reed, Mark L. "Wordsworth, Coleridge, and the 'Plan' of *The Lyrical Ballads*." *University of Toronto Quarterly* 34 (1965): 238–52.

Reiman, Donald H. "Keats and the Humanistic Paradox: Mythological History in *Lamia*." *Studies in English Literature, 1500–1900* 11 (1971): 659–69.

———. *Percy Bysshe Shelley*. The Griffin Author Series. New York: St. Martin's Press, 1969.

———, and Powers, Sharon, eds. *Shelley's Poetry and Prose*. W. W. Norton, 1977.

Reisner, Thomas. "Some Scientific Models for Shelley's Multitudinous Orb." *Keats-Shelley Journal* 23 (1973): 52–59.

Rieger, James. *The Mutiny Within: The Heresies of Percy Bysshe Shelley*. New York: George Braziller, 1967.

Robinson, Charles E. *Shelley and Byron: The Snake and Eagle Wreathed in Fight*. Baltimore: Johns Hopkins University Press, 1976.

Roche, Thomas. "Shakespeare and the Sonnet Sequence." In *English Poetry and Prose, 1540–1674*, pp. 101–18. History of Literature in the English Language. Vol. 2. London: Barrie and Jenkins, 1970.

Rogers, Neville. *Shelley at Work: A Critical Inquiry*. Oxford: Clarendon Press, 1967.

Rollins, Hyder Edward, ed. *The Keats Circle: Letters and Papers and More Letters and Poems of the Keats Circle*. 2 vols. 2d ed. Cambridge, Mass.: Harvard University Press, 1965.

______. *The Letters of John Keats, 1814–1821*. 2 vols. Cambridge, Mass.: Harvard University Press, 1958.

______. *Tottel's Miscellany, 1557–1587*. 2 vols. Rev. ed. Cambridge, Mass.: Harvard University Press, 1965.

Rose, H. J. *A Handbook of Greek Literature: From Homer to the Age of Lucian*. 4th ed. rev. London: Methuen, 1954.

Rosenthal, M. L., and Gall, Sally M. *The Modern Poetic Sequence: The Genius of Modern Poetry*. Oxford: Oxford University Press, 1983.

Ross, Donald, Jr. "Poems, 'Bound Each to Each' in the 1815 Edition of Wordsworth." *Wordsworth Circle* 12 (1981): 133–40.

Ruoff, Gene W. "Critical Implications of Wordsworth's 1815 Categorization, with Some Animadversions on Binaristic Commentary." *Wordsworth Circle* 9 (1978): 75–82.

St. Clair, F. Y. "Drayton's First Revision of His Sonnets." *Studies in Philology* 36 (1939): 40–59.

St. George, Priscilla. "The Styles of Good and Evil in 'The Sensitive Plant.'" *Journal of English and Germanic Philology* 64 (1965): 479–88.

Santirocco, Matthew S. "Horace's Odes and the Ancient Poetry Book." *Arethusa* 13 (1980): 43–57.

Saunders, J. W. "The Stigma of Print: A Note on the Social Bases of Tudor Poetry." *Essays in Criticism* 1 (1951): 139–64.

Schulz, Max F. *The Poetic Voices of Coleridge: A Study of His Desire for Spontaneity and Passion for Order*. Detroit: Wayne State University Press, 1963.

Scoggins, James. *Imagination and Fancy: Complementary Modes in the Poetry of Wordsworth*. Lincoln: University of Nebraska Press, 1966.

Scrivener, Michael. *Radical Shelley: The Philosophical Anarchism and Utopian Thought of Percy Bysshe Shelley*. Princeton, N.J.: Princeton University Press, 1982.

Segal, Charles P. "Ancient Texts and Modern Literary Criticism." *Arethusa* 1 (1968): 1–25.

Sharrock, Roger. "Keats and the Young Lovers." *Review of English Literature* 2 (1961): 76–86.

Shaver, Chester L., and Shaver, Alice C. *Wordsworth's Library: A Catalogue*. New York: Garland Publishing, 1979.

Shawcross, John, ed. *Biographia Literaria*. 2 vols. London: Oxford University Press, 1907.

Sheats, Paul. "The *Lyrical Ballads*." In *English Romantic Poets: Modern Essays in Criticism*, edited by M. H. Abrams, pp. 133–48. 2d ed. London: Oxford University Press, 1975.

Sheavyn, Phoebe. *The Literary Profession in the Elizabethan Age*. 2d ed., revised by J. W. Saunders. Manchester: Manchester University Press, 1967.

Shilstone, Frederick W. "The Lyric Collection as Genre: Byron's *Hebrew Melodies*." *Concerning Poetry* 12 (1979): 45–52.

Smith, Barbara Herrnstein. *Poetic Closure: A Study of How Poems End*. Chicago: University of Chicago Press, 1968.

Sperry, Stuart. *Keats the Poet*. Princeton, N.J.: Princeton University Press, 1973.

———. "Necessity and the Role of the Hero in Shelley's *Prometheus Unbound*." *Publications of the Modern Language Association* 96 (1981): 242–54.

Spurgeon, Caroline. *Keats's Shakespeare: A Descriptive Study Based on New Material*. London: Oxford University Press, 1969.

Stewart, Garrett. "*Lamia* and the Language of Metamorphosis." *Studies in Romanticism* 15 (1976): 3–41.

Stillinger, Jack. *The Hoodwinking of Madeline, and Other Essays on Keats's Poems*. Urbana, Ill.: University of Illinois Press, 1971.

———. *The Texts of Keats's Poems*. Cambridge, Mass.: Harvard University Press, 1974.

———, ed. *The Poems of John Keats*. Cambridge, Mass.: Harvard University Press, Belknap Press, 1978.

Storch, R. F. "Wordsworth's Experimental Ballads: The Radical Uses of Intelligence and Comedy." *Studies in English Literature, 1500–1900* 11 (1971): 621–39.

Sturm-Maddox, Sara. "Transformations of Courtly Love Poetry: *Vita Nuova* and *Canzoniere*." In *The Expansion and Transformations of Courtly Literature*, edited by Nathaniel B. Smith and Joseph T. Snow, pp. 128–40. Athens: University of Georgia Press, 1980.

Swingle, L. J. "Wordsworth's Contrarieties: A Prelude to Wordsworthian Complexity." *Journal of English Literary History* 44 (1977): 337–53.

Tibble, J. W., and Tibble, Anne, eds. *The Letters of John Clare*. 1951. Reprint. London: Routledge and Kegan Paul, 1970.

Van Sickle, John. "The Book-Roll and Some Conventions of the Poetic Book." *Arethusa* 13 (1980): 5–42.

Waddington, Raymond B. "Milton among the Carolines." In *The Age of Milton: Background to Seventeenth-Century Literature*, edited by C. A. Patrides and Raymond B. Waddington, pp. 338–64. Manchester: University of Manchester Press, 1980.

Wasserman, Earl R. *The Finer Tone: Keats' Major Poems*. Baltimore: Johns Hopkins University Press, 1953.

———. *Shelley: A Critical Reading*. Baltimore: Johns Hopkins University Press, 1971.

Weaver, Bennett. "*Prometheus Bound* and *Prometheus Unbound*." *Publications of the Modern Language Association* 64 (1949): 115–33.

Webb, Timothy. *Shelley: A Voice Not Understood*. Atlantic Highlands, N.J.: Humanities Press, 1977.

Whalley, George. "Coleridge's Poetical Canon: Selection and Arrangement." *Review of English Literature* 7 (1966): 9–24.

White, Newman Ivey. *Shelley*. 2 vols. New York: Alfred A. Knopf, 1940.

Wilkie, Brian. *Romantic Poets and Epic Tradition*. Madison: University of Wisconsin Press, 1965.

Wilkins, Ernest Hatch. *The Making of the "Canzoniere," and Other Petrarchan Studies*. Rome: Edizioni di Storia e litteratura, 1951.

Wittreich, Joseph Anthony, Jr. *Visionary Poetics: Milton's Tradition and His Legacy*. San Marino, Calif.: Huntington Library Press, 1979.

———, ed. *The Romantics on Milton: Formal Essays and Critical Asides*. Cleveland: Case Western Reserve University Press, 1970.

Wolfson, Susan J. "The Speaker as Questioner in *Lyrical Ballads*." *Journal of English and Germanic Philology* 77 (1978): 546–68.

Wordsworth, Jonathan. *The Music of Humanity: A Critical Study of Wordsworth's "Ruined Cottage," Incorporating Texts from a Manuscript of 1798–1800*. London: Thomas Nelson, 1969.

Wright, Herbert G. *Boccaccio in England from Chaucer to Tennyson*. London: University of London, Athlone Press, 1957.

Zillman, Lawrence John, ed. *Shelley's "Prometheus Unbound": A Variorum Edition*. Seattle: University of Washington Press, 1959.

Index